AFRICA IN FRAGMENTS

ESSAYS ON NIGERIA, AFRICA, AND GLOBAL AFRICANITY

AFRICA IN FRAGMENTS

ESSAYS ON NIGERIA, AFRICA, AND GLOBAL AFRICANITY

MOSES E OCHONU

DIASPORIC AFRICA PRESS
NEW YORK

This book is a publication of

DIASPORIC AFRICA PRESS
NEW YORK | WWW.DAFRICAPRESS.COM

Copyright © 2014 Diasporic Africa Press, Inc.

Cover artwork by Victor Ehikhamenor.

ISBN-13: 978-1-937306-33-5
Library of Congress Control Number: 2014945068

CONTENTS

Acknowledgements   *i*

Introduction Of Africa's Fragments and Polemics   *iii*

SECTION I: NIGERIA (NATION AND POLITICS)

1   How Nigeria Can Survive   *1*

2   The Other Problems of Corruption   *11*

3   The Case for Real Constitutional Reform   *21*

4   Nigerians' Love–Hate Relationship with Government   *35*

5   The "Federal Character" Conundrum   *39*

6   Can Nigeria Afford (Literally) This Democracy?   *47*

7   Northern Elites and Northern Economic Backwardness   *63*

8   The Limits of Electoral Reform   *67*

SECTION II: NIGERIA (SOCIETY AND LETTERS)

9   My Oga Is Bigger Than Yours   *75*

10 Anti-Intellectualism and Book People   *81*

11 Bongos Ikwue and Idoma Cultural Cosmopolitanism   *87*

12 Names and Naming in Nigeria   *93*

13 Helicopter Escapes and the Common Good   *101*

14 The Patriotism Blackmail   *107*

SECTION III: AFRICA AND THE WORLD

15 Africa, Corruption, Poverty, and Moral Consequence   115

16 Abuja Millennium Tower and the Problem of Explaining Africa   125

17 Arab Racism against Black Africans: Toward an Understanding   131

18 Boko Haram, African Islam, and Foreign Islamic Heterodoxy   151

19 African Participation in the Atlantic Slave Trade: A Deconstructionist Approach   183

20 Why Do Africans Migrate to the West?   195

21 Immigrants, Uprising, and the Revenge of History   205

22 Of African Immigrants and African Americans   209

23 Debt Cancellation, Aid, and Africa: A Moral Response to Critics   231

24 Race, Racism, and the Immigrant Black Experience in Euro-America   243

25 Nollywood and the Functional Logic of Mediocrity   259

26 Toward a New African Renaissance   267

Conclusion   277

Select Bibliography   283

Notes   287

Index   293

ACKNOWLEDGEMENTS

This book materialized because of the generous efforts of many people. I am indebted to them all. Some of these people should be acknowledged by name.

I am grateful to the editors of *Pambazuka, Kilimanjaro,* and several other magazines and newsletters for publishing earlier, much shorter versions of some of the essays in this volume. I particularly salute Philip Adekunle and Omoyele Sowore, who published earlier versions of a few of the essays as op-eds on their websites, *Nigeriavillagesquare.com* and *Saharareporters.com.* Without that initial gesture, many of those short essays may never have seen the light of day, let alone transition into longer, more developed chapters of this volume.

Dr. Farooq Kperogi helped me to refine, revise, and nurture many of the thoughts that went into these essays or crystallized in the positions expressed in them. He listened to my loud thinking, contributed his own informed opinions, and added nuance and clarity when I approached him with my evolving arguments. At other times, our numerous conversations on Nigeria, Africa, and global blackness spurred further thoughts and alerted me to new polemical and analytical possibilities. I am in his debt.

Other people who helped to sharpen my thoughts through critique, affirmation, or by offering sympathetic attention or supplying intellectual inspiration include Professor Toyin Falola, Professors Okpeh Okpeh Jnr., Dennis Dickerson, Thomas Schwartz, Devin Fergus, Trica Keaton, Pius Adesanmi, Steve Nwabuzor, Steven Pierce, Paul Zeleza, Douglas Anthony, Okey Ndibe, Clapperton Mavhunga, Peter Hudson, Adebayo Oyebade, Apollo Amoko, Clifton Crais, Edward Kissi, Mobolaji Aluko, Jemima Pierre, Shobana Shankar, Darren Kew, Fonkem Achankeng, and Jean Herskovits.

I thank all members of the USAfricadialogue discussion group, a vibrant community of scholars and intellectuals who daily discuss and debate African and African diaspora issues. Some of the contentions and ideas in these essays made their debut on that discussion list. I thank members who critiqued, corrected, expanded, and nuanced some of my contributions to the list, enabling me to see new analytical and polemical possibilities.

I need to acknowledge the informal contributions of intellectual interlocutors and friends to this book. Ikhide Ikheloa, Mohammed Dahiru Aminu, Rudolf Okonkwo, Adagbo Onoja, Joan Osa Oviawe, John Mbugua Gakau, Abdulrahman Muhammad, Abiodun Adamu, Emmanuel Taeger, Kanayo Odoe, Samaila Yandaki, Abdullahi Sken Ogu, Hyacinth Odogujeh, Monday Onwe, Aliyu Ma'aji, Basil Ugochukwu, Abdulaziz Abdullahi, and many others made comments or responded to my musings in ways that, unknown to them, prompted further thoughts and reflections that influenced the accents and slants in some of the essays. Some of the aforementioned inspired me by simply being good, listening friends. Okibe Agbese and Lucky Onmonya, intellectuals in their own rights, offered a diverse array of support to me during the period and process of this book's maturation.

Jonathan Hansen helped me with early proofreading and formatting. Carol A. Kennedy carried out further proofreading on the emerging manuscript.

I thank all three anonymous reviewers for offering comments, critiques, and suggestions. They did not just offer comments; they made it easy for me to implement and incorporate these comments into the manuscript by pointing to specific areas and essays needing revision and improvement.

The editor in chief at Diasporic Africa Press (DAP), Professor Kwasi Konadu, and his editorial board embraced this book enthusiastically from the time I pitched it to them. This enthusiasm never waned as the book made its way from rough manuscript through revisions and, finally, to a clean copy awaiting publication. Their support and interest in the book gave me energy and motivation that were instrumental in this multi-stage process.

My wife, Margaret, daughters, Ene and Agbenu, and other members of my immediate and extended family played various direct and indirect motivational roles in seeing this book to fruition. In the spirit of Ubuntu, I say: I am because they are.

INTRODUCTION

OF AFRICA'S FRAGMENTS AND POLEMICS

I have reflected over the last decade on several aspects of Nigeria's postcolonial nationhood, on Nigeria's place within the African postcolonial fabric, and on the positions and fates of Africans, continental and diasporic, in a globalizing world. This volume is a compilation of a select group of these reflections.

Thinking about these three interwoven entities has produced ideas and positions, both abstract and instrumental. These ideas had a long mental incubation period before they made it into text, before I expressed them in any written form. I wrestled for many years with the question of sharing them beyond the casual circuits of Internet discussion forums and published opinion editorials. Many of the ideas and positions expanded with time and further thought, outgrowing the space of the op-ed and demanding a more systematized platform of existence. The book medium, with its connotations of seriousness and depth, and with its power to assemble and unite seemingly disparate bodies of writing, suggested itself as the best mechanism for inviting the world into these engagements with Nigeria, Africa, and the tensions and instabilities of global Africanity.

The topics covered in the essays include corruption and poverty; the impact of foreign aid on Africa; postcolonial nation building; the structure of the Nigerian state; the debate on African participation and possible complicity in the slave trade; the challenges of democracy in Africa; postcolonial African migration to the West; relations between African Africans and African immigrants in the United States; African Islam and Islamic extremism; Arab–African relations; and more.

These essays contain deep personal ruminations, well-considered opinions, and rigorous analyses and arguments about many of Nigeria's, Africa's and global Africans' challenges and opportunities. I used my skill as a scholar, teacher, researcher, and commentator to construct the analyses and arguments in the following essays. As a result, the imprints of these forms of intellectual engagement can be found in all the essays. These essays have been written in a deliberately free-flowing style and without a strict adherence to the protocols of academic writing. There are few footnotes and citations in this volume, and the progression of the prose is, in most of the essays, punchier than the erudite language of academic writing. I have made this conscious decision because I want the essays to have a didactic, provocative, and instrumental effect rather to simply inform and document. Yet, I want them to be substantive enough for scholars to engage with. This dual ambition of producing a text that is accessible to a general public but rich enough for academic engagement shapes—or plagues—the following essays. The approach is experimental, and so its success and failure should be judged with this caveat and disclaimer in mind.

Neither Africa (continental and diasporic) nor Nigeria is a settled conceptual or geographical entity, and that, precisely, is the point of the interrogations and arguments articulated in these essays. I have attempted to pry open the multiple issues confronting Nigerians, continental Africans, and global Africans in a way that compels readers to grapple with the questions posed and to ask their own questions. Many of these questions remain unresolved in these essays; others led me to advance new ways of approaching old problems, and to offer alternative modes of thought. Throughout, the overriding aim is to complicate our understanding of these issues and problems where there appears to be an oversimplification, and to simplify what has been overcomplicated.

Many of the essays in this manuscript have had other lives, having been published previously for smaller audiences and on narrower online and print platforms. I have revised and expanded most of them to update their content, to accommodate my own evolving positions, and to supply more informational backdrops and contexts for the benefit of nonspecialist audiences. Other essays are interventions written from scratch on topics I had wrestled with from time to time, but on which I had not previously been able to articulate publishable positions.

Several of the topics that these essays deal with are controversial and are routinely debated in the fields of Nigerian, African, and African diaspora history, culture, politics, and economics. Controversy and immediacy, as well as a hybrid of the two, are not only suited to the medium of rigorous scholarly research and writing; they sometimes demand a treatment rooted in the punchy intervention of the essay. In this medium, one can take extrapolative liberties for the purpose of polemical emphasis, and in order to clearly delineate the terrain of argumentation and contrast.

Africa's myriad of both depressing and uplifting realities inspire deep thinking that often manifests itself in punditry, oral or written. It is in this spirit of debating Africa and her issues and of questioning received and familiar explanations that these essays were conceived and written. As the most populous constituent of Africa, Nigeria invites lamentations and impassioned discussions on its familiar challenges and on the state of its troubled union. These reflections have often congealed naturally into a discussion of how Nigerians and Africans and their interests, mobility, and anxieties have become globalized, mirroring the interconnections of an increasingly wired world and the increased solidarities of race, common experience, and marginality between peoples with varying connections to the continent of Africa.

These connections, the conditions and narratives that they have spawned, and the peoples and communities that embody them are what I have termed *global Africanity*, for the purpose of analytical convenience. This globalization of Africa has intensified as Africa's woes, tensions, and triumphs have spilled over, literally and metaphorically, and have come to dominate global agendas, aided in part by the emergence of new, vibrant diasporas of voluntary immigrants, who not only vigorously engage with the continent but also demand reckoning and a stake in its future. Mapped onto old communities birthed by exile and the Atlantic slave trade, these new, emergent diasporas disrupt our definitions and understandings of notions of blackness, Africanness, and intra-racial interactions. What's more, as Nigerians, Africans, and diasporic Africans of different national and cultural affinities have moved between and within spaces defined as African, they have carried with them new technologies and vocabularies for talking about the problems and predicaments of people they see as their kind.

These discussions are often rancorous, loud, and even combative, ensuring that no Africanist or African intellectual can stand aside in observational neutrality and under the pretense of being a detached scholar. Every Africanist and African scholar, indeed every African, is a pundit on Africa's many issues, whether they consciously embrace that status or not. They are reservoirs of opinions and positions on African affairs and often only need to be prompted for their inner pundit to emerge. And every African intellectual in the West is inevitably called upon, now and then, to debate and ponder the many crises and predicaments that confront their individual countries, the African continent at large, and global blackness generally. My journey to the reflections contained in this book began similarly, as I yielded sporadically over the years to the internal and external urges to try to make some sense of Nigeria, Africa, and global blackness.

The function of an essay collection is to compress topics of longstanding and ongoing debates into easy-to-read and digestible pieces, giving an overview of the various positions through description, explanation, and analysis, and building a clear set of arguments belonging to the author. An essay text is also sometimes the nonspecialist's entry point into complex academic fields and into hotly debated issues. This is the spirit in which *Africa in Fragments* has been written.

The challenge then is to provide insight, overview, and arguments in ways that are profound enough to inspire further thought but not so reductive as to "dumb down" a complex topic. Articles in an essay reader of this nature free the author to use informal writing techniques—such as employing the first-person narrative, mixing the casual, the experiential, and the anecdotal with techniques and skills derived from formal academic reflection and training. The essays in this volume follow that tradition. Essays are also avenues for offering solutions and interventions to analyzed problems in a deliberately instrumental way. This imperative, too, runs through most of the essays. They do not shy away from prescriptive and didactic conclusions. In several, I simultaneously wear the hat of an analyst and that of a concerned African thinking aloud about how to make the world better for Africa, Africans, and global African communities, and how to improve the place of Africans in a complex, rapidly evolving world.

As a scholar of Africa and as a Nigerian, I often think about Nigeria and Africa. Many of these thoughts and the manner in which they occur to me involve me intimately in what I seek to understand, analyze, and explain, an intellectual relationship that is best expressed through the liberal and liberating medium of the analytical and polemical essay. On some levels, however, these scattered thoughts are no less important, no less provocative, and no less rigorous than my more esoteric academic outputs on Africa and Nigeria, outputs possessing obvious markers of formal academic prose, rigid citation techniques, and a methodical, narrative style.

The essays in this volume display the enduring tensions between the three geographical and conceptual entities covered here. The commentaries contain informational backdrops that may serve the purposes of information and reference. This combination of polemical argumentation and analysis on the one hand and narrative and informational description on the other resulted in a hybrid that straddles the lines between a position paper, a think piece, and an op-ed—with a sprinkling of academic rhetorical and methodological ingredients. Even my emotional investments in the travails and triumphs of Africa come through in some of these essays, a style of engagement that is consistent with this unabashedly intimate and polemical style.

The veneration of nuance and complexity, sometimes for their own sake, in more formal methods of intellection is unsuited for and would harm the flowing argumentative analysis of the following essays. The beauty of this style is flexibility, malleability, and an improvisational fluidity derived from the nature of the topic and what one wants to say about it. Accordingly, these essays employ nuance and complexity when the topic calls for them, but I strive for simple, digestible and even essentialist terms of analysis when that format helps clarify the topic or my position on it. I bring more complexity and nuance to Nigerian and African phenomena that have been oversimplified, and simplify topics that have been overcomplicated by a desire to intellectualize and render in specialized jargon what can be effectively presented in fairly simple terms. My aim is to alternately disturb both formal and popular understandings of some of the issues pertaining to the ongoing struggle for the souls of Nigeria, Africa, and Africa's multiple diasporas.

For the general audience of casual Nigeria and Africa enthusiasts and for the instrumentally minded community of NGOs, college students, interested Africans and Nigerians, and others who desire a more accessible rendering of some of the major debates on Nigeria and Africa's political and social predicaments, this volume serves as an introduction to a more specialized dimension of engagement. My aim has been to produce a reading experience that provokes as much as it instructs or informs.

Another disclaimer on style is in order. The reflections herein are at times autobiographical. I consciously embraced these autobiographical intrusions, as evidenced by first-person narration and personal ruminations in some of the essays. Yet ultimately, all writings are autobiographical. This means that our writings are unconscious extensions of our deeply personal thought processes, informed opinions, experiences, anxieties, and priorities. Our intellectual engagements are constituted not just by our formal professional training but also by our learned opinions, our experiential insights, and our shifting identities. The essay medium is particularly suited to this flexible, intimate narrative style, allowing an exchanged between the personal and the external.

The next aspect of the text that bears clarifying is the title. I do not intend to present Africa as a fragmented entity of peoples, places, and conditions any more than similar designations break down into smaller units of analysis or fracture further into a multiplicity of identities and signifiers. Primarily, I use the concept of fragments to suggest that Africa is a fragmented entity, understood to mean different things to different people. Africa is often reduced to its topical and geographical parts in popular discourse. Africa is approached through the issues and debates that routinely surface in regard to the continent, its people, or realities. These are fragments that, taken together, constitute meanings that come to define Africa in the minds of many. On one level Africa's fragments can be understood in starkly geographical terms. In this scenario Nigeria functions as one important fragment of the continental and diasporic entity baptized with the moniker of "Africa." On another level, Africa is an umbrella conceptual abstraction that conjures up multiple topics and phenomena. The familiar topical fragments of Africa are intensely contested and debated and include democracy, corruption, conflict, race, migration, postcolonial dysfunction, ethno-religious intolerance, bad governance, and intra-African tensions—all of which this book covers. The organizational challenge of *Africa in Fragments*, a challenge that is admittedly not fully overcome, is the meshing of Africa's geographic and topical fragments.

Nigeria cannot stand in for Africa—that much is clear. But Nigerians are a subset of Africans, the Nigerian diaspora a subset of a growing diaspora of postcolonial migration. Many essays in this book either are entirely set in Nigeria or display a Nigerian slant. Yet several of those essays are analyzed in a continental context, and discussions of Nigeria are extrapolated to speak to or to benefit from wider African trends. The challenge for me was to transition from this Nigeria-centric set of commentaries to African and diasporic issues, and also to bring Nigerian issues and Nigerian conditions into the same framework as the broader issues of Africa, its sociopolitical debates, and its place in the world. This tension between Africa's topical and geographic constituents defies and resists arbitrary resolution and is thus often left hanging in the text, inviting readers to see or question the cohesion between Nigeria and Nigeria-specific issues on the one hand and broader issues of continental and diasporic significance on the other.

The concept of Africa as fragments also has an obvious literal dimension. African peoples, cultures, realities, and struggles are located in multiple, fragmented spaces and in multiple narratives of identity. So profound is this conceptual and physical scattering that even the notion of an authentic cultural core in Africa that is reconstituted elsewhere in the diaspora is problematic, since sites of authenticity, however defined, and signs of hybridity, cosmopolitanism, intersections, and reinventions can be found in both Africa and in global African communities.

STRUCTURE OF THE BOOK

The book is divided into two sections. Section One—approximately half of the book—focuses on Nigeria. This first section is subdivided into two parts. The first contains essays and commentaries on Nigeria's precarious postcolonial politics, particularly its struggles with constitutional, electoral, identity, citizenship, resource, structural, and ethical questions. Essays in this section refuse to take Nigeria as a given. Instead, they interrogate the constitutional, structural, economic, and political architectures of the postcolonial Nigerian state, critiquing a troubled status quo, and in a few essays, pointing the way to a healthier union—or, failing that, a rethinking of the union itself. The second one tackles a number of sociocultural issues that are in the realm of everyday discourse, even if they bear tangential relationships to the realm of politics.

Section Two focuses on matters relating to continental Africa, the larger world of global Africanity, diaspora realities and tensions, and Africa's place in a globalizing neoliberal world. This section of the book includes an essay on Nigeria's Nollywood film industry. Although the essay is not wholly, empirically focused on Africa and explores some geographically neutral questions, it is relevant to how we understand key concepts that feature in debates on Africa's developmental predicament—productivity versus consumption, mediocrity versus excellence, value versus devaluation, and sophisticated aesthetic creativity versus crass aesthetic commercialization.

As diverse as the following essays may appear to be, their common thread is the idea that polemical engagement with Africa can both break down ubiquitous misunderstandings and stereotypes of Africa while making Africa and all its complexities and unsettled meanings accessible to a wider audience.

Africa is a place, a thing, a concept, a set of images, modes of acting, and ways of seeing—in short, Africa is many things, concrete and conceptual. In positing Africa and one of its important constituents, Nigeria, as fragments and as contested conditions, my objective is to open the term "Africa" and its constitutive elements up to be reinterpreted and understood differently. The provocative essays in *Africa in Fragments* will disturb some of the familiar tropes that are routinely deployed to make sense of Nigeria, Africa, and the global Africanity spawned by the forced and voluntary mobility of black bodies and things around the world. If this disruption culminates in productive debates and new controversies on Nigeria, Africa, and global Africanity, the objective of this book will have been accomplished.

The chapters are uneven in length. There is a simple, organizational reason for this. Some of the topics discussed here lend themselves to a punchy analytical and polemical treatment. The essays on these topics are necessarily short, and the emphasis in those essays is more on the argument than on the universe of information and events in which the argument is being made. In these essays, theses require little setup because the contours of the topic are generally well known. Other essays focus on topics that are so complex or so unfamiliar as to require elaborate research, background information, and techniques of foregrounding and contextualizing that are common in scholarly articles. The resulting movement from scholarly to polemical analysis, and sometimes the mixture of the two, add to the book's intellectual variety.

A NOTE ON TERMS AND TERMINOLOGY

Given that many of the terms I use in these essays have contested histories, etymologies, and political and intellectual uses today, it is important to clarify the sense in which my analyses invoke them. Take the term *black*. This is a term that is understood somewhat differently on the African continent, where it is often used in localized conversation to denote no more than skin pigmentation or as a descriptive term denoting self-identity in relation to those understood to be pigmented differently. This definition and understanding of blackness is different from understandings privileged in African diasporic settings where blackness has a valence and import beyond physical description, often connoting more than skin-deep identities, consciousness, and claims. Even so, in some parts of Africa, such as the Sudan, South Sudan, Mauritania, and other areas in the so-called Afro–Arab borderlands, a fairly politically charged understanding of blackness exists, and *black* carries political and social connotations that shape social relations and narratives of power, oppression, and victimhood. My copious use of the term in the second section of this book should thus be understood in the narrow contexts in which it occurs—contexts that determine what the term means and does not mean.

Similarly, what constitutes the African diaspora is not a settled question, since there are several types of diasporas and several diasporic political, economic, and cultural imaginations. Early African diasporic demographics are generally understood to have been produced and constituted by a multiplicity of factors; in Asia mainly by trade, labor migration, forms of servitude, and colonial military service; in Europe by enslavement and voluntary migration; and in the Americas mainly by slavery. Today, however, many other diasporas have emerged, products largely of strategic migrations and voluntary professional or existential mobility as well as economic and political displacement. Obviously, these multiple diasporas seep into one another, creating tensions; but they also mesh productively at important intersections. These intersections have made sharp distinctions between Africa and its diaspora increasingly difficult to sustain. Institutional and political practices that compel solidarity between and among divergent black communities and increasingly common personal, marital, and organizational connections between different self-proclaimed African communities make distinctions between, say, African Americans and African immigrants increasingly complicated. Moreover, on the continent of Africa itself and in many African nations, there are, and have always been, large diasporas of forced and voluntary ethnic and religious exiles who have helped to intermittently redefine the concepts of home, homeland, and even the idea of a motherland from which the idea of diaspora derives its meaning.

Given these realities, the notion of a native-born black American that I deploy in at least one essay in this book is a much more complex one than my polemical analysis might suggest; for at what point does an immigrant qualify for the symbolic and tangible privileges of native-born blackness? In the United States and in other parts of the Americas, slave ancestry is understood as the fulcrum of natal black identity—and sensibility—but one might ask whether a non-slave-descended black person of any origin could assimilate to this group even in an honorary capacity.

These are important intellectual questions that often get lost in passionate intra-racial conversations on authentic black consciousness and identity. The questions implicitly posit the trouble with trying to police bounded communitarian identities within the broad community of black people who come from multiple historical and cultural origins. They also implicitly suggest possibilities for bridging and dissolving intra-racial boundaries of identity and consciousness. Yet to elevate these possibilities above the powerful, quotidian, and ubiquitous intra-racial dichotomies and tensions through which people of African descent understand and critique one another is to deny the on-ground sociopolitical consequences of charged nomenclatures of difference. Since my aim in these essays is to intervene in debates that deploy these problematic terms, my analysis is largely faithful to the dichotomous and differentiating techniques, meanings, and terms that inform and underpin these intra-racial debates.

Another term that occurs here requires clarification. *Extremism*, as a word and as a category, is laden with misunderstanding and ambiguity. Islamic extremism is a foil that I rely on for at least one of the essays in this volume, although I use it interchangeably with the term heterodoxy. However, the question of who is an extremist Muslim and, for our purpose, an extremist African Muslim, defies a clear-cut resolution, since departure from doctrinal mainstreams and interpretive orthodoxy does not by itself make one an extremist. Moreover, "extremist" is often a term of contempt used by dominant religious or political orthodoxies to refer to marginal or insurgent groups. Furthermore, this type of labeling is often a practice of devaluation that fails to account for the historical processes by which certain previously heterodox and "extreme" theologies and sects gain ascendance, become the orthodox, mainstream system, and proceed to render previously dominant doctrinal corpuses marginal.

In discussing Islamic extremism in Nigeria and Africa then, the point of departure for me is not to reinforce the doctrinal tyranny of an African Muslim mainstream and its claims to religious truth, or to suggest that there is unanimity and homogeneity in African Islamic practice, which is being intermittently threatened from the outside by doctrines that violate and reject the tenets of this "African Islam." Rather, the point of positing an African Islamic baseline is to underline the fact that, given the status of certain theological consensuses in Africa and the widespread provenance of certain established doctrines, practices, and institutions of Islam in Africa, theological claims that depart from these and propose disruptive and radical heterodoxies are bound to be perceived as extreme, and their adherents isolated as dangerous extremists. Often these heterodox sects and theologies live up to those designations not because they are inherently dangerous or violent, but because in the struggle for power, visibility, and the commanding echelons of religious authority, these insecure, fringy heterodox groups often feel that they have no chance outside the use of threats, spectacular violence, and intolerance. The use of these instruments of coercion and intimidation then reinforces the claims to pacifism, order, stability, and tolerance by the mainstream, further marking out the insurgents as extremist, nihilist outliers.

In view of these declared nuances, the debated terms used in this book to designate groups, phenomena, and ideologies should be considered provisional and specific only to the polemical and analytical contexts in which I have used them.

A SYNOPTIC SURVEY

The first chapter of this book weighs in on the recurring question of Nigeria's fragility, its well-known vulnerability to dismemberment. Africa's most populous country has overcome existential threats to its organic wellbeing before, surviving a brutal three-year civil war. In the last two decades, however, the old questions about the superficiality and brittleness of the union have been intermittently posed as familiar contradictions, and tensions have escalated into alarming fissures.

Citizens and foreign observers are worried that a combination of lingering grievances among constituents and self-inflicted political and economic injuries might torpedo the country, and along with it, damage the stabilizing symbolic and instrumental effects that a large, united Nigerian nation has on Africa. The country is besieged by a proliferating constellation of grievances from its various units, and previously taboo questions about the continued existence of the nation are now being openly broached. Underpinning this existential crisis, I argue in the chapter, is a fundamental question of the failure of the Nigerian state to fulfill the diverse aspirations of its constituent units, leading to disaffection, separatism, and the imagining of alternative geopolitical spaces and structural arrangements.

The chapter argues that the instinctive reaction of the invested Nigerian political elite to this growth of separatist agitation, which is to dismiss, disavow, or crush the proponents of breakup and local autonomy, is the wrong approach. In contrast to this elite intolerance for legitimate disaffection, the chapter makes a set of arguments, namely that if managed properly centrifugal and separatist sentiments can have a refining, corrective impact on a fractured, troubled nation like Nigeria; that the troubles of Nigeria are traceable to the arbitrary colonial logic of its founding, which was carried over to independence; and that until Nigerians reinvent a new logic and purpose for their union to accommodate the diverse aspirations of the country's many nations—what I call the logic of functionality—the country will continue to teeter without purpose, perpetually dysfunctional and on the brink.

This chapter's contentions have obvious implications for the rest of Africa. These continental ramifications and the proliferating phenomenon of intra-national self-determination movements are taken up in the last chapter of the book. That chapter contends that African states facing similar existential threats and questions ought to disavow the Nigerian model of declaring the union an inviolable starting point of national structural and constitutional reform. Instead, they should be willing to pose questions about the functionality and legitimacy of the state itself. It is the right thing to do, the two chapters argue, even if, in some instances, it might produce a situation in which the state presides over its own partial or complete dissolution. African states should regard postcolonial political geographies, inherited economic paradigms, and colonially imposed constitutional orders as compromised transitional inevitabilities of rigged decolonization processes, not as sacred foundations for nation building.

In this business of reconfiguring the postcolonial state to make it more accommodating to the mutating aspirations of Africans, two interrelated problems need to be deconstructed, understood, and resolved. This is the argument of Chapter 26. The first problem is that Africa harbors several long-held but effectively ignored sub-nationalist aspirations. The second is the reality that there seems to be a growing fetish of the nation-state as a final, vertical end-point of political organization.

Two essays, Chapters 2 and 15, deal with the knotty issue of corruption and its role in the stunted economic trajectories and destinies of African countries and peoples. Corruption is a debilitating challenge standing in the way of African countries realizing their economic and political potentials, and corruption discourses, whether instrumental, explanatory, or polemical, are right to point to its toll on the humanities and economies of Africa. However, corruption, like other vices, can become a self-propelling, self-fulfilling obsession, generating mass hysteria, sensation, and self-righteous hyperbole where clarity and understanding are needed.

In the hands of internal and external entities who stand accused of ruining the economic and sociopolitical aspirations of African societies, corruption can transform from a universally despised vice to a tool of deflection. In this context, noise and lamentations about corruption in Africa can overpower sober efforts to isolate and understand the range of conditions, practices, and actions that the charge of corruption can explain, and those that it cannot. Such is the status of corruption in the explanatory toolkit of analysts, scholars, and policymakers that it now functions as an all-in-one explanation for all that is wrong with Africa—a trope invoked to explain a complex, polyvalent African crisis, of which corruption is only one aspect.

Corruption is now the go-to excuse for a number of actors who themselves may be implicated in the African developmental and political conundrum, deepening the problem of meaning and definitional clarity underlined above. Given the ubiquity of the corruption-as-alibi phenomenon, we can no longer be sure what corruption means in regard to Africa. And given the plethora of contexts and situations in which the term is deployed, the need to clarify what actually qualifies as corruption becomes a foundational task in identifying corrective actions and in advocacy. Such is the misuse of the term that even those Africans who are patently corrupt and are called to account routinely summon the idiom of corruption to explain their circumstances, even attributing their comeuppance to corruption! This conceptual confusion makes corruption one of the most abused terms in contemporary Africa. Needless invocation and de-contextualized usage has rendered the term almost meaningless, begging the question of what it is that we are designating when we say, "There is so much corruption in Africa," or in Nigeria.

The two chapters on corruption in this volume take up these questions from different angles. Chapter 2 calls attention to two growing problems of corruption discourse in Africa: the ways in which loyalties and affinities take precedence over legal and policy definitions in determining attitudes to corruption in Nigeria; and the depressingly negative impact of what I call a numerical quagmire on Nigerians' appreciation of the enormity of the corruption problem plaguing their country. This latter point revolves around a basic argument: that corruption, far from generating more outrage as its incidence increases, has the capacity to instead generate apathy, disengagement, indifference, misunderstanding, and thus civil society inertia. In other words, the very conditions that corruption creates, namely mass numerical and financial illiteracy, and the existential grind of daily survival tend to either numb citizens to public corruption or make it impossible for them to fully understand the enormous monetary figures involved in the scandals. Lacking the fiscal aptitude to make sense of huge amounts of stolen money and their social opportunity costs, citizens become generally apathetic and thus incapable of working up the outrage to challenge the problem.

For its part, Chapter 15 grapples with many of the myths, stereotypes, and pathologies that are recycled in the corruption discourse. It changes the trajectory of debates and discussions on corruption in Africa by arguing that instead of focusing on and obsessing over its frequency, a discussion which often descends into lazy pathologies and cynical, conscience-assuaging

Afropessimism, it is more productive to focus on the moral consequences of corruption in Africa, which are the very reasons that we care or should care about corruption on the continent in the first place.

In focusing on the opportunity costs and the social consequences of corruption rather than on its sensational appearances in local and international discussions, the two chapters underline two points. One is that corruption's greater toll on the common good in Africa is the proper locus of outrage, not an alleged but unproven notion that Africans are more likely to be corrupt. The other point is that until Africans affected by corruption's moral consequences come to fully understand and appreciate the tragic scope of the fiscal and social toll of corruption, the local moral momentum needed to defeat it will remain elusive.

Chapter 19 wades through the dead-end debate about whether or not Africans participated in the Atlantic slave trade, a debate reignited by Professor Henry Louis Gates's *New York Times* op-ed on the subject. Rather than dwell on the "participation or no participation" question, I identify and argue the implications of specific roles that certain groups on the African side played in the trade; the many contemporary implications of these past entanglements in the trade; the need for specificity in assigning participatory agency; the contemporary politics of slave trade denialism and victimhood in Africa; the differing politics of archiving and memory on the slave trade; and the messy business of restitution.

Controversial as it was, if Professor Gates's intervention in this debate has had any benefit, it is that it has awakened us to the marginalization of the histories and narratives of victimhood that have been percolating among the African communities repeatedly raided for slaves by more powerful African states and neighbors, as well as the ways in which this silencing is helped by the descendants of these powerful African kingdoms and states, who disavow their ancestors' participation in slave raids. Because of the unintended consequence of Gates's op-ed, those who are interested in a full accounting of Africans' role in and victimization by the Atlantic slave economy now have

a vast field of neglected and silenced African narratives of enslavement to explore.

Chapter 22 interrogates the relationship between African
immigrants in the US and African Americans, working from the
analytically useful but admittedly narrow definitions of "African
immigrant" and "African American." The chapter examines the
sources of intra-racial tensions, arguing that much of the friction between the two black communities in the United States
stems from the internalization of stereotypes of otherness and
difference that have little basis in reality and are at best exag-
gerations and simplifications of benignly commonplace realities.
In addition, I contend that the relationship is not one that sur-
vives on its own relational momentum but that it is mediated
by a complex process of external media narratives, portrayals,
stereotypes, and by the strategic and shifting consciousness of
African Americans and immigrant blacks in white society. The
relationship between the two communities is in short over-de-
termined by what one, following Tejumola Olaniyan, may call
a system of "external switchboards," whereby powerful forces
outside both communities inject self-fulfilling and powerful
narratives into how the two groups perceive each other.[1] These
perceptions then become ubiquitous, charge up the atmosphere
in which relations between the two communities occur, and become, for good measure, the baseline from which African Americans and immigrant blacks approach or relate with one another.

Other misperceptions abound in—and about—the African
world, with serious consequences. Africa can be misunderstood
in many ways. This misunderstanding is perpetuated by strategic intention and by ignorance. Misunderstanding can sometimes take the form of feel-good narratives about avuncular, redemptive Western interventions in Africa. Nowhere is this type
of narrative more intense than in the vast world of Western aid
and development practice. Chapter 23 explodes some of the
more popular aspects of these false Western aid narratives, such
as the notions that aid is free money given to African countries
by altruistic Western governments and institutions, that Western countries dedicate a significant percentage of their budgets
to aid in Africa, that aid does not benefit the giving country, and
that aid is undeserved and useless in Africa.

Contrary to these popular myths, the chapter argues that aid is not only deserved as a token restitutive gesture for hundreds of years of Western-inflicted economic and sociopolitical injuries on Africa; it is actually ultimately more beneficial to the so-called donor countries in the West than to the receiving African countries. What's more, there is a dual and somewhat contradictory Western narrative that perpetuates these myths of Western altruism and of African countries as undeserving basket cases.

One aspect of this narrative is the tiresome argument, advanced in different guises, genres, and by different authors in the growing Western Afropessimism industry, that Western governments' aid has been frittered away by African governments with nothing to show for it. It is not that this argument is entirely untrue. It is rather the fact that the argument conveniently neglects the self-interested reasons why Western countries give aid to governments with demonstrably leaky hands and known records of colluding with Western allies to transfer stolen money into private bank accounts in Western banks.

The other aspect is the self-serving sensationalizing of Western do-gooder interventions in Africa—the need to be seen to be "helping" a distressed continent. Western critics of aid to Africa, especially those on the political right, want to have it both ways. They are eager to advertise for domestic and global image points ongoing projects purportedly designed to save Africans from themselves and from the alleged dangers of their natural and sociopolitical environment. Africa is the perfect foil to restate or reinforce the self-image of the West as altruistic and as an entity animated by Christian charity. Yet some of these same critics argue that Western aid to Africa is passé, a failed policy that merely subsidizes corruption, waste, and underdevelopment on the continent. For good measure, these narratives deny the complicity of Western actors and institutions in this aid-corruption-waste conspiracy.

I have surveyed only a few of the topics and essays contained in this book, drawing a few connections between chapters. The book may be read as a whole or the essays may be read separately. Either way, the connections between the chapters will be apparent. The point of having many essays in one book is that topical variety can coexist with coherence. Those looking for either will find it, and those looking for both will find them and devise the appropriate technique to maximize the benefit of the reading experience.

SECTION I

NIGERIA (NATION AND POLITICS)

CHAPTER 1

HOW NIGERIA CAN SURVIVE

In 2007, as part of the fifth-year anniversary of nigeriavillag-esquare.com, the popular Nigerian web forum's management organized a podcast on the theme of Nigeria and thankfulness. I called in to the show to share my thoughts on thankfulness and Nigeria and came away deeply impressed with the persistence of the Nigerian idea even among the critics of the country's broken politics and social dysfunction. It was a profoundly enriching experience, one that has caused me to contemplate one particular aspect of the discussion.

One of the panelists, Nigerian public commentator Rudolf Okonkwo asked a question that goes to the heart of every discussion on the viability of Nigeria as a nation-state. He wanted to know if there has been any country in history—African or not—that has experienced the same challenges of nationhood that Nigeria has been grappling with and has come out of it intact, with its spatial integrity and tropes of nationhood secure. It is a question that invites deep reflection on the meaning, trajectory, and evolution of nationhood itself. In one poignant question, Rudolf brought to our discussion the knotty contradiction of simultaneously celebrating Nigeria and acknowledging its brittleness.

A few moments of introspection led me to settle on Britain as the closest approximation of a nation-state forged in the crucible of uncertain nationalist trajectories. Britain is an instructive example of a country that has overcome centuries of turbulence, political uncertainties, and structural indeterminacy to forge a pragmatic and workable, if tense, union. Britain was Nigeria's colonizer. It is ironic therefore that one would advance it as a prototype of a troubled but functional political union. But the parallels between Britain's political history and Nigeria's are as remarkable as the differences between the two countries.

The British have not always been a coherent, organic nation. In many ways, they are still not, as the ongoing discussions of Scottish independence demonstrate. Ask many Northern Irish citizens of Britain and they will tell you that Britain is an imposition that hardly approximates their aspirations for nationhood. For a long time, the idea of Great Britain was neither great nor even British. Others first saw the British as British before they saw themselves in those terms. As is the case with Nigeria, there is nothing natural about Britain. Yet, somehow, Britain is a nation that works for its constituents.

A small, vulnerable island, Britain was invaded and ruled for many centuries by the Romans. The "pagan" Saxons invaded in the fifth century from the Nordic plains. It was the commingling of the Saxons and semi-autochthonous "Angles" that produced the compound ethnic category of Anglo-Saxons, which some people today take for granted as the foundational ethnicity of England. Englishness, at least in its original narrow incarnation, was forged in these circumstances of invasion and acculturation. Even this process was marked by vicious, bloody wars between factions of the Saxon invaders, as well as between the Saxons and the English kingdoms on the island. The wars between the English kingdoms and Saxon invaders were as much over differences in religion and culture as they were over territory. From this historical reality, a nation seemed unimaginable.

Britain knew neither peace nor a discernible geopolitical trajectory for the next six centuries. The French invaded in the eleventh century, grafting yet another cultural influence onto the Anglo-Saxon tradition. Also inhabiting parts of the same island were the Welsh and the Scottish. Both were fiercely anti-English in their ways. Given this ethno-linguistic and religious chaos, a nation seemed impossible to imagine, let alone build.

When the French withdrew or were defeated (depending on which version of the history you believe), the momentary political unity that coalesced in the struggle against French imperialism was replaced by a retreat to the animosities and insular solidarities of old.

I have, of course, taken some temporal and empirical liberties with British history here, but the outline is basically correct. In fact, the British, like Nigerians, could never agree among themselves about which political system or national religion to adopt—or whether to adopt a national religion at all. Oliver Cromwell's effort to settle these questions through an antimonarchist revolution plunged Britain into a civil war. Britain is still a country divided about the role and influence of the monarchy, and by the Catholic–Protestant divide, which is a direct result of its encounters with Roman Catholicism and the Reformation.

The parallels between Nigeria and Britain are instructive. Like Britain, Nigeria was colonized. Nigerians, like Britons, share a common memory of resisting foreign colonial invaders and of being oppressed by these invaders. Like Britain, the nation-space called Nigeria was by and large bequeathed by and consummated through the self-interested actions of foreign invaders and imperial powers. Like the British, Nigerians argue eternally about what form of government to adopt to satisfy most of the country's constituents. Like the British, Nigerians duel about how to structure the relationship between the various ethno-national regions that constitute the country.

Like Britain, which is effectively a confederacy of several nations—Northern Ireland, Wales, Scotland, and England—Nigeria is a country of many nations, with each one striving to define its relationship to the tenuous symbols of Nigerian nationhood, and to maintain its residual cultural and political autonomy in the face of an increasingly unitary Nigerian state. Like the British, Nigerians argue about whether to adopt a national religion and about whether the Nigerian state can or should remain a neutral arbiter in religious matters. The Catholic–Protestant debate in Britain is just as volatile and as occasionally bloody as the Christian–Muslim divide in Nigeria.

Like Britain, Nigeria fought a devastating civil war. The constituent units in Britain fought several civil wars throughout the nation's history. The passionate rejection of the "imposition" called Britain by some Irish and Scots is strikingly similar to the repudiation of the Nigerian "imposition" by many segments of the Nigerian populace, especially constituents such as the ethnicities of the Niger Delta and the Igbo, whose sacrifices for Nigeria clearly outweigh their rewards from and investments in it.

Like Nigerians, Britons received a defective national contraption that was designed more by the interests of a succession of external invaders than by the interests and aspirations of Britons. In turn the British colonizers crafted Nigeria purely to fulfill a British imperial administrative and economic imperative. The

African peoples who would constitute the nation had no say in its emergence. Nigeria, in short, emerged outside and in spite of the multiple nationalist aspirations of its many ethnic nations, just as Britain emerged largely outside the free volition of many of its constituent populations, and even against the aspirations of some.

Yet the British overcame these historical handicaps to build themselves a workable union that, however imperfectly, offers more belonging than alienation to its constituent units. At the risk of valorizing British nation building, the British saw this task as a necessity and subsequently worked hard at it. They decided to use the outline of a received "foreign" homogenizing imposition to evolve a nation-state that united English, Welsh, Scot, and Irish in one diverse commonwealth of mutually shared symbols and aspirations. They did this so well that not only did they build a great nation, but they used it as a springboard to conquer almost half of the world. You cannot go out to conquer and colonize other nations if you are not a nation yourself.

How did Britain do this and what lessons can Nigeria learn from its experience?

The British people first made one crucial decision: to be pragmatic about their nation-building effort. Despite the policies of the British government being tilted in favor of the English and harsh toward the Irish and to a lesser extent the Scots, the idea of one Britain thrives on the pragmatism of not destroying Welsh, Irish, English, or Scot identities and autonomies as a prerequisite for evolving a British nation-state. British nation builders consciously refused to see these ethno-national identities and aspirations as enemies of the emerging British nation; instead they saw them as essential components of an emerging Britain. This is a crucial difference between Britain and Nigeria, where a stealthy unitary impulse has crept into standard elite narratives of Nigerian statehood.

It was a sound premise from which the idea of a new, representative Britain sprouted and won adherents. The British eventually adopted a political structure that allowed each people to hold on to practices, cultures, institutions, resources, and developmental aspirations that were dear to them. But they all came together under the Union Jack and the crown to transact political business that was mutually beneficial. One of these items of business was that of empire building and colonization. There was something in it for everyone. The impoverished Irish needed jobs and economic lifelines and were all too happy to be sent to govern colonized territories in Africa, Asia, and the Caribbean on behalf of the British crown. Empire was a job-creating enterprise from the Irish perspective.

The Welsh, English, and Scots fulfilled their mercantile, careerist, and missionary aspirations by serving as Christian missionaries, administrators, traders, and extractors of raw materials in the colonies. Some people argue that the "dominant" English offloaded the Irish to the colonies to uproot a growing Irish disavowal of the "British imposition" at home, and thus mute Irish discontent. This may be true, but the Irish were eager to represent the crown in the colonies because they felt British enough to do so, and because they craved the benefits and recognition of Britishness. So, through a common nationalist endeavor, the Irish, Scots, English, and Welsh came to subscribe to a tenuous, constructed British national identity. They did so primarily because, artificial as it may be, this identity offered opportunities and benefits that narrow ethno-national political imaginations did not. Again, there was a tangible reward for everyone who participated in Britishness. In other words, British solidarity—British identity, if you like—bestowed rewards on those who bought into it.

Whatever its faults then, the British nation represents a pragmatic model of nationhood. It recognizes that for a nation to work, its constituents have to see it as beneficial to their interests and aspirations while not perceiving it as a threat to their culture. Such a nation cannot be imagined in opposition to pre-existing ethno-national identities; it has to be imagined as coexisting with them. The British Empire and its attractions are no more, but more Britons still believe in the "imagined community"[2] called Britain than do not. This is because the foundational principles of cultural, political, and fiscal autonomy and of inclusion remain intact, and because Britain rewards ethnic nationalities that offer it loyalty and patriotic energy.

Some Northern Irish and some Scots will continue to call for the dissolution of Great Britain, but the overwhelming majority will continue to believe that they have more invested in the British project than they are willing to give up.

The lessons for Nigeria here are many.

First, no nation is a given. A nation is what the people who desire it make of it. The British inherited a defective union, imposed largely by externally determined circumstances and adversity, but they worked at it until it became fairly workable. Unlike Nigerians, the British did not do this by becoming more unitary, homogenizing, or intolerant to ethno-nationalist aspirations. They did it by allowing the expression of the nationalist autonomies that predated the idea of Britain. Homogeneity—to the extent that it exists—followed logically as a voluntary pragmatic process that saw Irish, Scot, and Welsh assimilate willingly in various degrees into English culture. Although today some Britons decry what they see as English cultural and linguistic imperialism over the rest of Britain, it is generally not a sentiment that threatens to obliterate the entrenched solidarities of the British Isles.

For a nation to survive it must be more than a concept to its constituent ethno-regional units; it must approximate their interests and aspirations while allowing them considerable autonomy over fiscal, cultural, and political affairs. The British made Britain such a nation. Nigeria's solution, on the other hand, has been to terrorize and homogenize everyone into a shared national ethos underwritten by a unitary political system that brooks no centrifugal agitation. History has shown that this approach does not work. You cannot corral the enormous aspirational plurality of Nigeria into a bucket of false patriotism and declare that you have a nation. Such an approach is counterproductive. The Nigerian idea will sell itself and win voluntary ethno-national subscription only if it functions on material and symbolic levels for those whose humanity and territory it needs in order to command legitimacy.

Second, nations, as Benedict Anderson posits, are imagined communities, not natural occurrences. You work to build a nation-state; you do not take it for granted or expect it to evolve of its own inexorable volition. If you desire a nation, you have to work hard at it. No nation is a finished product. Nations are therefore being constantly reimagined to remain relevant to the evolving aspirations and interests of their constituents. This should be especially true for Nigeria, which was set up since independence to function not for its constituent units but for the interest of a small multiethnic political collective.

It is for this reason that I find the expression "the unity of Nigeria is nonnegotiable" ludicrous and dangerous. Only documented divine revelations like the Bible and the Quran are settled, nonnegotiable subjects. Even these canons of belief are subject to diverse interpretations. How much more then must inherited architectures and myths of the state be negotiated in a nation that was conceived and created by a foreign European power without soliciting the input of its peoples? Conversely, it is disingenuous and ahistorical to contend, as many Nigerians do, that there is no historical basis for Nigeria; there is. But this historical solidarity is not the God-ordained manifest destiny that some invested pseudo-patriots like to advance. It is manmade, the product of human agency, of relational dynamics and interactions that were carefully and deliberately developed in pre-colonial times by a succession of kingdoms and states in the Nigerian area. These dynamics were not always stable, and they were threatened and rejected at different historical junctures. Their outlines are, however, visible to open-minded observers.

Various Nigerian pre-colonial polities related with one another largely by choice, but sometimes by sub-imperial coercion. These relations embraced the economic, cultural, marital, religious, and political realms. But they were undergirded by choice and mutual consent for the most part. The notion that these associations rested on a natural, inexorable brotherhood of neighbors and Africans is a romantic and historically inaccurate rendering of the historical basis of Nigerian nationhood. Relationships between ethnic nations and even the internal cohesion of the ethnic nations themselves were constantly consciously reimagined and reoriented in a pragmatic recognition of changing priorities and aspirations. When the imposed national administrative community of the colonial state and its inchoate fostering of functional, expedient political unity are factored into this pre-colonial relational solidarities, what results is a fairly legitimate basis upon which a nation can be imagined and built.

Let us return, for a moment, to the dangerous myth of Nigeria's inevitability. On the face of it the rhetoric of non-negotiability sounds lofty. But it is actually quite dangerous; for it forecloses the process of nation building in its proper sense of crafting and re-crafting a nation until it is acceptable, however tentatively, to its constituents. Instead of clearing a rhetorical space for remaking and re-legitimizing the nation to respond to the evolving aspirations of its constituents, the rhetoric of non-negotiability rejects the tweaking of the union to make for a more acceptable nation-state. It is thus tyrannical in the sense that it forces those who do not or no longer believe in Nigeria to refrain from imagining alternatives or creative structural solutions to the dysfunctional status quo. It also impels fanatical, self-interested believers in the Nigerian project into a complacency that prevents them from appreciating the ways in which many constituencies are being alienated from the project by the convenient alliances of invested elites.

What's more, complacent, fanatical Nigerian patriotism dismisses and demonizes the separatist agitations of ethno-nationalist pressure groups instead of celebrating them for, if nothing else, serving to remind Nigerians of what is wrong with the union. Separatist agitations are, contrary to popular perception, instruments of nation building, for they reflect legitimate disaffection and disillusionment with the union and should be taken seriously as a point of departure for reforming the nation's political arrangement. Unlike Britain, Nigeria does not brook discourses of secession and separation. The British not only tolerate such discourses, they use them to remind themselves of how hard they need to work to preserve their troubled union.

Third, to repeat an earlier point, a nation will never be a final product, but is constantly remade in the interests of its constituents. A nation has to work to be relevant and to endure. The difference between Nigeria and Britain is not that Britain is a more coherent or logical nation than Nigeria. The difference is that Britain functions for its constituent ethno-nations—however imperfectly—and Nigeria does not. If we imagine a nation as a social contract, it is easy to conclude that Nigeria has failed to fulfill that contract and that Britain tries to do so, however incompletely. No matter how logical a nation is, an enduring failure to deliver the social benefits of nationhood will, in time, erode its legitimacy and undermine the loyalty of its constituents. When a nation is as troubled and as "unnatural" as Nigeria, the challenge is greater and the state needs to fulfill its social obligations with more vigor to sustain the loyalty of its units.

The British national idea was partly birthed by external aggression and British empire building. Nigeria does not need to invade or be invaded to craft a workable Nigerian union. Like the British, they need to be pragmatic in their national aspirations. That would entail the difficult decision of doing away with the de facto unitary composition of Nigeria. Nigeria is presently founded on an erroneous view of nations as incubators of sameness and homogeneity. Homogeneity is not a precondition for functional efficiency and legitimacy—the two most foundational ingredients for nation building. Britain and many other diverse countries have demonstrated this. Nigerian elites who parade a fanatical, dated notion of patriotism have continued to equate state legitimacy with homogeneity, common aspiration, developmental uniformity, and a forced repudiation of preexisting loyalties. It is a tragic mindset.

Nigerians can, like the British, use their common memory of colonial oppression and pre-colonial relations as a basis for re-negotiating a union that works and is acceptable and meaningful to Nigeria's many constituents.

CHAPTER 2

THE OTHER PROBLEMS OF CORRUPTION

Nigerians are right to agonize over corruption. It is the single most important reason their country is comatose and lacks the capacity to fulfill even the most modest duties of a government. It is the cause of much preventable death and suffering.

But ask the same Nigerians what they consider corruption and you get a muddled, confusing set of definitions and explanations. Their understandings of corruption are often circumscribed and hijacked by a myriad of factors: personal loyalty, ethnic solidarity, complicity, and politics.

Corruption, for Nigerians, is perpetrated only by those outside one's social and political circle. Indict someone closer home and copious caveats, alibis, nuances, and equivocations emerge to clutter the picture. The vices and practices often included under the rubric of corruption are routinely projected onto an array of Others, while coreligionists, ethnic kinsmen, family members, political allies, and benefactors are spared the stigma.

Naming is thus a central component of this amoral system. For if citizens cannot call corruption by its appropriate name consistently, regardless of place, time, context, and who is involved, how can it be fought? If Nigerians cannot forge a consensus—forget unanimity—on how to name corruption, if they cannot agree on the indicators of malfeasance, how can they settle on strategies for combating it? Naming is thus one of the foundational problems in Nigeria's struggle against corruption.

The other is the fact that Nigerians seem to have become so desensitized to, and have almost made peace with, certain kinds of corruption that they now consider "small," while many of them cannot adequately comprehend the kinds they call "large." This occasions a dual dissonance in which one kind of corruption is willfully ignored because it is seen as inconsequential and the other is misunderstood because its magnitude it so far beyond the register of everyday malfeasance.

WHAT IS CORRUPTION AND WHEN DOES IT OCCUR?

The most basic difficulty is that of naming acts as "corruption," a difficulty that routinely manifests itself in the familiar scandals that are a staple of government business in Nigeria. In 2012, President Goodluck Jonathan was caught in a self-confessed pay-to-play scandal. He announced at the commissioning of a renovated church in his hometown of Otuoke that a government construction contractor, an Italian construction company by the name of Gitto Construzion, had renovated the church as a gift to him. Adding to the audacity of this announcement, he revealed that he had in fact told the managing director of the firm about the poor state of the church, a clear hint to the latter to use his resources as a construction contractor to spruce it up.

I read the report of this scandal on saharareporters.com, nigeriavillagesquare.com, and other Nigeria-focused online news sources. The reports included direct quotes from reporters who covered the church commissioning service. There is no ambiguity there. This was a clear conflict of interest on display: a sitting president asked a government contractor to do him a favor, a favor that was eventually done.

You would think that Nigerians would rise in unison to denounce this brazen display of corruption. Not so. When I went to the comment section of the story on saharareporters.com, as I do when I want to gauge the reactions of Nigerians to unfolding events, I was shocked that some Nigerians—enough to reaffirm this central problem of naming—found some wiggle room to defend, rationalize, and confuse the scandal. I came away firm in my belief that some Nigerians have the depressing capacity to deny even the most egregious and obvious act of corruption.

In early 2012, Nigerians were treated to a theatrical display of a case of dishonor among thieves in the spectacularly bungled and badly conceived probe of the failures of the Nigerian Stock Exchange and its regulator, the Nigerian Securities and Exchange Commission (SEC). Public hearings conducted by a special committee of the National Assembly rapidly congealed into a set of revelations about the profligacy and vulgar indulgences of the SEC's chairperson, Ms. Arunma Oteh. Among other revelations, documents displayed by the House Committee on the Stock Market indicated that Oteh had gorged herself on a daily menu of delicacies averaging about eighty thousand naira (1 naira= $160) daily. She had also spent 30 million naira on hotel accommodations. At the very least, this was misuse of government resources, abuse of office, and gross financial mismanagement—in short, corruption. Was she remorseful? No. Instead, she boasted about sacrifices she was making on the job, "managing" with two cars instead of the five she had been promised!

You would think that Ms. Oteh's in-your-face corruption would attract the unanimous censure of Nigerians. Again, not so. Soon after the revelations and supporting documents were released, some Nigerians launched a full-scale defense of her actions on Nigeria's vibrant cyberspace. Loud and relentless, Oteh's defenders parried the damning scandal she engineered with a simple, repetitive mantra: Leave Oteh alone! Unable to explain away Oteh's documented vices, her defenders repeated this slogan to muzzle and muddle the message of those insisting on accountability and redress. It was clear from the ethical prevarication that followed that even if you caught a thief red-handed, in Nigeria, it would be wrong to shout, "Stop, thief!" without first devising a strategy to answer those who might come to the thief's defense or seek to redefine what constitutes theft. And the longer the saga endures, the more elaborate the defense and rationalization become.

The chairman of the oversight committee, Herman Hembe, got a taste of his own accusatory medicine when Ms. Oteh fought back with her own explosive allegations. Hembe, Oteh charged, had approached her commission for 15 million naira as funding for the entire public hearing and was getting back at her for the commission's inability to remit the money. Here was an oversight committee purporting to be investigating a commission it oversaw and asking the same commission to finance the investigation. The quid pro quo implications were clear, as was the ethical conflict, not to mention the disregard for the oaths taken by the legislators. Every aspect of Hembe's committee's solicitations was corrupt. Then came another bombshell. Hembe had also requested and accepted a business class ticket and a huge per diem from the commission to attend a conference in the Dominican Republic. Not only was the solicitation corrupt, a clear conflict that undermined Hembe's oversight integrity, but after he did not attend the conference, he failed to return the largesse.

Nigerians had a clear case of corruption, right? Wrong, according to some Nigerians who curiously came to Hembe's defense. Like Ms. Oteh's defenders, Hembe's supporters waxed lyrical with their own catchphrase of "leave Hembe alone," as though Hembe's person, and not his odious conduct, were under scrutiny. They introduced annoyingly puerile red herrings and irrelevancies to dilute the narrative of Hembe's misbehavior. This curiously pro-Hembe crowd continued deflecting the flak he was getting even after documents surfaced to corroborate the allegation, and after Hembe's implausible reasons for why he neither attended the conference nor returned the cash advance to the SEC collapsed. In spite of the clear wrongdoing, the pro-Hembe crowd doubled down, insisting on the lawmaker's innocence and patriotic intentions.

Former minister of the Federal Capital Territory, Malam Nasir el-Rufai, was prosecuted by a court in Abuja for allegedly allocating choice Abuja lands seized from the Power Holding Company of Nigeria (PHCN) and other organizations to his wives, friends, and business associates. Testimony by the investigating police officer in the case traced some of the beneficiaries to el-Rufai's many business investments. El-Rufai's defense? He committed no wrongdoing because his wives, family members, and friends are Nigerians and are, like other Nigerians, qualified to receive land allocations in Abuja!

Lost on el-Rufai are pesky moral and legal constructs such as conflict of interest, nepotism, and abuse of office—all of which used to be unequivocally labeled corruption, even in Nigeria. El-Rufai's defense is remarkable for its lack of self-reflection, its lack of self-scrutiny. One is forced to wonder: Are Nigerians genuinely ignorant of the ethical and legal implications of the acts that they defend and rationalize, or are they simply rationally committed to confusing the issues by feigning a lack of awareness of culpability? In a labyrinth of competing amoral narratives, clear-cut notions of right and wrong get lost.

El-Rufai, of course, is biased as a directly interested party, and one would be shocked if he were to have chosen a less escapist tack of defense. But what about his supporters, who can be found in small but vocal formations on numerous Nigerian cyber-communities? They have, incredibly, repeatedly clobbered those who object to el-Rufai's self-confessed corruption with the same talking point: el-Rufai's wives and family are Nigerians and there is nothing wrong with el-Rufai, as the FCT minister, revoking other people's land allocations and allocating the same lands to his relatives and associates. The legal and ethical escapism is mindboggling. What does it say about Nigeria and its struggle with corruption when neither the corrupt nor his or her supporters are able or willing to recognize corruption and call it by its proper name?

In such a muddy ethical landscape, how is it possible to define and name wrongdoing? Nigeria has laws that should do the naming. These established legal instruments are neutral arbiters that should be unencumbered by the multiple loyalties and considerations that cause Nigerians to take curious ethical positions on clear-cut matters of misconduct. But laws are not standalone entities. They are a product of society and have to be summoned to do their job. It is not to be assumed that moving from making a law to invoking it in binding judicial pronouncements is a straightforward proposition. It is anything but, for that is the process by which ethical confusion is often paradoxically upheld by the institution designed to do the opposite. Laws have to be interpreted by judges and legal practitioners schooled in the prevailing ethical atmosphere of their societies and applied to particular cases by people dedicated to upholding a society defined by multiple self-interested loyalties. It is how people engage with the law that matters. And so, in this case, the law is almost useless as a definitive source for criminality and legality.

If the defenders of Jonathan, Oteh, el-Rufai, and Hembe believe that those they are defending did not violate any laws or the ethical prescriptions of public office, that indicates that the laws in Nigeria's law books have failed to shape some Nigerians' understanding of right and wrong, of proper standards of public ethics. That would be tragic, for it would mean that the law is no help in the effort to define corruption. If on the other hand, these defenders of vice believe that their heroes have indeed committed ethical violations and yet they are determined to defend and rationalize their actions, this would be even more tragic. It would mean that these folks know what the law and extant religious and cultural moral codes require or condemn, but have intentionally chosen to disregard legal or moral consensus in order to scuttle its application. In this scenario, too, the law becomes useless as an arbiter of ethical ambiguity because some Nigerians willfully and even maliciously ignore it.

A NUMERICAL QUAGMIRE

The second emerging problem in debates on graft in Nigeria is that corruption is now measured in billions of naira, well beyond the comprehension of most Nigerians. Nigerians have become obsessed with the numerical identity of corruption, and their outrage or lack thereof now correlates to whether the amount involved is "big" or "small."

Million-naira corruption schemes have lost their shock value. Nigerians used to be outraged by the theft or mismanagement of such sums. Not anymore. They have undergone a subconscious desensitization. They now react to corruption only when it is represented in billions of naira or dollars. Even the capacity to be shocked by wasted billions is wearing thin. A small case in point: When the House Committee on Power Sector Investments accused former president Olusegun Obasanjo of wasting $10–18 billion on the electricity sector with nothing but a diminished power generation capacity to show for it, one of his few defenders, Malam Nasir el-Rufai, argued that the amount spent was only $5 billion and not $10 or $18 billion as the committee's report and other independent assessments estimated. Five billion dollars is the entire annual budget of some countries. In Nigeria, the figure is little more than an exculpatory rhetorical number summoned to minimize a crime.

Soon, even billion-naira corruption scandals, which are proliferating across the country, will become so banal as to elicit only a shrug. Nigerians have traded principle, which says that it is not the amount that matters but the ethics, for an obsession with numbers. This will soon catch up to them, because they may soon run out of numerical capacity to capture their ever-escalating corruption problem. Nigerians who are literate in the

Roman or Arabic scripts may not notice this problem, but the unlettered, who number in the tens of millions across all regions of the country, will soon discover that they lack the monetary vocabulary in their languages to account for and quantify the wealth being stolen and mismanaged by politicians and bureaucrats at all levels of government.

Most Nigerian languages even struggle to grasp the numerical scope of a thousand, let alone a million. In many languages, there is neither a word nor a visual metaphor for a million naira, a million yams, or a million anything! Unlettered folk used to measure money and currency in bags (*akpo, apo, jekan kudi,* and *ekpa*) or in the form of mounds, as in mounds of earth prepared for the planting of yams, cassava, and other crops. These were visual representations carried over from pre-colonial and colonial currency regimes and from agricultural systems. Lacking equivalent monetary constructions in their lexicons, people made sense of large sums of money only in this way—and when I say "large" I am talking about hundreds or thousands of naira, not millions.

Because of this mental visual of bags and mounds, when they heard that someone stole or mismanaged thousands of naira, they went crazy with outrage and wondered: What is he going to do with those mounds of money? When corruption scandals graduated into the millions, rural folks could no longer comprehend the extent of the national problem of graft. Some Nigerian languages simply adopted and Africanized the word "million." Even so, only the speakers of those languages who were lettered in English really knew the arithmetic scope of a million. Unlettered rural speakers only learned to say "million" in inflected, flavored tongues because they could not imagine millions of naira as bags of alloy coins or cowries. How many bags would that kind of money fit into? They had no financial understanding of what constituted a million naira; it was for them in the realm of uncountable, unquantifiable money. Now, as billion-naira corruption scandals have become the norm, there is a large demographic group in Nigerian society whose members are incapable of wrapping their minds around, let alone articulating in local languages, what successive generations of rulers have been pilfering from their patrimony.

With understanding comes outrage and action. In the absence of widespread comprehension and in the context of increased desensitization to "small" corruption scandals involving millions of naira, the capacity to feel the fiscal pain of malfeasance and mobilize against it has receded. Only a few years ago, billion-naira scandals were rare and were the subject of nationwide sensation. Today, they are the norm, at least at the federal level. Those who are literate enough to understand "billions" should not rest easy; at this pace, it will get to the trillions, a threshold that I confess I have no capacity to fully quantify in concrete terms. Do you say: "Imagine a three bedroom house filled with cash from floor to ceiling?" What will happen when trillion-naira corruption scandals become as common as billion-naira ones? Will quotidian societal literacy prove adequate in equipping Nigerians with the financial knowledge to understand the scope of what is routinely happening to their country's revenue?

CONCLUSION

Nigerians need to overcome the bifurcated ethic that allows them, when confronted by the same corruption in two contexts, to offer radically different moral responses. You cannot call what is a crime in one situation a fair action in another. They also have to find a way to translate the numerical magnitude of the national corruption problem into locally understood idioms—tropes that can be expressed lucidly in Nigerian languages. This is the only way they can generate the outrage that will power the fight against corruption. If the idiom of mounds and bags will not do, or if it is outmoded for an increasingly literate and nonagricultural society, how about quantifying the thefts as classrooms, hospitals, roads, power generating plants, and water supply plants, infrastructures that the amounts involved would have built? Instead of saying that someone stole 5 billion naira—an abstract monetary construct that is beyond the arithmetic imagination of most Nigerians—one could say graphically that he stole twenty-five classrooms, two hospitals, two rural roads, one small IPP project, and one rural water scheme. Even more melodramatically, one could say this or that politician or bureaucrat stole the futures of three hundred children and the futures of these children's children. If the idea of futuristic theft seems too abstract, one could simply say that a certain corrupt politician has stolen the retirement and thus the post-work livelihood of ten thousand Nigerians. We need a framing device that helps us get past the numbing and confusing numbers and into the human opportunity cost of corruption.

CHAPTER 3

THE CASE FOR REAL CONSTITUTIONAL REFORM[3]

A few years ago, at a conference in New Orleans, Louisiana, USA, I was in the audience when a politician who is now a governor in a southwestern Nigerian state gave a well-received presentation on elections in Nigeria. His talk pivoted from the familiar diagnostics of the many layers of electoral fraud to the more complex question of electoral reform.

At the end of his presentation, I asked him a simple question: Is electoral malfeasance not a symptom of a larger malaise, namely constitutional and structural defects, which in turn nurture the electoral desperation that is the catalyst for electoral malpractice? Stated differently, my thinking was that Nigerians are merely engaging in the self-deceiving gimmick of remedial therapy, and that they are focusing on symptoms and neglecting causes. My contention was that perhaps all the talk about electoral reform signals a hesitation to confront and reform the unitary constitutional order in the country, which confers godlike resource appropriation and distribution powers on executive officeholders in Abuja and the states, highly coveted perches that fuel desperation and electoral fraud.

The politician's answer was a reasonable and understandable, if clichéd, reassertion of a widely held sentiment endorsing incremental change over radical, root-cause transformation. He understood and empathized with my position that the root of electoral malpractice is a unitary state fattened with excessive power over political outcomes and resource distribution. He also agreed that because the attainment of political power confers instant, unchecked control over vast resources, the struggle to get to Abuja or to any of the thirty-six state government houses is necessarily fraught with fraud and desperation, which have the capacity to defeat or compromise even the most determined stab at electoral reform.

The ideal solution, the presenter conceded, would be to institute a truly federal constitutional order in which power and control over resource distribution are decentralized, a system that departs from the current one where resources accrue to Abuja, which then uses its discretion to allocate these resources while using some of this revenue to compel anti-citizen, election-distorting alliances, cooperation, and acquiescence at the state level. The foundational solution to Nigeria's electoral crisis, he agreed, was to starve Abuja, giving it only what it needs for defense, immigration, and external affairs, thus reducing the intensity of the struggle for federal political office, and giving citizens at the state level a reason and the leeway to demand and enforce both financial and electoral transparency without having to contend with federally funded repressions, immunities, and impunities.

While my interlocutor supported a return to a true federal structure that could make the current debate about electoral reform moot, he cautioned that Nigerians should not "let the perfect become the enemy of the good." In other words, electoral reform that would improve Nigeria's electoral practice was better than no reform at all, and an insistence on addressing foundational issues that occasion electoral problems should not stand in the way of pursuing what was possible, doable, and practical: cleaning up how elections are conducted and making sure that electoral outcomes reflect the will of voters.

As presidential incompetence unfolds and as the nation faces threats from a combustive cocktail of corruption, terrorism, crime, and infrastructural decay, conversations and debates have turned, once again, to the recurring question of whether electoral transparency and its supposed product—accountability—are the remedies for the Nigerian malaise, or whether a more fundamental, revolutionary restructuring of the union is overdue.

The debate is still unfolding. Some continue to put their faith in electoral reform, arguing that rigged elections perpetuate corruption and incompetence, and hurt accountability and transparency in governance. Rigged elections, they also contend, beget more rigged elections, a self-replicating cycle of gloom that, over time, will imperil the union. Their thesis is that the problem lies not in the structures and institutions of the union but with electoral practice, which should be guided by better rules, laws, and procedures. In short, get elections right and all other things will fall gradually into place. To these Nigerians, it is not the current structural configuration of Nigeria—i.e., the unitary identity of the state—that is the problem, but rather the absence of true democracy, a problem marked most visibly by recurring electoral fraud.

I sympathize with this position as a mechanism of mitigation and I respect its proponents as well-meaning patriots, but I reject it as a first-order solution. Honest electoral reform may emplace meaningful ground rules and clean up the electoral system to some degree, but it is only a matter of time before such rules bow to the perverse creativity of Nigeria's political class. And this creativity grows as the union becomes even more unitary in its approach to resource appropriation and distribution. The political class has an infinite capacity for perverse innovation that is birthed by desperation, which in turn is anchored on a more fundamental desire for access to the all-conquering realms of power in Abuja and the states capitals. This is the conundrum that Nigeria needs to overcome. Electoral reform may indeed improve Nigeria's much-criticized democratic practice, but it would only be a Band-Aid on the gaping national wound. It would not solve the debilitating structural impasse of the nation.

THE UNITARY STATE IS THE ENEMY

Without a reform of the unitary structure of the Nigerian state, citizens, lacking a sense of investment in a distant government nurtured by a distant oil revenue source, will remain indifferent to how government business is conducted and how elections are executed—indifferent enough to unwittingly help sustain the status quo and its perennial offering of electoral malpractice. Without going back to and resolving the nation's existential questions, Abuja will continue to be a resource-sharing bazaar, and political fights over participation in that bazaar at the national and state levels will defeat any electoral reform initiative no matter how sophisticated and well-intentioned. Returning to a truly federal system will starve Abuja of funds and force corrupt state governors and their political and bureaucratic allies, who would no longer be protected by Abuja, to answer to the demands and pressure of their constituents. But such a fundamental reform has other benefits, which I will return to shortly.

First let me confront the argument that implementing a more transparent electoral system and continuing with an existing form of democracy is the cure that a fractured nation needs. Transparent elections will curtail the degree of corruption, willful incompetence, dereliction of governance, and other acts of impunity that have proliferated as part of the national repertoire of crises. If the electoral system became more transparent and rigging became difficult, political officeholders would rein in their theft, or at least be forced to steal more discreetly. They would do this in the knowledge that, with rigging no longer possible, they would not return to office if they could not at least pretend to govern responsibly. But this is where the good-elections-as-cure argument begins to weaken. The argument assumes that every officeholder would want to be reelected and that none would be content with a one-term looting spree. It assumes the best of human nature and the possibility of a mechanical moral reflex in those who govern. It is a naïve assumption anywhere, let alone in Nigeria, where the very object of public office in most cases is a desire to profit from it. It is more prudent to assume the worst and preempt it.

What if candidate Okorie Olufemi Kangiwa wins an election to the position of president, and under the current unitary system of almost unlimited executive power gets access to the treasury? What if he decides that reelection does not matter to him and that he would instead help himself to a lifetime of loot at the public's expense? What happens then? How does a good electoral system solve that? Voters can terminate his political life at the next election, but he has already set a precedent for his successor. Who is to say that the next president won't promise his or her way into power, and then commit the same crimes? What is the recourse then, other than the routine, repetitive, but substantively meaningless exercise of voting out erring officeholders?

The counterargument is of course that there is no guarantee in anything and that even in advanced democracies voters sometimes get it wrong in successive elections. That is true. The big difference is that, by virtue of real checks on executive power, strong institutions, and disaggregation of power, resources, and initiative to constituent units, these countries can afford to ride out successive electoral mistakes. Excessive presidential turnover as a result of incompetence will not hurt them because their countries have the foundational mettle to thrive in spite of their presidents' or governors' ineptitude. Nigeria is in such dire straits that the state cannot endure or survive several incompetent, corrupt, one-term presidencies. Not when the fiscal foundation of the union is built on a finite, exhaustible resource: oil. Not when the country and its infrastructures are already comatose and need to be radically rebuilt for a new beginning. Five successive or intermittent one-term looting sprees can obliterate what is left of the country. And this would entirely be possible even under the most transparent electoral system and in the absence of fundamental structural reform that would *compel,* and not simply trust, officeholders to be transparent and accountable superintendents of the people's resources.

One often hears the clichéd argument that the answer to a dysfunctional democracy is more democracy. But what if, as in Nigeria, the version of democracy that is practiced has itself become part of the problem rather than the solution? The argument that there is no problem that democracy or more democracy cannot solve assumes that democracy is inherently good, is independent of its practitioners' intentions and cannot be perverted, and that democracy can thrive in a failed state structure designed willfully or otherwise to perpetuate precisely the vices that democracy purports to cure: corruption, incompetence, nepotism, mediocrity, and strife. The argument also rests on an ambiguous, ill-defined, and monolithic concept of democracy. Practicing democracy in a matrix of structural and constitutional arrangements that by their very nature encourage waste, corruption, electoral desperation, and poor governance produces a plethora of democratic evils. In such a system, democracy itself helps legitimize acts of national destruction.

Let me explain. Today, the biggest threat to Nigeria is corruption, which is traceable, as I have argued, to the dominance of the Abuja resource-sharing rendezvous and its many nodes at the state level. We assume that corruption refers to acts of financial appropriation that occur outside of the law, outside of the realms of legitimacy. But in today's "democratic" Nigeria, the threat of what one may call "legitimate" corruption is perhaps greater than that of embezzlement, theft, and other obvious "illegal" acts deemed corruption. Under this democracy, embezzlements and other kinds of graft can be legitimized by simply packaging them as bills of the national or state assembly, bribing or blackmailing legislative allies to pass them into law, and then pocketing or misapplying the resulting financial appropriation. As long as it is given the force of law by being passed by one or both of Nigeria's legislative bodies, it becomes legitimate. It becomes recorded in fact as a democratic and legislative act, an integral, legitimate ritual of Nigeria's democratic system.

Legitimized corruption!

Democracy has now provided a larcenous political class with the perfect constitutional platform for corruption. That is not the fault of democracy per se. It is the result primarily of the absence of conditions that enable democracy in whatever form to thrive and self-correct—equity, justice, citizen vigilance and fiscal investment, and structural safeguards against the abuse of office in all its forms. This foundational absence makes mockery of the rhetoric and practice of democracy.

So, when I am told that democracy is a cure-all and that Nigeria needs to simply improve its democracy, my retort is that democracy can work only when enabling conditions exist, conditions that remove the mortal threats that may in fact torpedo democracy itself, rendering it a source of harm to the body politic. If this is what democracy looks like, how can we make the argument that Nigerians need more of it to cure the systemic ills plaguing their country? What democratic system, no matter how well crafted, can survive the temptations and perverse liberties of the Abuja resource-sharing market? Unless Nigeria reforms its constitution to give citizens a fiscal stake in the government and return all struggles over resources to the local level, this democracy will, instead of saving Nigerians, kill them. And this is not hyperbole. This democracy has expanded and legitimized Nigeria's stealing field, and its expensive procedural rituals are now threatening to bankrupt the country as well.

Another counterargument is the "good leader" proposition. Its premise is that the trouble with Nigeria, to parse novelist Chinua Achebe, is not with its structure, constitution, and institutions but with its leadership. Achebe makes a forceful argument bemoaning the dearth of good leadership. So great is his faith in the power of a good leader—or a group of leaders—to rectify structural and constitutional defects that his proposition has gained glamour, and been rendered into a little-scrutinized mantra for lamenting contemporary political and economic dysfunction in Nigeria. It does not hurt that Achebe had also been a conscience of the nation, a sage, and a committed patriot. His persona has fed into the seemingly inscrutable sacredness of the leadership argument.

It is repeated in every forum of Nigerian political discourse that a good leader or a succession of good, committed leaders would reverse the rot and set Nigeria on the path of progress. The problem with this argument, aside from its reductionism, is that it assumes that the good leader or leaders with a cleansing mission would emerge outside the system of political patronage that is lubricated by Abuja-dispensed resources—a system sustained by entrenched interests that have no incentive to subscribe to a program of national reclamation and have every reason to support the opposite proposition. Perhaps the leadership argument was valid three or four decades ago, when the patronage system had not coalesced and when oil and its revenues had not taken such a central place in Nigeria's political system. In today's Nigeria, a lone messianic leader would have a hard time emerging even in a fair, transparent electoral contest. And if he did, he would have a hard time governing according to his conscience, since he would have come to power on the back of interests and power brokers that are invested in the status quo and would seek to reap from their investment instead of overturning the current system. More crucially, such a lone messianic figure would be hamstrung by existing constitutional and legal norms, which legitimize acts that will continue to hobble the nation by stifling people who could liberate it.

A few examples are in order here. How will a messianic president prevent the national and state legislators from awarding themselves unconscionable perks of office that would dig holes in the national budget and scuttle social programs? How would he prevent them from using such perks as a bargaining chip or blackmailing leverage against him? Under the current democratic and constitutional norms, the messianic president will, willy-nilly, give in to many acts of legitimate corruption being perpetrated by legislators and their executive branch allies. Another example: How will this president prevent his supporters, aides, and those who funded his political ascent from accepting the spoils of office? How can a lone man of ethics survive in a government populated by thousands of rapacious supporters and cheerleaders baying for loot?

In yet another example, how does this president prevent the legitimized, constitutionally mandated larceny under the guise of what is misleadingly called security vote?[4] If he uses his discretion at the national level to redirect "his" security vote to other programs, can he do the same in all thirty-six states without overstepping the constitutional boundaries of his power? How does he prevent state assemblies from approving vulgar perks for themselves and the executive branches of their states? Under a fatally defective constitutional structure, the messianic president will be a messiah only in his head, his messianism isolated and rendered abstract. At best, he will quietly enjoy the aura and prestige of office while constitutional and unconstitutional looting goes on around him (Shehu Shagari, anyone?). At worst, he will, with time, join the looting and give up on his futile cleansing mission. That's the depressing impasse at which Nigeria has arrived. The "good leader" thesis makes an emotional appeal to Nigerians' sense of hope, to their thirst for miraculous and charismatic transformation. But one does not have to invoke Max Weber to understand the limit of charisma and personal character in a context of collapse. Personal charisma, character, and commitment make a discernible difference only when the structural and constitutional ingredients are in place.

To be sure, constitutional and structural reform will not magically cure all of the nation's ills. The depth of the Nigerian predicament forecloses that. But it will solve several of the familiar problems and begin the process of healing. Constitutional reform that begins from the existential questions of a troubled union will return Nigeria to a truly federal structure where control over the bulk of resource revenue, developmental initiative, accountability, and policymaking will reside with the regions or states, not with a bloated and overbearing federal government. Under this reform scenario a small pool of revenue will flow to Abuja to fund a diminished federal government. The exact formula for this process needs to be agreed upon. It seems to me that a 50:50 formula (with 50 percent of revenue going to derivation zones and the other 50 percent being shared between the federal government and the other states) is a good starting point, from where a movement toward a 60:40 or 70:30 ratio in favor of derivation areas can begin. There will be several advantages to this.

First, in the long run, it will produce grassroots interest and vigilance regarding the financial and political affairs of states and local governments. Admittedly, this may preserve and even exacerbate corruption at the state level in the short term. Yet the principle is simple and commonsensical: the closer an institution is to the people it is designed to serve, the more stake people develop in it. The bigger the stake—political, economic, and emotional—the sharper the vigilance of citizens and the more determined they will be to ensure that elected representatives and leaders are transparent stewards of public resources and trust.

Second, for oil-producing states and regions, the effect will be dramatic in terms of both revenue pool and the transformation of political dynamics. In the short term, contests for political office in those regions will escalate, as politicians will reposition themselves to secure supervisory access to the larger resource pool that will become available. Indeed, politicians from these regions will most certainly begin an epic migration from Abuja to participate in what they anticipate will be a regional oil-dollar feast. Beneath all this chaos, however, a quiet political dynamic will gradually take hold, as the citizens of these regions realize that their politicians can no longer rely on power and coercive instruments mobilized from Abuja to protect themselves against popular agitation or to put down clamor for accountability and responsible governance. A new sense of political empowerment and a new awareness of stake-holding will develop among the citizens of these states. Over time, this will crystallize into a formidable civil society that will insist on both fiscal and electoral accountability. Their ethnic and physical proximity to the politicians will intensify this citizen power, ensuring that politicians make themselves accountable to their constituents instead of using Abuja as a shield, alibi, and foil to deflect local clamor for good governance and transparency, as is currently the case. Politicians from the oil-rich Niger Delta who will flock "home" from Abuja in the hope of constituting themselves into a new, Abuja-type oligarchy will, over time and as their constituents exercise their new voice, find their operational liberties curtailed and their immunity and impunities challenged. This will be a seminal shift in the struggle for accountable governance and electoral integrity in the oil-producing states. These states will be much better for it.

Third, for non-oil-producing states, the benefits may be counterintuitive, but they are many. States without oil will be compelled to shop for revenue outside the assured purview of the federal allocation formula, which is guaranteed, for now, on a perennial oil revenue bonanza. New revenues do not come easy. Necessity will force these governments to explore previously neglected sources of extractive revenue. Taxes and levies will also have to be imposed on economically challenged citizens, a move that will result in both hard sacrifice and a sense of investment and involvement. This sense of participatory involvement will prove crucial. The citizens, by virtue of funding the government from their toil, will develop instant proprietary interest in the management of government finances, ensuring through their vigilance that those they elect to run the government put their tax money to good, prudent use. Again, the geographic and cultural proximity of the electorate's anger, the prospect of its eruption, and the new reality that local politicians can no longer call upon Abuja's might for political protection or use Abuja as an alibi for poor performance will ensure an appreciable degree of accountability from public officeholders.

Fourth, all of these should, over time, produce a culture of public vigilance, accountability, transparency, and healthy competition between states and regions.

Finally, true federalism will help construct the basis for an enduring union. At a time when the nation stands challenged on many fronts by movements that reject the social, political, and economic tyranny of the Nigerian state, the lazy, repetitively hollow assertion that the unity of Nigeria is nonnegotiable will no longer do. Nations are not harvesters of homogeneity. They are efficient managers of difference. Often they are patchworks of different groups and different primordial and aspirational interests that agree to pursue some common goals while retaining their values, differences, and cherished autonomies. Nigerians are afraid to broach the question of difference, primordial or otherwise, let alone confront it in an open national conversation. Yet the signs are there—and festering—that differences, real differences, exist in the values, aspirations, priorities, and worldviews of the different regions and ethno-religious clusters in the country. A true federal structure will accommodate these differences.

MATTERS ARISING

The Marxist and neo-Marxist claptrap that everyone is motivated by the same existential economic needs and that identity issues are felt by the masses only when manipulated by elite calculations is no longer tenable, and it has become part of the problem. It is deceptive and escapist, and stands disproved on many fronts. Most committed Marxists no longer believe in the exclusive primacy of economic or materialist motivation and now subscribe to a more holistic index of impulses and needs. Those who still believe the foundational Marxist mantra do so as a matter of doctrinal correctness, not of philosophical logic or empirical compulsion. In Nigeria, identity questions and desires have become as important as economic ones. They are real and heartfelt, and are part of Nigeria's slate of unresolved issues. They cannot be buried behind empty, pretentious slogans.

Take the Caliphate and Bornuan North (the Northwest and huge swaths of the Northeast). The Boko Haram Islamist insurgency, which was birthed in that part of the country, threatens the fabric of the nation. The movement obviously does not enjoy widespread support in this zone. The same cannot, however, be said of Sharia, which posed an existential challenge to Nigeria in the 2000s, when its constitutionality was debated and when Muslims and Christians clashed over its implementation. When Sharia fever gripped this zone in 2000, there were diverse views as to what catalyzed the grassroots clamor for Sharia as a legal, social, and political order. Some attributed it to bad governance and an attendant desire for a utopian religious alternative. Others pointed to the manipulation of politicians who saw in Sharia a means to easy political legitimacy and immunity. Yet others insisted that this was not a clamor produced by politics or ephemeral discontent with poor governance but a genuine religious awakening at the grass roots, a populist reformist eruption in the tradition of the Fulani Islamic reform movement of the early nineteenth century.

Today, more than a decade later, Sharia remains an unsettled question. Nigerians have not determined its constitutionality. Nor have Nigerians answered the question of whether it is a fleeting, emotive desire or a deeper matter of identity and values that needs to be addressed explicitly in the constitution to douse the dueling contentions on its constitutionality and its supposed threat to Nigeria. But how can Nigerians come to this resolution outside a serious discussion of regional, ethnic, and religious values and differences? How can Nigeria construct constitutional protections for those desirous of certain religious or social reforms and comforts and those fearful of such changes? In fact, how can Nigerians even determine whether Sharia is indeed the overarching political template preferred by the population of the Caliphate North if they are not willing to discuss and resolve the constellation of national questions that they are constantly reminded of during moments of national crisis?

For other regions and clusters, the touchstone of subnational aspiration may not be Sharia but a preoccupation with the autonomy to do things in other spheres without an intruding, overbearing federal government. In the Southwest, the desire for a state-controlled police force is strong, eliciting diverse views on its constitutionality. Given strong support for it in several Southern states, should Nigerians not discuss it seriously? What about the recurring decimal of citizenship—the question of whether the rights of indigenes should flow from residency or origin? Given its deadly centrality to many ethnic and ethno-religious conflicts in different parts of the country, does it not deserve a serious constitutional conversation that will settle it once and for all?

CONCLUSION

In the past those who advocated this path of true federalism couched it in the angry idiom of a nation saddled with incompatible differences. They expressed it in the vocabulary of blame. They posited that a section of the country is a leech and a drag on the rest, that it deserves expulsion, and that the other "productive" section deserves freedom from the burden of subsidizing its lazy appendage. That was and is still a counterproductive tactic for sparking structural political reform. Instead of advancing mutual gain and healthy, developmental competition as the basis for their advocacy of pristine federalism, many federalists spoke about parasites that needed to be banished or punished. That is why the idea of a serious, people-driven, everything-is-on-the-table constitutional conference never gained traction and spooked politicians and regular citizens alike (even the national conference of 2014 was undermined, *ab initio*, by the imposition of so-called no-go areas). The best case for reforming and rewriting Nigeria's unitary constitution is the logic of compatible differences—the conviction that Nigeria may be a bewildering congregation of different peoples, interests, aspirations, values, beliefs, and priorities, but that the differences are compatible and should be preserved through a pragmatic process of reimagining and reconstructing the very foundations of the nation. Nigeria will live or die by how Nigerians treat this foundational imperative.

CHAPTER 4

NIGERIANS' LOVE–HATE RELATIONSHIP
WITH GOVERNMENT

Nigerians harbor an ambivalent view of government. On one level, they are disgusted with the entity. They are even distrustful of it, preferring to be left outside its orbit to lick the wounds inflicted on them by those who call themselves leaders and bureaucrats.

Self-preservation in the face of consistent political torment is not a peculiarly Nigerian preoccupation. The way to preserve oneself against governmental abuse is to refuse to reward an abusive government with loyalty and trust. Nigerians treat the government with a disdain equal to that with which the government treats them. It is a justifiable tit for tat. That is one level of the relationship.

The other layer of the ambivalent engagement is that Nigerians continue to invest their hopes in government even as they take active steps to wean themselves from its predictable failures.

This contradictory perception of government is not only pragmatic but also completely understandable. Self-preservation is a weapon of the poor. However, if the poor are also desperate and continue to cling to the hope of redemption, they must, in spite of their cynicism, embrace a belief in the redemptive potential of government and its institutions. It is not an ideal situation. The ideal would be a situation in which the person who is distrustful of government steps completely out of its reach, declares himself a government unto himself, and upholds a consistent ethic of antigovernment critique. But consistency is a luxury of privilege. Nigeria's poor, dispossessed, and government-abused people have every reason to associate government with development-killing corruption, oppressive extortion, injustice, and maladministration. Once this association is made, it is a challenge to trust the entity that embodies these vices. But aloofness to government is also not a practical option, hence the contradiction.

Disengagement from the apparatuses of government is not only unrealistic; it is not in the interest of Nigerians. If you disengage from the government, the government will not return the gesture. If you run and hide in the hope of living in a private universe devoid of government-borne stresses and letdowns, the government will not respect your choice. Its agents will hunt you down and insist on sucking you into the nodes through which the state replenishes its authority. Bribe-seeking cops will not spare you from harassment because you've removed yourself from the yoke of government. Tax-collecting extortionists will insist that you meet your tax obligation to the government even when it has demonstrated poor stewardship over tax revenue. The Power Holding Company of Nigeria (PHCN), notorious for billing citizens heavily for electricity and giving them darkness, will not give you a pass, either. So, consistent rejection of government and absolute self-sufficiency is practically impossible. For the poor in particular, it is not an option; they are, for no fault of their own, ironically wedded to the failing institutions of government. This explains the ambivalence of their relationship to it, the fact that they loathe it but also root for it to work.

The tragedy of this existence is that, much as the poor Nigerian detests the government's intrusions into his life and its failure to live up to its obligations to him, he cannot realistically detach himself from the object of his disgust. His poverty and economic helplessness means that he is held captive to government; he is at the mercy of its incompetent and corrupt operatives. His poverty makes him vulnerable to the oppression and manipulation of the very entity that is responsible for his impoverishment. His economic desperation puts him in the vortex of the very institution that he detests, the institution that he would prefer to exit but cannot. He is paradoxically dependent on an incompetent, predatory state.

The other tragedy is that the politicians and bureaucrats who have given government a bad name know just how dependent Nigeria's poor are on government, and they manipulate this helplessness for political capital. They know that there is a pragmatic limit to Nigerians' capacity to forsake the government. Their interest is to keep the status quo of an impoverished populace that will remain dependent on the government no matter how incompetent the state is—or even because of its incompetency.

It is an interesting paradox. The more ravenous the state becomes, the more Nigerians depend on it. Nigerians are needy for governmental attention. This need grows even as the government shirks more of its responsibilities to them. Citizen dependence should be an incentive for improvement in the performance of leaders and bureaucrats. But it is not. Instead, it is a license for government officials to mismanage their portfolios in the knowledge that the more irresponsible the state becomes, the less inclined Nigerians will be to dismantle it because they will crave its dwindling attention more than ever. The incompetence of the state paradoxically becomes its protection, the corruption of the rulers (and the poverty and misery that it spreads) their insurance against the rejectionist anger of Nigerians.

Bad as this quandary may seem, it is not hopeless. Nigerians have it rough with their government and are justifiably indifferent to the workings of state institutions. But this is precisely the problem: You do not abandon the treasury to those who have robbed it. You don't remove yourself from an institution that, bad as it has been to you, may be instrumental to your economic comeback. That's the logic of electoral vigilance and citizen political activism. The plight of Nigerians is precisely why they cannot afford to surrender the government to the uncaring opportunists who currently run it. The failure of government is the most persuasive argument for the need to take an active interest in the processes by which government is constituted and held accountable. The failure of government is not an argument for apathy and disengagement.

There is nothing inherently bad in government; it is those who run it in Nigeria who have sown distrust and cynicism against it, which in turn allows the crooks and incompetents to consolidate their hold on the state and perpetuate their crimes against Nigerians. It is a self-perpetuating cycle.

Nigerians are not peculiar in their ambivalent relationship to government. In the United States, where I live, the right wing, especially members of its implacably libertarian axis, rail against the role of government in their lives and have patented the battle cry of small government. They want less government and more privatization of public life. They want government to withdraw from many spheres of their lives. In Nigeria, citizens want more, not less, government. They desire government resources, government's constructive intrusions. In the US, even the constructive, protective role of government is sometimes demonized as tyranny and an encroachment on natural freedoms. It is a narrative of luxury and privilege that will resonate little with Nigerians. Nigerians would gladly trade their privacy and some of their intimate freedoms for positive, ameliorative governmental interventions in their lives and communities. But even in the United States where the mantra of small government is fully developed, there is a whiff of hypocritical contradiction in the movement for less government. Many supporters of the small government ideology have a dependent relationship with government. Some of them are on welfare and are beneficiaries of the government-funded health and educational assistance they bash as symbols of government excess.

So, in some sense, Nigerians are more realistic in their perception of government—in rightly being disgusted at its failures and excesses but in also holding out hope that, if managed properly, government can be an instrument of social and economic redress.

CHAPTER 5

THE "FEDERAL CHARACTER" CONUNDRUM

Federal character. It's Nigeria's poor version of affirmative action, its effort, so say its proponents, to ensure that public institutions are peopled in a manner that reflects the country's diversity. On paper it is a mechanism for accessing public goods and privileges in a fashion consistent with the nation's ethno-regional plurality.

The ruling Peoples Democratic Party may be the architect of rotational presidency—a system of rotating the presidency between Nigeria's two main regions—but the ideological genealogy of rotation is traceable to the same thinking that is at the heart of federal character, a system of ethno-regional quotas conceived to ensure representational and allocative equity between Nigeria's multiple ethnic and political constituencies. As postcolonial Nigeria hopscotched its way from one existential crisis to another, federal character seemed a wise, timely mimicry of its American policy cousin.

There is little to quibble with in the effort to engineer fair, balanced representation. There is, however, something tragically wrong when this becomes an end in itself and when the federal character principle becomes the enemy of the very ideals that it purports to achieve: equity and fairness. Shutting down a citizen's aspiration or ambition for a position for which they are exceptionally qualified because of the need to achieve ethnic or state balancing seems ultimately self-defeating, solving a problem by creating a more consequential one. This is the problem Nigeria faces.

Equity: the principle does not denote equality, a utopian, unattainable ideal. Equity demands that everyone be given a fair shake and that everyone's reward mirror the volume of his or her contribution. That's fairness, not equality. Fairness is attainable. Equality, measured by outcomes, is a mirage. Nigerians seem to have the two confused in their obsession with the federal character principle, rotational presidency, and quota system.

If Nigeria's ruling class applied this understanding of equity in its constitution making efforts, it would not have a problem with the modest demand of the people of the Niger Delta for a 25-percent derivation payment. When this demand was broached at the National Conference charade organized by ex-president Olusegun Obasanjo, the proposition gained little traction. The rhetoric of the non–Niger Delta delegates found a convenient semiotic connection between equity and equality: many delegates from non-oil-producing states haughtily insisted that as equal federating units of Nigeria, all should have equal shares from oil revenue. Equality was conflated with equity. The existing 13-percent derivation payment was made to sound like discriminatory charity. Some even went so far as to call for its revocation.

Move the discussion to a different context. At stake is not access to oil revenue but the distribution of public office and placement spots in federal bureaucratic and educational institutions. You would expect consistency in the political elite's rhetoric. What one gets instead is an invocation of the federal character principle. Non–Niger Delta politicians are quick to switch scripts—from the trope of equality to that of regional balance—when the topic shifts from Niger Delta resource control demands. They endorse the discriminatory, unfair, and uncompetitive status quo; they support federal character in fanatical tones. But federal character directly violates the spirit of equality that is often advanced to discredit the Niger Delta struggle for fairness and equity in the distribution of oil revenue.

Yet this contradiction has not registered on politicians from the non–Niger Delta zones. The insistence on the implementation of a federal character principle, which claims to promote fairness and build toward equality but which actually undermines both, is the biggest indictment on Nigerians' collective hypocrisy. Nigerians pick and choose the issues on which to impose true equity as the baseline of deliberation and which ones to subject to the counterpoint of the federal quota system.

Then there is the issue of whether federal character is something that Nigeria still needs or whether it is yesterday's solution for today's problems. The country stands challenged on multiple fronts—political, economic, ethical, and technological. This epic national challenge demands that the nation turn to its best and brightest and that the best be determined through a fair, competitive scrutiny of claims. Nigeria's national challenges demand that those who claim to have what it takes to produce what Nigeria needs are made to demonstrate their expertise on an equal, competitive platform of evaluation. The last thing Nigeria needs at this critical juncture is a constitutional provision that venerates mediocrity. A comatose country courts excellence in order to recover; it does not cultivate mediocrity.

The urgency of the national problems makes the hypocritical search for equity through federal character and rotation an expensive, atavistic proposition. It is a political solution to a technocratic problem, an arrangement that harks back to a distant period when politics was held to be more important than economic survival because economic survival was a taken-for-granted fact of life. Nigeria needs technocratic competence, governmental efficiency, and an across-the-board meritocracy. What federal character fosters is mediocrity baptized in the argument of fair representation.

This truth has dawned on most Nigerians: that what matters to Nigeria's beleaguered people is not how many ministers come from a certain region or whether a certain state has any minister in the federal cabinet, but how effective these ministers are in making government work for the people. The only group not to have caught on to this pragmatic reality is the political elite. For them the distribution and allocation of federal political offices and other largesse outrank the commitment to effective governance and problem solving.

There was a time when the federal character principle was crucial to the very survival of the union, and sentimental investments in ethno-regional representation trumped the existential anxieties of Nigerians. This was the 1960s. The potency of identity politics in that immediate post-independence period was expressed dramatically and gruesomely in the vehement—and later violent—opposition to Aguiyi-Ironsi's unification decree.

But that was then. The economic comforts of the 1960s, which cushioned the stomachs of citizens and gave them the luxury of indulging exclusively in the crude politics of representation, have evaporated. Today, a predatory cohort of politicians and bureaucrats has besieged Nigerians and their livelihoods, reducing existence to a scavenging adventure. In this crisis of survival, the politics of representation is a secondary concern of most Nigerians. What they desire is a government that meets its obligations to its citizens while working to foster their potentials. The human faces of such of a government and their ethno-regional labels have come to mean less and less as the country has slid more and more into a developmental abyss.

The federal character principle is understood, in this new political atmosphere, as a mere conduit for elite patronage and for the circulation of public privileges. It bears little or no relevance to the needs of the suffering peoples of Nigeria. The global political economy has transformed before our eyes, imposing new, competitive imperatives on all nations—burdens that cannot coexist with pandering to mediocrity in the name of balanced representation. We live in a globalized world, where the uncompetitive becomes a victim, not a beneficiary, of this unprecedented human and ideational mobility. The challenges of this new world call for the patronage and cultivation of excellence and merit at all levels, not shoo-in arrangements that stifle competition and innovation.

A persuasive argument could be made in the 1960s and 1970s about the educational backwardness of the North, the disproportionate historical disposition of Southern Nigeria to Western education, and the potential for that to trouble the waters of national cohesion without a deliberate policy intervention to skew the levers of equal competition. Today, such an argument would be passé. It would even be patronizing to the North. The most effective way to boost Northern educational aspirations is not to guarantee the region a quota of representation in federal institutions but to act out a tough-love, hands-off policy of noninterference in which the best man or woman wins. Competition is a more effective stimulant than quota patronage in a context such as Nigeria where there is no history of systematic exclusion of or discrimination against a group of people.

Finally, the ideal that underpins federal character does not square with a widely shared and expressed ideal: the preference for residency rather than ancestral origin as the supreme marker of citizenship/indigene rights. In the wake of recent ethno-religious crises, this ideal has gained currency across the political and intellectual spectrums. Conversely, there has been widespread outrage at the practical consequences of the indigene–settler divide.

But where is a similar outrage at the consequences of federal character, which, like the indigene–settler model, excludes and denies access and participation on the basis not of incompetence and lack of ability but of origin? Selective outrage won't cut it. The reform of citizenship rights, which is widely endorsed across Nigeria, violates and is violated by the federal character principle, which not only recognizes, codifies, and consolidates ethno-regional and ancestral origin and citizenship but also encourages its use as a basis to make claims over federal privileges and positions. It is disingenuous to advance a reform that seeks to disavow identity-based entitlement in one arena and turn around to uphold a principle (federal character) that canonizes and rewards same in another.

Nigerians can't have it both ways. If they want to keep a retrogressive and outdated constitutional invention like federal character, then let them stop pontificating about a cosmopolitan, identity-neutral universe of fair competition and fair reward as every pundit did in the wake of recent crises.

On the other hand, if they agree that the constitutional codification of ethno-regional representation (in the form of indigene-based federal character) is counterproductive and outmoded, the reasonable thing to do is to expunge it from the constitution. This would make it easier to move against the incendiary indigene–settler dichotomy, rotational presidency, and quota system without being open to charges of hypocrisy and selective rejection of identity politics.

This brings us to the question of what should be done. Ideas are floating around, but there is no easy answer. Some have suggested that fixing the leadership crisis in Nigeria, making life better for the Nigerians, growing the proverbial pie, and multiplying the number of opportunities will sentence indigene-based access to resources and opportunities to a slow, natural death, as the practice of protecting privileged access while denying the same to "settlers" would lose its appeal.

However, of all the strategies of remediation advanced so far, the constitutional amendment option appears to be the most progressive and proactive, for it will simply abolish the allocation of rights and resources based on claims of indigeneity. For that reason, it appears to be the most popular among progressive Nigerians. But the constitutional strategy, too, has its problems.

For one, it would most certainly face opposition in the North, where it will be construed with the fear of Southern domination in the North in mind, a fear that has a long history in the North going back to colonial and early postcolonial times, when educationally disadvantaged Northerners felt that their institutions were being swamped by educated Southerners. Former head of state General Aguiyi-Ironsi's unification decree exacerbated this feeling and ultimately led to a bloody backlash. Aliyu Tilde, a well-known Northern Nigerian pundit, argued in a blog that there remains some of this feeling in the North, especially in the Muslim-majority areas. I myself have seen, heard, and experienced this oppositional construction of southern (and Middle Belt Christian) migrants and settlers in the North as opportunity-taking interlopers. One needs to overcome this at a practical and psychological level before one can realistically implement any policy that departs from the current indigene/settler/federal character framework.

Secondly, a constitutional or legislative initiative that supplants or replaces the current constitutional endorsement of indigene-based federal character with a more heritage-neutral system will likely fail on the ground because politicians invested in current identity political permutations will simply ignore the law or find a way around it, knowing that members of the political cleavage that they rode to power, who themselves are beneficiaries of such exclusionary practices, will back them as defenders of indigenous and/or majority rights. A putative constitutional remedy will most likely be ignored on the ground as folks devise creative ways to preserve their privileged access to scarce resources and opportunities while closing same to non-indigenes or so-called settlers.

I recognize that these concerns and issues are valid especially since I am very close experientially and professionally to the arenas in which these realities manifest—the grass roots where the ugly consequences of parochial and exclusionary practices are felt. My sense is that too much water may have passed under the bridge and that folks may have settled into a certain uncomfortable status quo, such that constitutional reversals of federal character that may have worked two or three decades ago will no longer have any impact and will be overwhelmed and rendered irrelevant by actual practice on the ground. I do not therefore know of a cure-all, fail-proof solution.

What I do know is that a serious national conversation on this is necessary, as well as on other issues plaguing Nigeria. This is long overdue. Every potential solution has to be given serious attention and discussed in the spirit of reconstructive nation building, and the remedial consensus that emerges from this national conversation should at the very least minimize the negative, retrogressive consequences of federal character, promoting excellence and competence above mediocrity and the meaningless satisfaction of equitable representation. It should also minimize associated practices of indigeneity-based rights and access.

CHAPTER 6

CAN NIGERIA AFFORD (LITERALLY) THIS DEMOCRACY?

I have sensed a disturbing complacency in Nigerian politicians and intellectuals as they try to explicate democracy for their compatriots. They assume erroneously that democracy is its own justification—that simply being baptized with the moniker of "democracy" is sufficient. And that Nigerians, dispossessed they may be, will be satisfied with a political concept that, as currently practiced in Nigeria, stands empty of its substance.

This tragic misunderstanding is troubling because the assumption is that even as Nigerians groan under the weight of multiple deprivations, they can take solace in the knowledge that they have democracy and that democracy will soothe their pain. How wrong! The proper retort should be a classic Nigerian pidgin-English putdown: *Na democracy we go chop?* (Is democracy edible?) But let's not trivialize an important issue.

My good friend Ikhide Ikheloa, a literary critic and former *Next* newspaper columnist, has been on a personal mission. His aim: to orchestrate the demise of Nigeria's current "democracy." He is so convinced that democracy, as currently practiced, is a mortal danger to Nigerians that he equates its dissolution with an epic struggle for political liberation: liberation from predation and legalized, "democratic" oppression.

For Ikhide, democracy has, far from doing Nigeria good, set the country back decades and provided a perfect alibi for the political class to bankrupt the country once and for all. Tough words, but those who know Ikhide know that he can be unapologetically melodramatic and passionate in his opinions.

Melodrama aside, what Ikhide is saying is the stuff of dinner table discussions and long-distance telephone and e-mail conversations among Nigerians at home and abroad. Stripped of all provocative rhetorical devices, what Ikhide is advancing is pretty basic: the democracy practiced by Abuja is fractured beyond redemption—beyond mere course correction. It is not what Nigerians signed up for in 1999 when the country returned to civilian rule after a decade and half of military dictatorship; and if they do not act urgently, it will consume them all.

Let me break it down through a process of crude itemization.

First, the material promise of democracy, that is, the supposed correlation between democracy and improved standards of living, has yet to materialize for Nigerians in fifteen unbroken years of "democracy." Democracy has not improved the prospect of development, and in some instances has been a hindrance to it.

Second, even advertised abstract benefits such as press freedom, human rights, the right to free political choice, and the right to make deliberative input in governance have all been denied Nigerians under this democracy. While Nigerians saw glimpses of these benefits in the wake of military disengagement in 1999, today's "democratic" environment resembles, in some respects, the regimented, freedom-less days of military rule.

Third, "democracy" has provided the perfect cover for corruption—massive corruption. "Democracy" has—forgive the redundancy—democratized corruption. Under the military, corruption was a quasi-monopoly; it was tightly controlled by a small cohort. Under the current "democratic" regime, the need to cultivate political support and immunity means that the loot has to circulate. Democracy has legitimatized certain kinds of corruption. In the days of the military, the zones of licit and illicit monetary appropriation were clearly demarcated, so one could tell easily when an act of corrupt self-enrichment had occurred. Not anymore. Under current "democratic" practice, public officials steal legally. They only have to underwrite what they steal as a licit item in the budget bill. This can be done in a few choreographed, taxpayer-funded legislative committee sittings and a hurried process that circumvents debate en route to approval. Political officeholders can even steal in anticipation, carefully documenting future thefts and including them as budgetary earmarks or exculpatory footnotes in legislations. And it's all legal—and perfectly within the procedural norms of this "democracy." Where the law did not exist to legitimize the theft, legislators have enacted or been goaded by executive carrots and sticks into enacting one-off bills to authorize acts of pillage deemed in the pecuniary interest of legislators and their executive partners. Democracy has licensed and unleashed novel evils in the country. Consider this: The Borno State House of Assembly passed a bill awarding stupendous severance perks worth tens of millions of naira annually to the governor and his deputy—for life! Many other state legislatures, notably Akwa Ibom, Kwara, Lagos, Zamfara, Gombe, and Rivers State have followed the same path, awarding unconscionably vulgar lifetime perks to governors who finish their terms in office. And it's all legal and within the rules of this "democracy."

Fourth, the bill for this destructive "democracy" is now being paid for with the lives and limbs of Nigerians. I'll explain. A recent report confirmed what many Nigerians have suspected all along: Nigerian public officeholders at all levels are the highest paid in the world. Together with their string of assistants and advisers (who sometimes also have their own paid advisers), Nigerian public officers gobble up at least half of nation's revenue and budgetary appropriations in legitimate rewards. And we have not accounted for the unbridled stealing that is now a legitimized staple of patrimonial politics in Nigeria. Add that to the math and we may be talking about 70 percent of the national revenue being spent on the maintenance of "democratic" personnel—on running this "democracy." This prohibitive overhead has left the country with a smaller pool of funds than ever to invest in the things that matter to Nigerians: roads, healthcare, school, water, electricity, and food. This odd financial state of low return on "democratic" investment is unsustainable. Something has to give.

Fifth, this "democracy" has intensified ethno-regional bickering while bequeathing an unfolding legacy of costly national political gridlocks. The quagmire occasioned by Yar'Adua's health crisis in 2010 is a perfect illustration. Try quantifying the financial and political cost of this long-running farce and you'll see how expensive "democracy" really is. The country teetered precariously because the ritualistic niceties of democracy stood in the way of pragmatic, decisive, patriotic action. This preference for process over productive outcomes is one reason democracy is losing its appeal with many Nigerians. Most political gridlocks are resolved quicker than the one brought on by Yar'Adua's health problems and at less political cost, but that is not much comfort, either. For when routine political disagreements are settled, they often involve enacting political solutions that entail graft, which is just as costly to Nigerians as prolonged impasses.

Sixth, elected officials often do not play by the rules that brought them to power; they seek instead to subvert laws and constitutions to secure longer tenures. Think Obasanjo of Nigeria, but also think Mamadou Tandja of Niger, Yahyah Jammeh of Gambia, Yoweri Museveni of Uganda, and many other African leaders whose fickle commitment to democracy has led them into tenure-extending adventures that have thrown their countries into costly political crises. The irritant for many Nigerians is that "democracy" has been reduced in practice to—and accepted as being constituted by—only one of its many elements: the ritualistic conduct of periodic, incumbent-rigged elections. Every other benefit of democracy has eluded Nigerians.

Seventh and finally, in this "democracy" every government action is conceived through the lens of politics, not of patriotism. Instead of asking if a policy or initiative is good for the Nigerian people, elected officials ask if it would look good politically. Instead of asking how a policy might help Nigerians, officials ask how it would help them win the next election—how it would enrich campaign donors and party godfathers and how much it would generate for the election war chest. This permanent campaign culture is a costly drawback of democracy and has reached a head in the United States, the prototypical practitioner of the presidential system of government. The difference is that America's robust economy can absorb the cost; Nigeria's cannot.

DEMOCRATIC DISAPPOINTMENT

With such a low dividend on democracy, and with "democracy" being so costly and toxic to the body politic, it is no surprise that many Nigerians have begun to question their loyalty to the received wisdom that democracy is superior to its alternatives.

For many Nigerians and Africans, democracy has failed. It has failed to live up to its publicized benefits—tangible and intangible. So glaring is this failure and so painful are the betrayals of Africa's "democrats" that ten thousand Nigeriens poured into the streets of Niamey to rally in support of the new military regime there in 2010. Westerners may be scrambling to comprehend this dramatic reversal of public opinion from a craving for a democratic overthrow of a military dictatorship more than a decade ago to an enthusiastic embrace of a military overthrow of a "democratic" regime today. But this is something that people in neighboring Nigeria can explain and understand. The Nigeriens at the rally were not expressing a preference for military autocracy. They were voicing their disillusionment with a failed democracy.

Nigeria's democratic setbacks may not yet entitle Nigerians to reject democracy altogether or to be receptive to military rule. But Nigeria is at a crossroads, and if the country continues with this charade, a Niger-like scenario of democratic disillusionment may be on the horizon. Nigeria cannot continue along this path: abusing democracy, invoking it to legitimize all that is abhorrent, but neglecting to fulfill its utilitarian promises to Nigerians.

America and the rest of the West have the luxury of evaluating democracy from a purely idealistic standpoint. They can afford the long wait necessary for democracy to register—the gestation period needed for democracy's more visible benefits to trickle down and permeate society. They can comfortably absorb the overhead cost of democracy and the financial and political burdens of partisan gridlock. Their economy is big enough to soak up the imperfections and dysfunctions of democracy—which are many. Their political system is decentralized enough to withstand partisan and procedural impasse at the political center. In America, political dysfunction, the byproduct of liberal democracy, is not necessarily fatal to the body politic.

Not so in Nigeria—or in the rest of Africa.

Nigerians' perception of democracy is a purely utilitarian one. Americans obsess intellectually about what democracy means; Nigerians ask what it can deliver to them. Americans bicker about the ideational and philosophical contours of democracy; Nigerians prefer to ask more tangible questions of democracy. Nigerians evaluate democratic practice not in abstract or futuristic terms but in terms of its immediate benefits to their lives. Democracy will be only as popular as the results it delivers to

Nigerians. They want democracy to deliver quantifiable rewards, and they cannot wait too long for these. Fifteen years seems a long enough wait.

It is not the fault of Nigerians, either. The rhetoric of democratic advocacy in the military era made glib, enticing connections between Nigerians' economic plight and the lack of democracy in their country. The suggestion was clear: Democracy brings development and improved living. Nigerians' expectation of democracy rests on this promise. It is time they began to see some of the promised returns. If they don't, they have a right to question the assumed connection between democracy and development, and to become disillusioned.

It is unrealistic to expect that in a developmentally challenged country where poverty is an inescapable companion, citizens would perceive democratic governance from a non-materialist perspective. Their needs are tangible, and so are their expectations from democracy. Nigerians should not be expected to muster the idealism and patience required for a drawn-out process of democratic maturity while their bellies are empty. The idea of the politics of the belly, which French anthropologist, Jean-Francois Bayart coined,[5] is not just a metaphor for corruption and the politics of patronage in Africa; it is also a literal guide for understanding the way Nigerians relate to democracy.

WHERE DO WE GO FROM HERE?

There is no innate or sacred loyalty to democracy in Nigerians— or, for that matter, in any other people. The degree of Nigerians' attachment to the concept corresponds to the benefits that they see it delivering or the damage it is doing to their lives. This is why democracy is suffering setbacks across Africa.

So what's the alternative to a broken, dangerous democracy?

It's not so simple. Dambisa Moyo, the Oxford-educated Zambian author of Dead Aid, offers one of the most eloquent critiques of democratic practice in Africa. Democracy—multiparty democracy—prevents timely action that may be the difference between a life-saving economic initiative and life-taking inaction, gridlock, or disaster. Democracy fosters costly ethno-partisan impasses that stifle development and productive economic change. She climaxes her critique by prescribing "benevolent dictatorships" as the practical model for Africa. At least dictatorships get things done—if they want to, and are capable of pushing needed reforms through without the costly and time-consuming observance of democratic rules and processes. The procedural red tape of democracy is an enemy of development, she argues.

It is hard to disagree with Moyo's critique of democracy in Africa. But it's equally hard to sympathize with her prescription because benevolence and dictatorships rarely coexist in Africa, or anywhere, and it takes a certain amount of willful naïveté to assume that they could. Nonetheless, Moyo deserves commendation for going against the grain of universal democratic orthodoxy—the unquestioned dogma that democracy can simply be transplanted to Africa in its Western form with its stifling multiparty squabbles, expensive electoral rituals, and costly, divisive deliberative quagmires. In Nigeria and much of Africa, the price of democracy is not simply the opportunity cost of observing the niceties of democratic practice. Sometimes the price can be literal, in the sense that, already reeling from fiscal troubles occasioned by debt and dysfunction, several African states simply cannot afford the cost of running big legislatures, a large cabinet peopled by members of ruling political alliances, and the financial cost of providing logistics for periodic elections. These burdens and luxuries of democracy become even more glaring when juxtaposed against the enormous developmental needs of these states. Some of these developmental deficits can be solved with the resources devoted to aping the democratic models of the West, resources squandered in a fraudulent effort to *appear* democratic while taking advantage of this contrived appearance to fleece the national patrimony.

Here is the bottom line: This democracy is fatally broken. The country is headed for an implosion if Nigerians fail to do something about this troubled system of governance they call democracy. Ikhide Ikheloa may be hyperbolic in his characterization, but the disenchantment with democracy and its many failures is real. Nigerians ignore this reality at their collective peril.

Much as Nigerians are inclined to defer the discussion and to toe the politically correct line of advancing democracy as its own cure, they are frequently confronted with political crises that threaten the very foundation of the Nigerian union—political crises that partly emanate from a pretend democracy and its complications. The question is: What is democracy's worth if the way it is practiced imperils a country and its people and widens the crevices that divide its citizens? Would Nigerians rather preserve a pretentious democracy and lose the nation in the process?

What, then, are the choices before Nigeria?

Earlier, I introduced Dambisa Moyo's prescription of "benevolent dictatorship." It's not a new idea. It has floated around since the 1960s. It used to be called one party developmental dictatorship, or more euphemistically, the developmental state. The poster country of that model today is China. But China is China and Nigeria is Nigeria. Because of Nigeria's history of military rule and because of strong elite unanimity in opposing non-representative political templates, this model would only heighten the current crisis of governance and stifle development. In other words, it would be a dictatorship but it would be anything but developmental.

How about military rule?

I have found that most Nigerians do not share the irreconcilable hostility of the schooled elite to military rule. Much of this hostility is founded on abstract, theoretical objections, not on crude or even enlightened interests. Most Nigerians are more pragmatic. They would prefer an effective military regime that improves their lives to a "democratic" regime that is preoccupied with a systematic violation of their rights.

Nigerians are not the only ones who entertain episodic fantasies about the virtues of decisive autocracies during moments of democratic disappointments and stalemates. Even the Americans occasionally bemoan the problems of democracy and its elevation of bickering above action. Frustrated that some of his agendas were stuck in the traffic of congressional partisanship, former president George W. Bush famously remarked that "a dictatorship would be a heck of a lot easier." He was joking, of course. But he was also expressing a genuine frustration at the slow pace of democracy—at the roadblocks that democratic rules and procedures place in the way of policy, initiative, and problem solving. And yet, the frustrations of democracy are more intense, more burdensome, and more consequential in Nigeria than they are in America.

Nigeria's intellectual and political elites are fond of saying that the worst democratic regime is better than the best military regime. This is elitist, out-of-touch rhetoric, a talking point of pro-democracy advocacy. Most Nigerians would reject this proposition outright. The poor, anguished farmer in my village who desires the positive physical presence of government in his community would disagree with it. So would the slum-dwelling day laborer in Kurmin Gwari, Kaduna. He would gladly accept a performing government of any stripe.

This is, of course, a false-choice scenario. Most Nigerians would prefer the ideal: a democratic government that is also an effective governing machine, a prudent, fair, and humane allocator of resources. In the absence of the ideal, however, they would settle for a regime—any regime—that gives them the roads, schools, water, healthcare, electricity, and food security they crave.

A critique of democracy is not an endorsement of military rule. It need not be. The enlightened segments of Nigerian society are firm in their agreement that democracy is inherently better than military rule. Because these segments—and not the brutalized and desperate masses—are the drivers of political paradigm shifts, we can take the military rule option off the table. But that does not mean that Nigerians have to engage in the fatalism of accepting the invidious, "democratic" status quo. It means, rather, that, (1) Nigerians and indeed all Africans need to engage in an honest conversation about the ways in which the democracy foisted on them by the Washington Consensus and by the "democratization" rhetoric of donor countries is actually a mockery of the tenets of democracy—representation, legitimacy, and accountability; and (2) that we have to craft something in its place.

On the first point, it is clear that liberal democracy is, *ab initio*, a flawed concept that in practice results in elitism, oligarchic imposition, bad representation, and corruption. In a liberal democratic setup the process is rigged from the beginning to elevate people who, judging by their social and economic orientations,

are not representative of the socioeconomic profiles of a majority of the population—elites who are wealthier, better educated,
and thus unrepresentative of the people the aspire to govern.
That's not the only problem; because of the fundamentally elitist
nature of the political system, the existing political parties and
platforms inevitably send up two or more elitist, unrepresentative choices that, in other, more democratized circumstances,
would be rejected as disconnected elites by the majority of citizens. But liberal democratic practice is a fait accompli in many
ways, so that once the system pushes these choices through primacy election contests that are guaranteed to favor members of
a small upper crust of elites, the masses are forced, in the name
of democracy, to vote for one of these unrepresentative choices.

Obviously, this is a fundamental problem of liberal democratic practice, one which should cause those who advance it as a
sacrosanct political product to become more willing to tweak,
amend, and domesticate the practice of democracy to meet the
peculiar needs and circumstances of individual countries and
peoples. In the West, the aforementioned flaws are, to the extent
possible, mitigated by strong judicial institutions and by well-es-
tablished systems of checks, balances, and accountability. In Nigeria—and Africa—the absence or weakness of these institutions
means that the people are saddled with a democratic system in
which elites not beholden to and unrepresentative of the anxieties, needs, and interests of a vast majority of citizens can ride
roughshod over their compatriots. As long as they organize the
periodic ritual of elections, they can brutalize their compatriots,
abuse the organs of "democracy" to line their pockets, and perform the perfunctory dance of "democracy" to remain in good
standing with Western democratic evaluators and donors. This
is the sham that is proliferating across Africa in the name of democratization and democracy.

The other layer of the problem is the foundational argument,
now approaching a consensus, that liberal democracy functions
poorly in an environment saturated with poverty and lack, and
that obsessions over the causal connection between democracy
on the one hand and economic growth and wealth distribution
on the other miss the salient factors that catalyze the expansion
of economic opportunities for citizens.[6] In Nigeria and much of

Africa, this contention is even more poignant, given the depressing reality that poverty, along with and the existential grind that it spawns, works against democracy in two ways—preventing citizen activism and civil society vigilance, and enabling corrupt politicians to use their loot to buy off the votes of poor, desperate compatriots.

This disconnect between liberal democracy and ordinary Nigerians is at the heart of the latter's frustrations with what continues to be described to them as democracy. This democratic frustration does not mean that redemption can only come outside the ideas and practices that privilege representation, legitimacy, and accountability—outside the generic rubric of democracy. But it does mean that countries like Nigeria should be free to craft their own kind of democracy to suit their circumstances and address their peculiar vulnerabilities. And if one begins from the premise outlined above, that liberal democracy is an imperfect object that is by its very nature fraught with pragmatic compromises, it becomes much easier to visualize and articulate creative, pragmatic, and locally relevant *democratic* alternatives to it.

For starters, why can't Nigerians modify this unwieldy American presidential system that is undermining their country? Even the Americans, with all their wealth and strong institutions, are complaining about the financial cost (or *transaction cost*, to use chic political science jargon) of their democracy, and its divisive, do-nothing, hyper-partisan gridlocks. Nigeria's gridlocks are more costly because not only are they partisan, they are complicated by ethno-religious and regional fissures.

Why does Nigeria need to have two money-guzzling legislative chambers instead of one lean, inexpensive one? Why, in the name of all that is good, does the constitution require that each state have three senators when it could have one, saving the country money and compelling the senator to actually work? Even the Americans, whom Nigeria imitates, have only two senators representing each state.

INSTITUTIONAL MISFITS

Many African cultures are authoritarian in nature. The figure of the big man who sits atop the political food chain with magisterial command, taking care of his subjects' needs but demanding total subservience from them, is seductive. When the American executive power system and this preexisting cultural reality converge, you end up with the kind of vulgar abuses of power that are the routine of Nigeria's executive officeholders across the country. Nigeria does not need a system that intensifies this basic authoritarian cultural disposition. It needs a system that attenuates it, such as a parliamentary system or any other arrangement that approximates its virtues.

These are just a few examples of how one could reform and recalibrate Nigeria's democratic practice to fit Nigerians' peculiar needs, problems, and pocket. The choice is not between military rule and the unsustainable status quo.

Abuja will understandably oppose reforms that will reduce executive power and its abuse, shrink the stealing field, and expand the pool of resources available for developing the lives of Nigerians. Already, its answer to the problem of dwindling developmental revenue (caused by excessive democracy expenses and corruption) is to inflict more taxes and levies on Nigeria's economically beleaguered middle and lower classes.

This is a welcome blunder. It should backfire with a positive outcome. With taxation comes the clamor for accountability, hostility to government recklessness, and demands for effective representation. With taxation comes citizen vigilance. Maybe the failures of this democracy and Abuja's frantic reaction to them will fertilize the ground for corrective action and for the installation of a true, concrete democracy.

A one-country lamentation on the state of democratic practice in Nigeria is only a window into a larger continental problem, one that calls for reflections beyond country-specific details. The realist, pragmatic sentiment expressed in this essay is finding reception among a new, youthful breed of African thinkers and leaders, even if the space for expressing it remains largely closed off by the discursive tyranny of the liberal democratic orthodoxy. It is not only Dambisa Moyo who has bucked the liberal democratic consensus when it comes to Africa. Swaady Martin-Leke, a former child refugee from Liberia, an entrepreneur, a successful businesswoman, and a recent Desmond Tutu Fellow, appeared on the Aljazeera Television talk program *South2North* and offered the following unconventional take on Africa's political predicament:

> We are not really ready for democracy but it's not acceptable in the current global context to actually say that we are not ready for democracy. So what's happening is until we get benevolent dictators like in Rwanda we are basically at the mercy of our governments and in the meantime we're just almost victims of democracy.[7]

This may seem a little exaggerated in its indictment of liberal democracy in Africa and the "democratic consensus" that enables it. But if anything it is a restrained verdict. Africans are not "almost victims" of liberal democracy (or "copycat democracy," as I like to call it); they are victims, period. Folks in the West would be scandalized to see the depravity that passes for "democracy" in many African countries as well as the damage it is causing. As I stated earlier, I am not sure that the oxymoronic concoction of "benevolent dictatorship" is the answer, as a dictatorship by its very nature cannot be benevolent, and Rwanda is, at present and in spite of its remarkable if tense stability, hardly a good example of a "benevolent dictatorship." However, at the very least, the failure—yes, failure!—of liberal democracy in Africa calls for a new paradigm that allows an unfettered conversation on alternative models of democracy, which may be more suited to the sociopolitical, economic, and cultural realities of African countries. This conversation cannot happen under the current tyranny of the liberal democratic orthodoxy. This is what I understand to be the overarching, takeaway point from Martin-Leke's argument.

Democracy is not forced down on a people from the top through the instrumentality of a scarcely representative and ad hoc consensus of political elites. Democracy has to evolve organically from conditions in a particular country, driven by the desire of an economically situated, educated, and politically conscious coalition of professionals, entrepreneurs, workers, traders—in short, civil society groups—for governing efficiency, legitimate leadership, and accountability, and for rights and enlightened representation. In many African countries, education and economic foundations are poor. Infrastructures have decayed or are nonexistent. The result is that even if there is a civil society in the crude demographic sense, it does not have the critical mass of educated, economically independent citizens willing to use their economic and social leverage to force a democratic agenda on the political elite. Furthermore, infrastructural deficits mean that professionals, workers, and entrepreneurs spend the bulk of their time surviving and making a living, with little spare time to invest in grassroots and urban organizations that generate pressures for homegrown democratic practices.

Then there is the foundational reality of mass poverty, economic disenfranchisement, and illiteracy, which renders a large pool of the population, including those living in rural areas as farmers and artisans, largely apolitical and thus incapable of generating the bottom-up momentum for legitimate democratic institutions, for representations, for basic human rights and dignities, and for effective, accountable governance.

In the absence of these ingredients, the fad has been for Africa's small political class to simply reach a consensus on adopting some mode of liberal democracy available to them in the form of Western examples in practice, and in the form of academic and democratic advocacy literature in theory.

As a result of this undemocratic "democratic" history, what have emerged in the more than two decades of liberal democratic practice in various African countries are depressing political caricatures posing as democracies, which nevertheless garner approval from Western democracy advocates. These advocates would be horrified to learn that the liberal democracy they pushed and funded in Africa is now little more than a feel-good political device for political elites to violate their citizens and escape consequential Western scrutiny or reprimand. The "democracies" that have emerged are expensive, conflicted, dysfunctional, and massively corrupt.

The idea that only liberal democracy constitutes democratic practice and that it should be adopted even in places where the sociopolitical, cultural, economic, and judicial conditions for it do not exist is perhaps the greatest political danger to Africa today. You cannot have a functional liberal democratic system without the foundational sociopolitical, economic, and cultural ferment outlined above. To insist on having it imposed in the absence of these conditions is to turn the logic of democratic evolution on its head. It is tyrannical, and not democratic, which is the ultimate irony.

CHAPTER 7

NORTHERN ELITES AND NORTHERN
ECONOMIC BACKWARDNESS

The Lugardian creation that materialized as Northern Nigeria is not a product of mythmaking, but its elites have constructed elaborate myths around it. One such myth is the narrative of North–South economic parity. This claim bears no resemblance to the region's reality. Nonetheless, it has been a useful rhetorical device for Northern political elites who desire an excuse for their failure to bring about actual, rather than mythical, economic parity between the North and the South.

The story of Northern economic backwardness is partly a creation of the confluence of colonial arrangement and disparities in natural economic endowment. Colonialism and its economic priorities dealt the region a bad hand from the beginning. The centrality of oceanic shipments to the colonial economy and the higher value of Southern export crops such as cocoa, rubber, and palm produce meant an economic downgrade for the North in the colonial scheme. The North lacked access to the ocean and its shipping revenue. It produced export crops that, compared to Southern ones, did not fetch much value in the international commodities market. Consequently, the North played second fiddle to the South in the colonial revenue-generation system. For long stretches in the colonial period, the North's administrative costs were partly subsidized by Southern-derived revenues.

There have been several attempts by Northern politicians and intellectuals to parry and deny the reality of Southern economic ascendance vis-à-vis Northern economic decline. Some of the deniers are sincere, well-intentioned observers, who reckon that admitting that the North is in a subordinate economic position to the South reflects poorly on the reputation of the region and puts it in a weak political bargaining position.

The late Dr. Bala Usman belongs in this category. An erudite historian of the highest repute, he subscribed, later in his career, to some wild pseudo-deconstructionist postulations apparently designed to challenge the narrative of Southern Nigerian economic and resource advantage. Not only that, but he went so far as to concoct a bizarre theory claiming that Southern petroleum endowments are actually Northern in geological origin! Anything is preferable to admitting the truth of Northern economic disadvantage. As with all revisionist claims that one has to strain to make, the farcical nature of his attempt to refute the Southern economic head start actually discredited it, while reinforcing that which it sought to challenge.

Other deniers are less innocent and honorable, avoiding the question of Northern economic collapse because any honest assessment of this history of loss, corruption, and economic myopia might implicate them. But facts are facts. Today, Northern Nigeria, however defined, is in economic free fall. Its industrial hubs are long gone, and surviving industries have lost their luster. Northern Nigerian unemployment statistics bear the staggering imprints of years of economic complacency. The Northern economic picture will depress even the most incurable of optimists. The North has failed to recapture its pre-colonial economic prosperity.

The biggest legacy of the colonial reality of assessing Northern economic productivity in relation to the South's was that the British colonial authorities understood North and South as competing economic zones, whose revenues and productivity were constantly compared. Another legacy—a function of the North–South economic competition that colonialism set in motion—is that one cannot contemplate Northern economic realities without referencing their Southern analogues. For good or ill, the North and the South are economic competitors. The sooner Northern economic planners realize this reality, the better for the region's collective and fragmented economic futures. Colonial intertwinement has bequeathed a legacy of friendly economic competition and comparison between the two regions. It is not something to be denied or decried. It is something to be recognized and factored into the ways that Northern elites imagine the economic future of their region.

Interregional economic competition is not necessarily a bad thing, colonial legacy or not. Everyone needs someone to look up to or down on. It is the reality of life. There is nothing wrong with looking to the South for a model of postcolonial economic and commercial vibrancy. There is also nothing wrong in trying to locate and address the source of the asymmetrical economic fortunes of North and South.

The South has nurtured and encouraged the entrepreneurial spirit of its people since independence, weaning them off the government-is-our-father mentality. The North, by contrast, has nurtured a government dependency that cannot be sustained for much longer. The legendary enterprise of Northern Nigerians, displayed in pre-colonial and colonial times, has been neglected. It has been sacrificed for a politics of patronage that has trained Northerners to tie their needs to government financial intervention and the occasional "generosity" of ethically challenged Northern politicians and bureaucrats.

The irony of Northern economic backwardness is that it is a product of the North's greater access to political power in a country where there is a de facto correlation between political power and access to national resources. Northern political elites have done very little with so much political power and are the real villains of this unfolding story of economic failure. Their default inclination has been to simply maintain access to political power and the temporary economic blessings that it bestows. But this cannot substitute for deliberate regional economic planning. It is, in fact, counterproductive because the facts show a correlation between Northern political ascendance and Northern economic deterioration.

As we approach the eve of the post-oil economy, the gloom of the Northern economic picture is more compelling—or depressing. Northern political leaders may be using state resources to practice crude patrimonial politics in the hope of preventing total economic collapse and a revolt by economically dispossessed Northerners. And they may succeed in this for now. This, however, is not a substitute for visionary thinking or for crafting a regional economic roadmap to the impending post-oil economy.

The end of oil is upon us. Oil is a finite resource that may run out before Nigerians have a chance to prepare for that eventuality. But Nigerians may not even have the luxury of waiting for the oil wells to dry up, as the development of energy alternatives by global energy consumers may settle the issue for them, catching citizens and leaders flatfooted. The question is: What are those who employ fiery rhetoric in defense of "Northern interests" doing to prepare their region for this inevitable reality?

The South, the oil-producing region that should stand to lose more from the transition from oil, already has a head start in preparing for a future without oil. It is an irony that would not be lost on so-called Northern leaders that the region of Nigeria that one might expect to be more complacent in the orgy of oil revenue is the one that is better positioned to survive and perhaps thrive in the post-oil future.

Those who want to be seen as champions of the Northern cause and have built their political careers purportedly defending the North should put their money where their proverbial mouths are. They should devise and finance a plan for Northern economic recovery, a plan to wean Northern peoples off the destructive patronage of their elites and unleash their creative energies for the post-oil economic future.

CHAPTER 8

THE LIMITS OF ELECTORAL REFORM

I was at an African Studies Association conference in New York, where one of the panels deliberated on the chaotic April 2007 presidential elections and the subsequent election reform process inaugurated by then president Umaru Musa Yar'Adua. The roundtable discussion was rich and insightful, each speaker analyzing what led us to this democratic quagmire and what should be done to extricate us from it.

The discussion got me thinking about the committee set up by late President Musa Yar'Adua to reform the electoral process, the report of which is generally seen as a solid blueprint for electoral reform in Nigeria. Can this document, if implemented, deliver a workable, problem-proof electoral formula to Nigeria? In reflecting on this question, I have also been considering the limits of electoral reform. I am doing so not only because I suspect that electoral reform is being gradually advanced as a stand-in for other kinds of reforms, but also because Nigerian political leaders are exciting citizens' collective democratic hope in a reform of the electoral system but have not stepped back to take stock of its limitations.

There is no doubt that the electoral system and other institutions of democracy need to be deepened and made less amenable to manipulation by politicians. Such institutional reforms could render the self-interested and illegal interventions of powerful politicians, especially the president, less injurious to Nigeria's democracy, if not completely impotent. I would argue, however, that no electoral reform can stop a determined president from engineering the kind of electoral outcome that they prefer, at least not under the current political structure of an overbearing executive branch.

And this is where I must begin. Nigerians seem to assume that credible electoral reform will remove the underlying motivation for vote-rigging. It will not. Rigging and other forms of election fraud come from a political desperation that, if backed by executive power, cannot be stopped by the most formidable of electoral laws. Some politicians' only province of expertise is finding creative ways around laws that stand in the way of their political interests. This is true not just for Nigerian politicians but for politicians everywhere. A desperate, determined, and conceited politician is a fitting match for any good electoral law.

Let us not forget that what got Nigeria here is not just a bad electoral system. In addition to bad electoral laws and systems, the democratic setbacks that Nigeria has suffered in the last ten years were largely the result of the machinations of a group of narcissistic politicians led by Olusegun Obasanjo. This group of people had no qualms about breaking, ignoring, or strategically misinterpreting electoral laws. Many members of this group are still active in politics at the federal executive level. If they had no hesitation in participating in the abuse of porous electoral laws, why should they behave any differently with better electoral laws and a better system? My cynical instincts tell me that a better electoral law will simply bring out the best of these politicians' criminal ingenuity.

As laudable as these reforms are, the quest for a credible, enduring democratic culture must then go beyond electoral reforms. Nigeria must devise a mechanism that prevents politicians with executive power from scrapping the electoral conventions of the land, or at least makes it unprofitable for them to do so. To do this, Nigerians must remove the basis of desperation from the political calculus. This entails preventing any group of people from having too much power, access to national resources, or privileges that outweigh the compulsion to respect electoral and institutional conventions. Nigerians must prevent these politicians from becoming invested in the national political system to the point of doing illegal, unconstitutional, and unconscionable things to keep and nurture their jobs.

The example of Olusegun Obasanjo and his allies who hijacked the Nigerian state is instructive. Part of Obasanjo's perverse brilliance is his ability to deploy a discourse of "economic reform" to seduce the West and to engineer international consent and admiration while destroying democracy at home—the same democracy that the West is purportedly committed to nurturing. How did Obasanjo manage to achieve such an incredible feat?

Simple: He initiated a set of reforms palatable to the IMF and the World Bank and recruited Nigerian technocrats committed to the visions of these organizations to superintend the reforms. To go along with this, a stable rhetorical diet of "reform" and respect for "technocratic competence" was served to the West.

This political sleight of hand muted and mitigated Western democratic vigilance, allowing Obasanjo and his allies to subvert democracy and free enterprise locally, while pretending to be committed to the free market and democracy. Without international outrage and repercussions, Obasanjo was able to break Nigeria's admittedly faulty electoral laws and manipulate institutions to his heart's content.

My fear is that even if electoral reforms succeed in fashioning an electoral system that is formidable, future presidents may simply deploy Obasanjo's playbook, initiating pro-Western reforms to deflect Western criticism and to extract Western consent, while engineering dubious electoral outcomes to their own benefit. If other presidents choose to imitate Obasanjo's perversely brilliant politics, and there is evidence that they have chosen that path, then Nigeria's democracy may be doomed, no matter how sound the country's electoral system may be.

In Nigeria, as in much of Africa, there is a strong motivation to hold on to power, exclude one's opponents from the democratic space, and flout electoral and constitutional conventions in the process. Backed by the overreaching executive power of the Obasanjo presidency, the PDP and its corporate allies sought to inaugurate a political dynasty of control over the state and its resources, with some of them even gleefully declaring that the PDP was set for a hundred-year rule. Yet any other political party or political class would have done the same thing. This includes the defunct ANPP and ACN, the newly formed APC, or any other political tendency in Nigeria. They would also probably have sought to subvert the electoral process and the laws of the land to retain their privileged perch in power, for longevity is the supreme logic of political power in Africa because it guarantees access to the spoils of office. The problem is not the electoral system or laws per se, but the facts that (1) the federal executive government is too lucratively attractive, and (2) the federal executive government is too powerful.

The two facts reinforce each other. The attractiveness of federal executive power is a function of the immense access to resources that it bestows on those who wield that power. In the same vein, executive power enables the president to subvert the electoral system and to undertake unethical and undemocratic acts in order to preserve access to resources. It is a depressing duo, a perfect recipe for political desperation, the type that can make nonsense of any electoral laws or system, no matter how well crafted. In such a climate, power and the access to resources that it confers must be maintained at all cost. This leads to the sort of reform talk and the repressive and unconstitutional acts that characterized the Obasanjo presidency. A lot of people were too deeply invested (literally and figuratively) in power to let go; to let the electoral laws and conventions hold sway; to let the constitution mediate the electoral process. From PDP chieftains to pro-Obasanjo business moguls dependent on state patronage, to political appointees, to international lobbyists—a whole slew of interests and groups of people became so invested in the Obasanjo presidency and/or its reforms that they either participated in or acquiesced to the wanton dismemberment of the electoral system in the quest for so-called continuity.

Continuity and reform became intertwined slogans authorizing the most brazen electoral frauds and the most insensitive subversion of democracy in Nigeria. The culmination of this process was Obasanjo's undemocratic declaration that he would not hand over power to anyone not committed to continuing his "reforms." Curiously but understandably, this scandalous declaration did not attract even a whimper of criticism from the self-appointed monitors of democracy in the West. "Continuity" and "reform" were deeply implicated in the electoral fraud of April 2007 and in the numerous undemocratic and unconstitutional actions that led to it.

To recap, electoral reform is laudable, but it is powerless in the face of any dogged political group intent on maintaining the status quo and their privileged access to state resources and power. This is why electoral reforms must not skirt or precede the resolution of the fundamental issue of the structure of the Nigerian state: the fact that the federal government controls too much resource revenue and has too much power over its distribution. This is the root of political desperation, which has doomed Nigeria's presidential electoral contests to date.

Without reducing the attractiveness of the presidency and of other elective federal offices through the institution of fiscal federalism and without the devolution of control over resources to Nigeria's constituent units, electoral contests will remain contests for access to resources, and the desperation and greed that fuel these contests will continue to undermine Nigeria's electoral system.

Along with fiscal federalism, a comprehensive constitutional review should whittle down the power, reach, and influence of the presidency, devolving power, developmental initiative, and the most consequential electoral contests to the local levels where the Nigerian people can best mobilize to counter the election-rigging and democracy-subverting actions of politicians. Because people have a direct stake and investment in the politics of their constituencies, the determination of politicians to trash electoral laws and conventions are unlikely to succeed at those levels.

It is hard to imagine how electoral reform can succeed when an overarching executive power fueled by the desperation and greed that follow logically from the enormous resources controlled by the state can override any electoral convention. Nigerians seem to be putting the cart of electoral reforms before the horse of constitutional reforms. The latter, if carried out properly to reduce the economic attractiveness of public office, especially of federal elective office, can constitute the most important electoral reform and thus make the type of electoral reform that was initiated by President Yar'Adua either unnecessary or simply complementary.

SECTION II

NIGERIA (SOCIETY AND LETTERS)

CHAPTER 9

MY OGA IS BIGGER THAN YOURS

Most Nigerians love to be called *Oga*. Even if they don't care for the actual term, they like what it connotes. They like it not only because it projects relevance but also because it entitles the bearer to the natural or forced subservience of his interlocutors. To be called Oga is a reassurance that one has subordinates and social inferiors who are willing to confer on or concede to one the symbolic trappings of socioeconomic distinction. Oga bespeaks respect, except, of course, when peppered with sarcasm.

But the Oga phenomenon is also an allegory for Nigeria's many afflictions as a nation. At the heart of the Nigerian crisis of values, bad leadership, and social decay is an obsession with a distorted, vulgar notion of what it means to be important, to be an Oga.

There is nothing inherently wrong with coveting Ogahood. The quest for Ogahood is at some level the expression of a can-do, ambitious spirit that ought to be harnessed to positive ends. That is a subject for another essay.

Everyone desires recognition. A philosopher once described the object of most social movements and struggles as the quest for recognition and redistribution.[8] We all desire to have our humanity, identity, and rights respected, but we also want to obtain tangible material benefits that we feel entitled to. This proposition assumes that society produces and distributes benefits and that members sometimes seek these benefits through the leverage of status and identity recognitions. The problem in Nigeria is that citizens desire status and want to be able to deploy that status for personal pecuniary gains, but they shirk the responsibility of contributing to the production of the material benefits they covet—the benefits that come with Ogahood. Theirs is an insatiable desire for the benefits of Ogahood and a corresponding disdain for its responsibilities.

In its fullest realization, Oga is the Nigerian rendition of the popular figure of the African big man. The original African big man is a father and a patriarch, a servant, a caregiver. He is a compassionate do-gooder who may occasionally consume conspicuously and partake in bizarre rituals of power but who nonetheless deprives himself for the community's sake.

Nigerians have divested the big man concept of its connotations of servitude and selflessness. In its banal expression through the Oga phenomenon, it now signifies a desire to be served and attended to but not to serve or sacrifice for country or community. This is why some Nigerians would give and do anything to be reckoned with as an Oga. They would kill, defraud, steal, rig elections, lie, and deceive. In this twisted moral universe, the attainment of Ogahood trumps the observance of mores and values that are rooted in the noble ethics of African big-manhood.

Nigerian politicians have no moral limits or restraint; armed robbers observe no sympathetic endpoint in the infliction of harm; security forces heed no procedural limits on brutality; and citizens swoon adoringly over the amoral—and immoral—Ogas in their midst. It is one vast network of mutually reinforcing idioms of vanity and moral compromise. The worst Oga, the most depraved big man, is treated as the best role model. And yet, the Oga wants to be an even bigger Oga and would do anything at the expense of society and other citizens to ascend. Keenly observing the moral recklessness of the Oga are his studious underlings. They have watched as their Oga has successfully navigated his way to the top, breaking laws, greasing palms, swindling, wheeling, and dealing along the way. Without the punitive deterrence of enforced law, the Oga's immoral ways become a blueprint instead of a cautionary tale.

Everyone wants to be an Oga; no one wants to serve, to be an ethical, hard-working citizen. Everyone wants to consume, conspicuously of course, but no one wants to bear the burden of producing. It would be interesting to see the day when Nigerians all become Ogas and there is no one to call anyone Oga because Ogas don't call each other Oga—the day when the Oga title loses its aura and becomes an empty, banal sign. Yet this day will never come in a society of limited resources and zero-sum realities.

The Oga's possessions and social status are their own justifications. This is a fundamental ethical distinction that transcends the cliché of the end justifying the means. In the peculiar world of Ogahood, the end is both the end and the means. Even pedestrian routines in the life of an Oga are a part of his public persona—a carefully cultivated self-portrayal.

Even those of us in the diaspora have the Oga bug. In the narratives we construct for the consumption of our Euro-American friends, colleagues, and acquaintances, we are princes and princesses. I have yet to meet a Nigerian resident in Europe or North America who is not a prince or princess in their public script—a descendant of common African folk like me. Most of us see no nobility in statuses like peasant, laborer, craftsman, civil servant, or other pedestrian, if dignified, vocations. So we tell our Euro-American interlocutors that we are princes and princesses. We are willing to lie to get Oga-like recognition in foreign lands. Yet we never stop to think about the implausibility of an exodus of Nigerian princes and princesses who would curiously prefer various forms of laborious servitudes in Euro-America to the princely pleasures of their realms in Nigeria. Or that our Euro-American friends may call this narrative into question as stories of royal origins proliferate among us, and wonder if Nigerian kingdoms had only kings and princes and not subjects.

There is a troubling irony in this diasporic self-portrayal. In a quest to secure a legal foothold in Western countries, immigrants who impersonate princes and princesses are as likely as any others to have told tales of undistinguished and dispossessed beginnings, of destitution, and of desperate escape from home, from economic lack and suffering. The dissonance between a biographical narrative of princely pedigree and a tale of difficult escape from Africa sits in perpetual judgment over us. For what sort of privileged prince abandons his realm and its perks to embrace a life of servitude and toil abroad?

Yet, there is a case to be made for Nigerian immigrants who give up personal honor, or Ogahood, in one arena—in the lawyerly precinct of the Western immigration bureaucracy—only to reassert it in the quotidian rituals of immigrant–native interactions. Once the business of immigration papers is settled in favor of the immigrant, what is the incentive to renounce an ethic of honor that accords recognition only to those who advance to be recognized, to those who seek and cultivate honor and prestige through inventive techniques of self-imaging?

This is why the trope of Ogahood is embedded in the aesthetic repertoires of Nigerians abroad. Their writings bear it out, whether as verbose speech designed to impress and confound or as robust prose interlaced with needless referents to modernity. But this bold negotiation for honor tends to retreat in the face of the law, replaced by a narrative cowardice that seeks to curry pity, and by a tale that satiates Western liberal humanism and Western conservative humanitarianism. This momentary cowardice is rational and calculated, though. The desperate immigrant does not tell the interviewing immigration official that he is a prince. Doing so would result in denial of legal status and truncate his chances of attaining Ogahood in the future—the very essence of the migratory adventure. So, from beginning to end, the Nigerian immigrant's journey is calibrated to achieve Ogahood. Even when he is actively disavowing his aristocratic aspirations (or origins) before the immigration judge, he is ironically doing so with an eye to regaining that coveted pedestal on the shoulders of legal immigration status. It's a sophisticated script, and it requires a measure of self-immolation.

Think about it. The immigrant is in the West to pursue the signs of personal importance, the accouterments of modernity that confer the prestige of Ogahood. Yet the protocols of the immigration system require that he remains silent about his real intentions. He is compelled, instead, to proclaim that he is in the West to merely eke out survival in the orbit of Western capitalism, away from the horrors of a dysfunctional Africa.

Some of these discursive maneuvers are products of the generic anxiety of an immigrant. No immigrant, especially a stereotyped African one, wants to be branded a refugee, an economic migrant. So we invent fables of princely origin to both impress our Euro-American friends and distinguish ourselves from black Euro-Americans of the slave trade diaspora. But much of it is inspired by our love of status and by our aversion to non-Oga statuses and the boring, monotonous virtues associated with them: hard work, just reward, and moral restraint.

Afrocentric African Americans, our cousins in America, have constructed an epistemological and literary tradition around the concept of princely ancestry. The emphasis in Afrocentric discourse on slave ancestors' pre-slavery privilege in Africa is a variant of the motif of respect, the ethic of Ogahood. In this case, the effort is restorative, seeking to recover respect and status denied to slaves and their descendants. It is also, unlike the Nigerian variant, escapist. It seeks exit from an overpowering Eurocentric narrative. This hegemonic narrative denies history and respect to Africans forced to America as slaves and stamps anonymity on them and their descendants.

In claiming that their enslaved ancestors had been kings and queens in Africa, African Americans are seeking to restore themselves to a respectable status in history, to restore themselves to a culture of respect from which Eurocentric discourses have excluded them. This is a clear divergence from the Nigerian narrative claims on Ogahood and princely pedigree. Nonetheless, there is a connection between the two scripts, as both are animated and reference the same cultural idioms of honor and respect. Afrocentric claim on R-E-S-P-E-C-T, to quote Aretha Franklin's soulful hit song, and its corollary insistence on prestigious heritage, much like the Nigerian quest for Ogahood, constitute a subtle demand for status change, for recognition, and for the right to project a sense of importance in a context in which one's status has to be staked out, worked out, asserted, and cannot be taken for granted.

In the Nigerian homeland, the attractions of Ogahood are the core of many artistic genres. They are the staple of an aesthetic culture expressed through a reference to loud displays of self-importance. There is hardly a fictionalized Nigerian story without the archetypal big man or big madam. Cyprian Ekwensi's Jagua Nana in the novel of the same title, Chinua Achebe's Chief Nanga in *Man of the People,* and numerous similarly flat and predictable characters of ostentation, ambition, and honorific display all embody the Oga ethic. Even Okonkwo, Achebe's famous figure of African anti-colonial rage in *Things Fall Apart,* is driven to his rampage against the institutional and human signifiers of colonial violence by an encrypted yet widely understood code of personal importance.

Nollywood has since moved to audio-visually codify the ubiquitous scramble by Nigerians to attain the statuses that matter.
The descent into fetish, the melodramatic portrayal of vice, the
glamorization of vulgar political patronage, the commercialization of Pentecostal Christianity, and the reverential adulation of
men and women of wealth—all of these familiar motifs of Nollywood add to the overwhelming presence of the idiom of personal importance, of Ogahood in postcolonial Nigeria.

As a new capitalist culture of entrepreneurial aggression
struggles for space among men and women with political clout,
Nigeria's growing literary corpus and the expansive reflective
mirror of Nollywood are running out of representational tools
to capture the ever-growing frontiers of Ogahood. Will there be
room, still, in this emerging ethical universe for the old, respectable bromide of Ogahood, the one that is coterminous with honest quest and its symbolic rewards?

CHAPTER 10

ANTI-INTELLECTUALISM AND BOOK PEOPLE

Expertise. Every country needs it. Some countries cultivate and nurture it; others denigrate it. Expertise used to be revered in Nigeria. Today, the learned and the informed are scorned as bookish idealists who, in spite of their mastery over their subject areas, are unschooled in the ways of Nigerian life. This disdain for book people, for competence and intellectual capital, has crept into the realm of politics. That's the arena in which it is doing the most damage to the country.

Nigerians are prone to amnesia. Some of it is self-cushioning, willful forgetting, some of it an expression of the national malaise of shortsightedness. Most Nigerians seem to have forgotten the time when people who knew what they were talking about were encouraged to talk about it. Nigeria's oft-repeated national attitudinal distortion is a function of this failure to remember when national values were different and when those values defined how Nigerians conducted personal and public affairs. One of those values used to be the pursuit and expression of knowledge and expertise.

The elevation of quackery and street smarts to high national arts makes it hard for some Nigerians to imagine a time when the country valued their opposite: the mastery of a knowledge area or technical subject. But it doesn't take a distant excursion into history to get to a recent past in which learning, expertise, and knowledge were the gold standards at all levels of life. There were those who breached this national ethos, of course. But back then, knowledge possession was its own reward, a target of admiration and a source of inspiration.

Knowledge used to be celebrated, if not always put to use, from top down and vice versa. Its acquisition and the access and importance that it conferred dominated the counsel of parents and guardians to their wards. Pep talks in other social settings venerated people of expertise and projected them to young Nigerians as models of accomplishment and heroism. Men of intellect, unique qualification, and expertise were widely consulted for their superior insights. They were sought out to comment on burning national issues in their areas of expertise. They were prodded to intervene in policy debates that fell within their intellectual province. Their competence and jurisdiction over matters of public good gave them a social and intellectual capital that entitled them to reverence and moral authority.

Remember when Professor Chike Obi, the famed late mathematician, was consulted for his expert opinion on the question of what constitutes two-thirds of votes in two-thirds of states during the 1983 presidential elections? This was standard practice when Nigeria, though sliding, still valued expertise and book knowledge.

Placed in the same situation, today's politicians would, far from seeking the verdict of an expert, transform into overnight mathematical geniuses and proclaim with authoritarian fervor what they believe the constitutional criteria on two-thirds means. Their self-serving declaration would subsume and override the opinion of any professional mathematician, no matter how learned, no matter how grounded in the settled logics of the field.

Another solution to a numerical impasse in today's politics would be a peculiarly Nigerian invention called "a political solution." It is a political consensus usually consummated by quid pro quo accords, shady deals, the active fear of class suicide, or all three. It is applied when the constitution is breached or when a political event fails the constitutional muster. Extra-constitutional interpretations and compromised opinions are summoned to supplant the informed opinion and advice of actual experts.

Sometimes the goal is to put the issue beyond the intervention of experts, to deny the experts a say on the matter. Political events are manipulated and controlled to yield predetermined outcomes and to preempt ambiguities that may call for the intervention of experts. This last method alienates expertise and enthrones mediocrity. With the other methods, politicians impersonate experts or disregard their informed opinions. Here, they avoid having to seek out informed pronouncement, shutting out the book people altogether.

Unlike the know-all, conceited politicians of today, yesterday's politicians respected experts and craved their pronouncements over difficult national issues. It's not that they enjoyed doing so or implemented expert recommendations consistently. But they had to seek out experts because society still regarded the talented and the trained as consultants of first and last resorts, and this ethos impressed on politicians the imperative of recognizing where their knowledge ended and that of trained personnel began.

There was still some value to being a trained, knowledgeable formal or informal consultant on certain specialized matters. Some of the politicians themselves, unlike today's flaky public officials, had been experts—proud experts—in various higher vocations and fields and had parlayed the prestige of their professional and intellectual accomplishments into political ascendancy. Their residual respect for book knowledge therefore moderated their disdain for the idealism and technical expertise of book people. It was also in their own self-interest as men of expertise who found themselves in politics to demonstrate the importance of knowledge to policy formulation and political decision-making. Their patronage of experts added luster to their own political standing among their less intellectual peers.

Then something shifted in Nigeria's national mores. This tectonic shift was mostly political; perhaps it was a deeper moral shift that merely manifested first in the realm of politics. No matter, the shift has erased the relevance of experts in national life. Today's experts and intellectuals are called dreamy-eyed idealists who live in the unrealistic worlds created by their own textbooks, unable to grasp or participate in the morally perverted world of Nigerian political and economic transactions. Now normalized as the realistic alternative to an academic utopia, this is a world in which there are few rules and moral restraints; it's a world in which street smarts trump reason and intellect.

Nigeria is saddled with a national assembly that rarely if ever calls expert witnesses to factually and intellectually foreground its hearings on key national policy issues. Even technical and esoteric committee hearings rarely solicit expertise. They prefer the cacophonous deliberations of uninformed legislators whose only point of reference is how much money is at stake in a particular bill. When experts are called, it is usually for show. Their advice is discarded as rapidly as bribe-backed non-expert interventions are proposed to the committee.

An allied problem is the veneration of Euro-American and Asian expertise, even when it is inferior to its Nigerian counterpart at home or in the diaspora. One political joke when Olusegun Obasanjo was president was that if one wanted his approval on any project or policy proposal, all one had to do was recruit a white or Asian "expert" and introduce them to him as the foreign technical partner or consultant for the project. It worked every time. Today, even sincere, competent entrepreneurs now have to play the game of lining up behind a foreign face—any foreign face—to attract serious attention from the government or its agencies of service delivery.

Nigeria is in this mess partly because it has routinely failed to harness the brains of its experts in policymaking, project planning, and infrastructural endeavors. Nigerians' growing antipathy to intellectual subjects and objects is a consequence of the canonization of mediocrity and ignorance in the nation's affairs. It reflects a growing devaluation of intellectual engagements as meritorious pursuits in their own right and as paths to national redemption. This devaluation is itself a product of a perverse, mercantile folk wisdom that tends to commoditize and commercialize everything in its sight, measuring its value by how much it is worth monetarily or in terms of the instant gratification it can confer. In such a starkly materialist universe, the pleasures of the mind, the intangible benefits of sound knowledge, and intellectual exchange recede in importance.

Nigeria's anti-intellectualism is also anchored on rational, deliberate, and self-interested projects of politically powerful elites; it is not happenstance. Political and policy regimes governed at critical junctures by expert opinions and respect for specialized knowledge tend to generate a culture in which verification, proof, substantiation, and debate are privileged and in which unfounded claims are dismissed. Such a culture, if allowed to take root, can threaten the existing order and force its superintendents to explain, justify, and account for their actions and policy pronouncements. This would be a tall order for those accustomed to reaping rewards without performing intellectual labor in the process.

There is a final, related aspect to Nigerian elites' anti-intellectual indulgences. A society in which book knowledge, technical and technocratic competence, and the humanizing practices of the mind enjoy a growing profile inevitably generates a social momentum for more investments in the means for nurturing intellectual talents and acquiring knowledge. With investments in education, especially in foundational education, already lagging and with public agitation for free basic education growing, the least desirable societal transformation, from the perspective of Nigeria's ruling elites, is one which results in greater public demand for more investments in education. The anti-intellectual status quo has endured therefore because it is profitable to Nigeria's ruling elite and to those who aspire to its membership.

CHAPTER 11

BONGOS IKWUE AND IDOMA CULTURAL COSMOPOLITANISM

A few years ago, I had the distinct privilege of meeting a musical idol of mine, the irrepressible Bongos Ikwue. I sat in on his rehearsal for a concert he gave in Abuja in 2009. I was a first-row witness to a performance of this legend's signature songs, which were interspersed with sumptuous new compositions that have coalesced into an album that now heralds his musical comeback. After the rehearsal, Bongos gave me an exclusive taste of some of the songs in his evolving album. I also met his backups—his two talented daughters, who, like their father, have taken to music as a calming, refreshing sideshow to their professional and educational engagements. It was the highpoint of my visit to Otukpo, our common ancestral urban center.

Bongos Ikwue has come full circle. After taking a detour from his musical habitat to fulfill his professional calling as an engineer, he has returned to the turf on which he amassed his overpowering—and enduring—cultural influence. He is back to composing and performing. That should hearten a generation of Nigerians who were culturally nurtured by the aesthetic and pedagogical pleasures of his timeless musical compositions.

There are two audiences for Bongos's musical genre, a unique alchemy of folk, country, and jazzy sounds, smoothly integrated to offer inspiring songs that soothe as they morally instruct. He courts and satisfies both audiences, transitioning dexterously between satisfying two fairly diverse appetites for the philosophical treasures he communicates through music. In a sense he has had to translate his own musical products and the philosophical nuggets encased in them to and from two different linguistic formations: Idoma and English. He has been his own literary translator, which is an uncommon feat in the arts. It is a mark of his cosmopolitan literary sensibilities that he has navigated this tension without losing much in translation and without displacing his two loyal groups of artistic interlocutors.

On one side, there are the connoisseurs of locally produced Afro-Nigerian sounds who have celebrated Bongos's English language offerings. "What's Gonna Be Is Gonna Be," "Amen," and the iconic television soundtrack, "Cock Crow at Dawn," are staples that speak to Bongos's pan-Nigerian followers.

Then there are Bongos's Idoma kinsfolk, for whom his Idoma language musical renditions offer an experience deeper than an ephemeral musical pleasure. To the Idoma, Bongos is at once a *griot* in the most pristine tradition of African cultural repositories and a philosopher offering intimate communion with the rhythms and dramas of the Idoma world. For those of us who by choice or parental influence were culturally nurtured on Bongos's stream of musical wisdom, listening to his Idoma language songs transported us to a symbolic world that was pure and ennobling, distant yet realizable. Bongos was a philosopher, our philosopher, a gift to us from our ancestors and a gift from us to the world. He interpreted our world and gave substance and stability to the shifty concepts of home, ancestry, and community.

In those days, the lyrics of Bongos's Idoma folk songs and his own original Idoma-language compositions filled the gap created by the dizzying urban transformation which undermined the consistency and efficacy of parental moral instruction. Our musical encounters with values and moral systems that draw on lived Idoma experiences—ones etched in the material and symbolic universes of the Idoma people—constituted a reaffirming cultural immersion. It made one more surefooted, more certain in one's identity and in the cultural verities that produced what one might, casting aside all postmodern anxieties, call the Idoma essence.

Bongos has been concerned with interpreting the world of the Idoma to outsiders while recalibrating familiar universal values to fit the milieu of the Idoma. He inserts the instrumental truths of universal philosophies into the lived virtues of the Idoma world and vice versa, merging, in the process, the global and the local, the cosmopolitan and the parochial. Bongos's main musical medium for conveying this "glocal" vision is the instructive proverb, on which many African artistic genres thrive.

Besides preaching instrumental staples like altruism, humility, industry, hard work, unity, love, and communal cohesion,

Bongos's music has an organizing undertone that anticipates and challenges the smug universalism inherent in Eurocentric cultural offerings. His musical worldview also disrupts the anti-essentialism of the postmodernist consensus, which brooks no localized, settled idioms of understanding and living. He sees no abiding friction between the universal and the local. His musical facility in the language of the cosmopolitan "outside" (English) and that of the organic "inside" (Idoma) has enabled him to transcend the chic but simplistic dichotomies which posit a paradigmatic universal that purports to be independent of localized experiences. Bongos's entire musical philosophy has been one of bridging the artificial, facile chasm between the Idoma world and the universal abstractions that it contributes to and is enriched by.

The philosophical implication of Bongos's music is that universal values are not independent of their constitutive elements; they are instead coextensive with their divergent parts. They are empowered and substantiated by the material and abstract worlds of disparate people living in localized, sometimes remote, milieus in different corners of the world. Idomaland is one such constituent of the universal. Its quotidian realities, cosmological landscape, and incantatory messages mirror and feed into the universal axioms that we take for granted in speech and gestures, and that some of us adopt as moral instructions. Not only are universal concepts minted in European linguistic systems analogous to similar concepts in the worlds of the Idoma and other non-hegemonic cultural formations; they sometimes derive their credibility and persuasive appeal from the fact that they are ultimately rooted in the material and symbolic inventions and adaptations of peoples—like the Idoma—who are often theorized as peripheries of the world.

Bongos has resolved this universal–local conundrum in his musical productions. From his earliest musical adventures, he saw no debilitating tension between the essentialist notions that bind the Idoma to their lived truths and values and the indeterminacy and perpetual transformation of the world encapsulated in so-called universal philosophies. A universal truism, which is a sum of its parts, cannot claim superiority over the provincial parts that constitute it. Keenly sensitized to this, Bongos's music has appealed to eclectic palates and relied on a variety of techniques and instruments that defy the binaries that seek to untangle the modern from the traditional, the universal from the local. Yet Bongos has always recognized the limits of the Idoma literary and symbolic world that has provided him with an infinitely fertile arena for musical creativity and of which he has been a foremost ambassador. He has never stepped on the slippery slope of reductive and stifling nativism. For Bongos, the wisdom expressed through the medium of the European language is not a self-sustaining truth but a hegemonic congealing—and manifestation—of parallel truths lived, sung, performed, and recited for centuries by Africa's wise peoples, of which the Idoma are one.

This convergence of the universal and the local in Bongos's musical system is borne out by several of his songs.

What's gonna be is gonna be
What goes up must come down

These are the opening lines of his English language hit, "What's Gonna Be Is Gonna Be." These lines are familiar, elemental universal truths. Beyond expressing the physical logic of gravity, they convey the fundamental instability that underpins our world and the human endeavors that propel it. They also express, for the religious and superstitious, a certain non-fatalistic wisdom in yielding to the inexorable, sometimes predetermined, march of life.

Let us now step into an analogous axiomatic construction in the Idoma value system and examine Bongos's apparent appropriation of an Idoma social idiom to speak to a recognizable, even commonsensical, universal truth. In his song, "Eche Une" (The World Is a Swing), Bongos presents the Idoma analogue to the English-language "What's Gonna Be Is Gonna Be." The allegorical invocation of the up-down/forward-backward motion of the swing is a synthesis of the instability of the human condition and the brittle control that humans have over their destinies and trajectories. In these two analogous songs, Bongos is able to bring into dialogue the philosophical treasures of the Idoma spoken word and the rational/scientific and metaphysical/religious foundations of universal thought. This is just one example of the productive and edifying interface between the "local" world of the Idoma and the outside world with which it is in continuous symbiotic communion.

The Idoma folk song genre, owned, perfected, and universalized by Bongos, did not speak solely to the world that produced it. No. It also spoke to the world "outside"—the world seeking an authentic Idoma input into its own regeneration and evolution. For the Idoma who belong in both worlds, the lyrics of Bongos's songs speak with a peculiar potency. This is why Bongos's music was instrumental, especially for the Idoma who grew up outside the homeland, in shaping the evolution of youthful consciousness and in helping to inspire cultural nostalgia and emotions of identity. Bongos's Idoma language compositions were, to paraphrase Barack Obama, the soundtracks of our youthful cultural discoveries and quests.

Adagbo Onoja, a compelling voice of Idoma cultural narration in his own right, is spot-on in describing Bongos as a pioneer translator of Idoma culture to the world. Bongos's cultural relevance to the Idoma, his primary artistic constituency, reaches even deeper. He has also made universal modes of understanding and contemplation intelligible to the Idoma, enhancing the cultural conversation between the Idoma and the larger world.

CHAPTER 12

NAMES AND NAMING IN NIGERIA

The subject of names has fascinated me for a long time. I read an article in Nigeria's *Newswatch* magazine many years ago that sparked my interest in the politics and sociology of naming. This piece is in some ways an extension of that brilliant, humorous piece.

What's in a name? A lot, especially in Nigeria. Nigerian names are particularly revealing. They amuse, shock, outrage, enlighten, ennoble, and empower.

Take the name Longshack, which—believe it or not—is a Nigerian name, not a British or American place name. The name is fairly common among my compatriots on the Jos Plateau. At first encounter one wonders if the name is a product of colonial Anglicization, a curious relic of colonial social encounters. One also wonders, on the lighter side, whether there might be a Shortshack to complement Longshack.

What about the monosyllabic names for which our Plateau brothers and sisters are also known? In Nigeria, Pam is not short for Pamela. It certainly is not the popular culinary oil substitute known to Americans. Pams are living, breathing humans from Plateau State, Nigeria. Lar may be a less common name on the Plateau, but what it lacks in number of bearers it makes up for in the prominence of its few bearers. Remember Solomon Lar, the second republic governor of Plateau State?

Then there is Dung. It's the last name of my high school classmate. From—you guessed it—Plateau State. I am sure Ms. Dung—if her last name has not changed—would resist any comparison of her last name to a certain undesirable byproduct of the metabolic processes of a popular domestic animal.

In the Hausa-speaking parts of the country, it is quite common for people to take on the name of their trade. This is not a way of drawing attention to their competencies, or a strategy of—let's use a fancy postmodern term—business branding, but a legal identification. Inuwa Maidoya (literally translated as Inu-

wa seller of yams) would not be a strange nomenclatural occur-
rence in these parts. Nor would Ibrahim Maishayi (Ibrahim the
tea salesman) be uncommon. These are dignified vocations in
the Hausa-speaking milieus of Nigeria, where modesty of ambition and dignity in lowly labor are celebrated, if dying, virtues.
Hausa men harbor no shame about engaging in trades that men
in other parts of the country would shirk as "women's work."
These adopted trade names show the social boundaries of the
permissible, the tolerable, and the acceptable.

I often wonder why it is hard to find a *Maitaba* (tobacco salesman) in the Hausa states. There are, of course, plenty of *maitabas*
in the generic sense of tobacco seller. Smoking is, after all, tolerated in Hausaland and violates no mainstream Islamic precepts.
But where in the name of nicotine are the Garba Maitabas and
Lawal Maitabas? Is the dearth of Maitaba legal names a reflection of the ambivalent status of tobacco in the region? Does it
say something about tobacco's existence at the hazy interstic-
es of Hausa social life, or about the fact that tobacco straddles
the social territory of de facto social toleration and timid con-
demnation? The transition from an occupational honorific to a
formal, registered name is fraught with considerations that are
often complicated by a society's norms as well as its boundaries
of the acceptable and tolerable.

In other words, it may be fine to sell tobacco and/or smoke
it, but taking a tobacco-associated name pushes the envelope of
social acceptability too far. What does this tell us about the place
of tobacco in Hausa society? Perhaps it is that tobacco exists un-
easily in the ill-defined and murky zone between socio-religious
permissiveness and social resentment of habits that are tolerated but not encouraged.

If we can't find a Maitaba in Hausa society, we can't even con-
ceive of a *Maigiya* (alcohol salesman). For no Hausa Muslim—or
any Muslim for that matter—would associate their name with
a product outlawed by their religion. Not as a trade name, and
certainly not as a proper, legal name.

In the same Hausa context, individuals, especially the successful, like to adopt the names of their hometowns as their
legal last names. Aminu Kano, Abubakar Tafawa Balewa, Shehu
Shagari, Kabiru Gaya, Shehu Usman Katsina are all names that

boldly and proudly proclaim the ancestral origins of their prominent bearers. Through individuals' adoption of place names, five-hut villages have found instant fame, etched into Nigerian history and our social consciousness.

But there is the occasional aberration—even in Northern Nigeria, where the obsession with adopting the hometown's name is more fully realized. For instance, Sadiq Mamman Lagos is not a Lagosian. He is a popular Kaduna businessman, a member of a prominent Hausa family from Kaduna state, whose patriarch is said to have made his fortune in Lagos. Here is therefore an adopted place name that announces not the bearer's ancestry but his abbreviated economic biography.

Still, identifying with the place of origin or adopted place of origin is a strong factor in the politics of naming among the Hausa. So strong is this relationship between naming and identity that even those who are suspected of having *become* Hausa through a process of voluntary assimilation have to try to establish a verifiable link to a hometown or village in Hausaland. For instance, several years ago, some "disgruntled opponents" of Governor Rabiu Musa Kwankwaso of Kano state displayed their gripe by questioning the governor's Kano identity. All the governor had to do was remind them that his last name was the same as that of a small, dusty village a few miles from Kano city. It doesn't get more Kano than that. That shut the "disgruntled elements" up, or ought to have.

Even among the Hausa, one comes across the odd, accidentally Anglicized name. For instance, Ujudud Sheriff is a prominent journalist and has had, to my knowledge, no association with American law enforcement. Sheriff is actually a product of Anglicization—some would say corruption. The original form of the name is Shariff, a fairly common Islamic name applied to descendants of the Prophet. In Southern Nigeria, Osa Director is neither a movie director nor a director of a company. He is a newspaper editor whose directorial experience, if any, is limited to directing reporters under him on what subjects and stories to investigate or what kind of reports to write.

There is a pan-Nigerian dimension to this rich naming culture. Names encapsulate statements of wealth and proud accomplishment across Nigeria's cultural and ethnic spectrum. Maikudi (the rich, or owner of wealth) is popular among the Hausa as first and last name. Alhaji Maikudi Daneji is a prominent Kano businessman. Kabir Maikudi may be made up, but it is not implausible.

Olowo (owner of wealth) is a fairly ubiquitous name among the Yoruba, both as a praise name and a legal name. I knew an Alhaji Abdullahi Olowo, who was the chief of the Yoruba community in Kano for a time. Ironically, when I knew him, he was a financially troubled man who bore only traces of a once-wealthy existence. Similarly, in his peak as a wealthy, if notorious, moneyman, Victor Okafor preferred to be known as Eze Ego (king of money). He named his popular Lagos high-rise Eze Ego Plaza to underscore his preference for this expressive, more declaratory name.

Yet certain names must be silenced in certain spaces as a ritual of subservience to higher authority. But this silencing also honors the bearer of the name, for the silencing—the inability to say a particular name within a particular spatial and temporal configuration—signals a new, if temporary, status for the name and by extension for the bearer. This silencing also announces certain connections and coincidences between two individuals occupying different status positions in society. A good example is the name Maisuna, in the Hausa caliphate culture of Northern Nigeria.

Maisuna is a shortened version of Maisunan Sarki (one who bears the king's name). This is a nomenclatural invention among the Hausa-Fulani of Nigeria to preserve the exclusivity of a king's given name in and around his court. My own first encounter with this phenomenon was about twenty years ago, when, as an undergraduate at Bayero University, Kano, Nigeria, my classmates and I went for a tour of the palace of the emir (Muslim king) of Kano, the late Ado Bayero, as part of a field trip organized by one of our history professors.

On arrival at the palace, we stopped at the office of the palace secretary to confirm our appointment before being taken on the tour. While the bureaucratic process of appointment confirmation continued, an elderly worker at the office, a messenger by designation, carried messages between the secretary and a different wing of the palace where the emir lived and worked. I noticed that they called him Maisuna. As a fluent speaker of Hausa but one who was ignorant of Kano's esoteric royal traditions, it didn't make much sense, since Maisuna simply means possessor or bearer of a name—what name is that, I wondered. It was one of my classmates, an ethnic Hausa and a son of a Kano aristocrat versed in the vernacular of royalty, who explained to me that, as a sign of respect for the king or Sarki, no one named Ado (the king's given name) who lived or worked within an earshot of the palace could be called by that name. They were instead called Maisunan Sarki (the king's namesake), or Maisuna for short.

I thought and still think that this little nomenclatural invention is a rich window into the ethics of royal respect and kingly prerogative in this part of Nigeria. Kano, of course, was part of the defunct Sokoto Caliphate and remains a part of the post-caliphate Hausa world of Northern Nigeria, so to understand its royal naming tradition and its social import is to be enlightened on a wider system of royal prestige dating back more than two centuries. The provenance of Maisuna is a metaphor for the changes that the emergence of a king might bring to his court and its environs. It is not only the case that the king, once he ascends the throne, can no longer be called by his given name, even by his closest friends or contemporaries—for the name is, as long as he is king, retired, as one might retire a jersey in professional American sports; it is also that this change and its honor reverberate through the immediate vicinity of the royal court. So that the royal staffer or palace occupant who has to essentially give up his name to take a new, more anonymous one partakes in the honorifics of this tradition, in the changes that kingly succession can introduce. This is why those who bear the name Maisuna tend to command reverence in the former caliphate areas, and their descendants typically continue with the name, usually as a last name, long after the king who brought about the renaming has died. Much later during my stay in Kano, I personally came to know one Yusuf Maisuna, at the time a medical student at Bayero University.

Nigerians want their name to do much more than identify them. They want it to supply a crisp, catchy summary of what they are about, what makes them unique. How else do you explain the immodesty and vulgarity of proclaiming your wealth through your name? The Euro-American rich have their conspicuous consumption. The Nigeria rich have their immodest names that bespeak their wealth and accomplishments. It is not that Nigerian big men do not also consume conspicuously. They do. But why stop at showy materialism when you can inscribe your status eternally onto your name—onto your formal, legal identity? It's a rare chance not to be missed.

Nigerians understand the politics and significance of naming. That is why few Nigerian names betray the random, whimsical vanity of Euro-American naming cultures. Names are called upon to bear the anxieties, both momentary and enduring, of parents, families, and communities into which children are born. Many names offer clues about the circumstances of a birth; the socioeconomic conditions of the family at the time of the birth, good or bad familial events proximate to the birth, and even national and global events that the child's birth coincides with. The immense charisma, promise, and tragic assassination of American President John F. Kennedy produced an outpouring of emotions that resulted in a few male children being named Kennedy in the 1960s and 1970s. I personally know some of these Kennedys. At the height of ex-Head of State Yakubu Gowon's popularity as a youthful leader in the pre- and post-Civil War oil boom era, many Nigerian babies emerged from their mothers' wombs into that era of profligate military populism to be named Gowon.

In 1974, when the Gowon regime paid government workers the accumulated arrears of a recommended doubling of the national minimum wage, the oil-fueled delusions of fiscal abundance produced a national frenzy of conspicuous consumption and recreational spending that resulted in many more male babies being christened Gowon. A cursory inquiry into the biographies of these Gowons will reveal that their parents were direct or vicarious beneficiaries of Gowon's largesse. Shortly thereafter, Gowon was overthrown, and the disastrous implications of his profligate fiscal regime unraveled before a sobered nation. Gowon soon lost its popular appeal as a baby name.

Nigerian English names like Endurance, Blessing, Comfort, and Patience are indicative of a family's mood and emotions, which the name is supposed to capture, archive, and communicate. Other names like Godspower, Thankgod, and Godswill have distinctly Christian flavors that at once convey a family's religious devotion and the Christian fads, sensibilities, and vocabularies prevalent at the time of the bearer's birth. One of the major militants in Nigeria's oil-rich Niger Delta region, who has now renounced militancy and assumed a lucrative position in the oil and maritime sectors of the Nigerian economy, is named Government Ekpenumolo. A name like Government is something of an outlier, but it might bespeak the bearer's parents' outsized dream for their child. The government is understood in Nigeria as an omnipresent, all-powerful entity, capable of mobilizing and wielding limitless resources and power. This understanding is articulated in sayings and proverbs in several Nigerian languages. In these sayings, we are told that "you cannot fight the government," "the government does what it wants," and the question is posed rhetorically, "Who can fight the government and win?" The government thus represents the culmination of all aspirations to wealth, power, and influence. Government is a metaphor for abundance and potency, and so the name Government may be intended to capture the parental hope for a child growing up to attain commensurate power.

Other Nigerian names are more transparently aspirational, expressing a hope that the birth of the bearer, itself a mark of good fortune, would signal more good luck and providential favor, hence the name Goodluck, as in Goodluck Jonathan, the current president of Nigeria. The pattern is similar in many of Nigerian indigenous languages, where names are summoned to store and activate memories of important signposts and landmarks in a family's history and struggle, or to underpin new aspirations and beginnings.

In Muslim families and communities, names are similarly crafted to announce virtue and religious devotion, or to denounce vice and ungodly conduct. Some names go even further to announce promises and pledges meant to be kept to God, as though by inscribing the promise in a proximate living being, the name-giver is constantly reminded of the obligation.

Many Nigerian names carry the weight of abridged familial and communal histories, suggesting descent from a line of warriors or traders or priests—or providing clues to rich narratives about the familial or communal self. To get at this hidden narrative, the name encapsulating its essence has to be decoded and unlocked to reveal the stories, acts, and deliberations that informed the name in the first place. In this way, Nigerian names are windows into a realm of social reality and symbolic action that might otherwise remain inaccessible.

CHAPTER 13

HELICOPTER ESCAPES AND THE COMMON GOOD

Rich Nigerians recently reached a new height—literally—in their struggle to stay above the poverty and chaos that plague their country and besiege their homes and workplaces. The new fad for the country's superrich is to commute around Lagos, arguably Africa's most chaotic and traffic-plagued city, in helicopters. Faced with a daily grind of crippling traffic, rich Nigerians did what the rich always do: they bought their way around the problem. Helipads now adorn (or disfigure, depending on your perspective) the roofs of high-rise buildings that house the workspaces of Nigeria's growing class of super-wealthy businessmen and women.

Regardless of geographical location, the rich almost always find a way to stay above the quotidian struggles of their societies. They are adept at not letting the minor irritants of daily life get in the way of their business and pleasure. There is nothing wrong with a man of means deploying his means to avoid the unsavory but avoidable experiences of life. The problem, however, is that the Nigerian superrich are not merely caught up in the imperative of insulating themselves from the pesky banalities of life in a challenging social milieu. They thrive on perpetually extending and policing the social boundaries that mark wealth from poverty, and separate the world of the rich from that of the poor. The Nigerian moneyed class is obsessed with obliterating the few levelers that remain in the Nigerian society.

It used to be that, whatever your income level or the size of your bank account, there was a set of comforting social equalizers that everyone had to navigate. One of those reminders of our common humanity and shared limitations was the traffic experience, unpalatable and humiliating as it always is. Not a few Nigerians have chuckled with self-comforting humor at seeing the convoy of billionaires Mike Adenuga or Aliko Dangote trapped in Lagos's notorious traffic alongside their own *molue* (commercial intra-city bus) or rickety private automobile. Most Nigerians will deny ever taking such perversely vengeful delight in seeing the rich "sweat it out" in traffic along with their less moneyed compatriots. But it is true that when the superrich are occasionally compelled by traffic or some other common quotidian adversity to endure some of the unpalatable sights and sounds of the Nigerian street, they draw many welcome-to-my-world stares from regular folks. Though cooled by the cold air oozing from the refrigerated orifices of their luxury cars, the rich complain, fidget, and fume through the traffic experience like the rest of their compatriots. Their experience is even more harrowing, given that they are used to plowing through life with ease and alacrity. Being unschooled in the dirty art of surviving the familiar struggles of the urban jungle, and unused to encountering situations they cannot control or defeat, the rich are made miserable and forced to join the fleeting fraternity of suffering and grumbling people.

To watch these privileged commuters order their drivers, orderlies, escorts, and aides to clear the road to no avail is a delightful lesson in the limits of money and power, a reminder of our common humanity. It is, above all, an invitation to contemplate the humanness of those who sometimes carry an air of immortality. Those are moments of pure existential joy for the oppressed commoner, moments in which rich and poor join the chorus of antigovernment critique, forming a fragile, fleeting solidarity of citizens mad at their government for failing to devise a way out of a perennial public transportation problem. The impotence and paralysis of the rich in the face of Lagos traffic serve to console the poor, rekindle their sense of contentment, and reaffirm the folly of correlating wealth with happiness or quality of life. The moment in which the rich man's money is no good and cannot separate him from the vagaries of the Nigerian experience is precisely the moment that reaffirms the poor man's narratives of self-consolation.

The traffic was one effective leveler in Nigerian society. For the superrich, it was humbling and humanizing. Traffic jams, as they are called them in Nigeria, forced them to behold the images of poverty that they would otherwise avoid by breezing around in their tint-windowed automobiles. For the poor, the traffic was a fortuitous rendezvous for beholding the momentary social impotence of poor and rich alike, and to laugh at the rich man's discomfort at encountering the inconveniences that mark the poor man's daily life. More important, it was an opportunity in adversity to compel the rich to contend with the poor, with the odd chance that, in this small spatial and temporal context, the poor man's plight might overcome or match the rich man's money and privileges. Having a predicament in common had an almost soothing effect on the polity.

That was then.

The superrich have now removed this residual social equalizer. Short on innovative business and technological practices, the Nigerian financial and industrial aristocracy excels in the art of getting around the incompetence of government and the dearth of social infrastructure. They have already brought such perverse resourcefulness to bear on several domains. Like the traffic situation, the absence or decay of key public infrastructure and services—pipe-borne water, electricity, education, and healthcare—unleashed self-preservationist creativity in the Nigerian upper class. They mounted monstrous electricity generators that doubled as noisemaking machines. They drilled sophisticated boreholes in their expansive residencies and installed small water treatment and pumping facilities to help bring potable water to every corner of their homes. To get around the decay in the health sector, they carry foreign health insurance cards and routinely fly abroad to be treated for the slightest of infirmities. To wean themselves off dependence on Nigeria's decaying educational system, the rich looked abroad and to Nigeria's emerging but offensively expensive private educational sector.

The Nigerian superrich can afford all of these escapes from government's incompetence and infrastructural failures. But they have not merely escaped; they have also rubbed it in and stuck it to the poor man who used to mock them in the days when they, like everyone else, depended on and suffered through Nigeria's poor infrastructure. The helicopter gambit is the latest evidence of the superrich's determination to protect themselves from the daily injuries that a failing state inflicts on its citizens; to reassert their social status; and to stick it to the jealous, angry masses.

What is happening is a fundamental fragmentation of the Nigerian citizenry along a new fissure: those who depend on and are subjected to the daily trauma of depending on Nigeria's decaying infrastructure and those who have exited this dependence. Its implications are potentially profound.

What the Nigerian superrich are doing amounts to surrendering to governmental incompetence and failure. It is depleting the vestigial emotional investment that Nigerians have in their government. When the rich remove themselves from the state system and craft an alternative domain of existence, one funded by private resources, some may celebrate it as a triumph of free enterprise, resilience, and individual resourcefulness. That may be partly true, although the prohibitive exclusivity of this class makes such capitalist triumphalism an overblown conclusion.

The truth is that, for all its ideological merits, such behavior by the Nigerian superrich emboldens the incompetents who superintend the Nigerian state and its resources, and threatens to trigger a cynicism that will deter Nigerian youth from reforming the system or reversing the infrastructural rot; and instead, inspire them only to seek escape from their nation's egregious failures. What's more, as the Nigerian economy has expanded due to the telecom revolution, the explosion of homegrown visual and audio entertainment, and other entrepreneurial innovations in the service sector, the number of those who are able to fund their expensive escape from Nigeria's everyday dysfunctions has soared. Along with those who have prospered in these new spaces of innovation and private enterprise we have seen an increase in the number of new dollar millionaires and billionaires with the familiar oligarchic connections to the sinews of power.

The trend of millionaires emerging from state-awarded largesse, privilege, and monopoly persists. This swelling in the number of Nigerians who own private jets and helicopters translates to a direct or indirect shrinkage in resources available for public infrastructural investment. This patrimonial space connecting the public and private sectors is either unethical or outright corrupt, transferring capital from the public to the private sector in non-competitive exchanges that add little or no value to the commonwealth and common good. There is, then, a correlation between an expansion in what one might call the private governmental industry and the gradual incapacitation of the public governmental space. Nigerians cannot be celebrating the number of their compatriots who own private jets and other means of escape from Nigeria's infrastructural morass—acquisitions for the most part financed indirectly through favors and unearned privileges from the government—and sustain a serious critique of government's inability to build and maintain social infrastructures. That would be contradictory. They cannot glamorize and aspire to the conspicuous consumption of compatriots whose success can be located in state failure and in corrupt processes of patronage and then turn around to demand that a state fiscally hobbled by such patrimonial entanglements fulfill its infrastructural obligations to citizens.

Moreover, if every urban-dwelling, credentialed, and entrepreneurial Nigerian is merely seeking to join the boastful ranks of those who delight in circumventing Nigerian society as we know it, then who will hold the government accountable for the mass of voiceless, illiterate, and rural-dwelling Nigerians who will always depend on some form of government infrastructure? If we all desire to live in this parallel Nigerian society of helicopters and privately funded infrastructure, what is the incentive for preventing a failing state from sinking into irredeemable calamity?

The solution to state failure, incompetence, and the collapse of social infrastructure is not the utopian advancement of a world without government or of a society of privately empowered, self-sufficient, and independent citizens—as idealistically seductive as that may be. The solution is for the rich to use their influence and resources to push for change and for a more accountable and responsible government that provides infrastructure and social services for *everyone*.

The question is: are Nigerians determined to build a Nigerians that upholds and promotes the common good or are they seeking to build little enclaves—little Nigerias—where they can hide from the harsh realities of life in the country? To put it bluntly, are Nigerians content to have a country in which everyone's goal is to become a state unto himself?

CHAPTER 14

THE PATRIOTISM BLACKMAIL

It has become faddish for supporters of the status quo in Nigeria to attack its critics as unpatriotic, or to at least insinuate this critique of the critics into their commentary. Paradoxically, this stealthy attempt to monopolize the patriotic label and the rhetoric of patriotic devotion for a few unquestioning and vocal supporters of the government is more dangerous than the pessimistic criticism that it purports to detest. So vocal have these accusations become that it is necessary to reiterate, even if for a purely intellectual purpose, that the uncritical, self-declared patriot and the perennial critic and pessimist are actually motivated by the same patriotic instincts. The patriotic space is as vast as it is diverse.

Let's dwell a little on these increasingly vehement preachments on patriotism. In the first place, patriotism is not a finished product, a settled state of being. It is a progressive emotional evolution toward the love of country. Therefore, for a group of people to claim that they have attained a patriotic place of comfort, where the love of country is without reservation and pessimistic interludes, is insincere. This kind of patriotic proclamation is usually a strategy of claim making, of strategically projecting a sentiment for political and self-interested purposes. Patriotism can be expressed in degrees, not in absolutes. The degree of its expression corresponds naturally to one's endearment to the object of that patriotic feeling. In most cases this object is a nation-state.

Secondly, if a patriot feels the need to declare his/her patriotism, and to construct it in opposition to the views of people he regards as unpatriotic, the self-consecrated patriot inadvertently makes himself the object of skepticism. For if you are a true patriot, why would you advertise it at every turn? Would your patriotism not be obvious from your intellectual and programmatic engagement with your country and its affairs? In other words, as Nobel Laureate Wole Soyinka aptly said, why should a tiger project its tigeritude when its attributes and physiological qualities already identify it as such? Patriotism, like threats of violence, can become tired, boring, and ineffective when constantly declared rather than performed. That is one of the problems of self-declared patriotism: It is louder than it is practical and tangible.

Understandably, those directly invested in the status quo, that is, those in government, are usually the most vocal in demanding unbridled patriotic commitment from Nigerians. They are also the ones who routinely accuse those who disagree with their policies, conducts, and priorities of a lack of patriotism, as if Nigeria's rulers' interests are coextensive with Nigeria's. But this appeal for a patriotic citizenry is, as many perceptive Nigerians have pointed out, often unaccompanied by recognition that patriotism usually follows from a sense of gratitude and pride. None of this is easy to express in today's Nigeria because the state has deprived Nigerians of the reasons to be grateful and proud.

Having underscored the flaws of self-declared patriotism, let us scrutinize the ideological and intellectual basis of the sentiments that underlie such posturing. Self-declared patriots claim that they are optimists, and that they are able to visualize the brighter side of things, no matter how bleak the picture may appear. They take the glass-half-full view on Nigerians' affairs. Conversely, they claim that non-patriots are pessimists and cynics who see nothing good in Nigeria and are quick to focus on the negative. There is no serious dispute here. In broad terms, patriots are optimists, sometimes unrealistic optimists, while so-called non-patriots tend to deliberately embrace skepticism.

But this is only a fraction of the truth. Some so-called non-patriots are cynics, but most are not: they are pessimists or cautious optimists. This clarification is in order because self-declared patriots exaggerate the pessimism of the so-called non-patriots to the point of branding them as aloof and indifferent to the affairs of their country, a mendacious claim.

Self-professed patriots also exaggerate the difference between themselves and those they regard as pessimistic non-patriots. For instance, the patriots ignore an instructive point of convergence and intersection between their sentiments and those of the non-patriots. Their motivation is the same as those of the non-patriots that they attack. Both groups of Nigerians want things to get better in their country. They are motivated by the same underlying commitment to Nigeria's progress. The pessimistic critic criticizes because he wants those in power to change course and do the right thing for the country. The optimistic patriot supports and praises the status quo and those in power in the hope that such support will motivate the leaders to do the right thing for Nigeria. The premise, for both groups of Nigerians, is thus the same. It is empty rhetoric, then, for self-declared patriots to claim that they love Nigeria more than the pessimistic critics.

The only difference between the two groups is that critics are more impatient with the pace of progress or with the lack thereof. The underbelly of these two persuasions is, however, the same: a level of love for one's country that motivates one to take active interest in its fate and plight. Contrary to the optimists' claim, then, the pessimists are not aloof to their country and its affairs. They criticize and ventilate their frustration and disappointment precisely because they are not aloof. Indifference produces disengagement and apathy, not active critical engagement, and certainly not the tough love that critical pessimists shower on their country.

Two groups of people constitute important caveats to the foregoing analysis. Sycophants and cynics occupy the extremes of the patriotism spectrum. Sycophants are quick to substitute their sycophancy and opportunism for patriotism. They also glibly attack those unwilling to display a similar subservience to power in the interest of personal gain. The patriotism of such sycophantic opportunists is questionable, as they are more loyal to their political patrons than they are to Nigeria's interests. Cynics, on the other hand, are afflicted with an enduring unwillingness to accommodate or admit any prospect of progress and development in Nigeria. For some cynics, a justifiable hatred for the incumbent administration can quickly morph into a blanket criticism of all things Nigerian. But not all self-declared patriots are sycophants and not all pessimistic critics are cynics.

Still, the point needs to be made that cynicism is not a productive conduit for patriotic sensibilities, and pessimistic critics must be vigilant enough not to slide into the realm of cynical disengagement.

Let me use an analogous debate to illustrate this point. For about a decade now, there has been a discussion among African scholars on the ramifications of what has come to be known as Afro-pessimism. Afro-pessimist thinking comes in different guises and generally denotes the pervasive notion that Africa is a lost cause, doomed to the congenital deficits of its peoples and the natural drawbacks of its landscape. For much of the 1990s, Afro-pessimism was defined in these terms, making it the exclusive expressive domain of Caucasian racists and self-hating Africans. More recently, the definition has been broadened to include any harsh and unfair criticism of Africa's affairs.

With this definitional revision, it is now possible and indeed common to associate many African critics of conditions in Africa with Afro-pessimism. It is also possible now to clearly separate these African critics and pessimists from those (mostly non-Africans) who do not associate Africa with anything good and discount any possibility of African progress. One should not even dignify the latter group of Afro-pessimists and their attitudes to Africa by analyzing their views. Their verdicts on and criticisms of Africa are rooted in racial hatred, a sense of evolutionary superiority, or inexplicable self-loathing. Their aim is to spite and put down Africa and its peoples.

Most African critics and Afro-pessimists, on the other hand, criticize conditions and the state of leadership on the continent precisely because they love and care about it. Their Afro-pessimism is thus rooted not in self-hatred or cynicism but in their almost insatiable desire for African progress. Their caustic style of criticism and their damning verdicts on the continent's affairs do not invalidate this underlying commitment to Africa. They instead underline the intensity of their emotional engagement with Africa.

But the line between Afro-pessimism and Afro-cynicism is a thin one, so these critical Afro-pessimists, like their Nigerian counterparts in the business of critical, skeptical engagement, must be careful not to breach it.

In the final analysis, then, we are all patriots. The flowering of citizens' patriotic praise or anger may take different forms, but the nationalist commitment that informs their critical or for-giving engagement with Nigeria is undeniable. The self-serving lectures on patriotism that are regularly delivered to us by bad Nigerian leaders about patriotism deceive as much as they conceal the egregious failures of leadership at all levels.

SECTION III

AFRICA AND THE WORLD

CHAPTER 15

AFRICA, CORRUPTION, POVERTY, AND MORAL CONSEQUENCE

Corruption has acquired the status of a continental emergency in Africa. But this is not another pontification on corruption. Rather, it is a polemical disavowal of some popular fallacies on corruption on the continent.

One of the most insightful attempts to explain the cultural basis of political corruption in Africa contends that patronage ties between regular Africans and political elites place informal obligations and demands on the latter, obligations that are often fulfilled through corrupt enrichment. Corruption in this explanation has many participants besides the politician or bureaucrat who engages in the act. It is an explanation that understands corruption through the prism of mass complicity and cultural toleration.

This paradigm captures some of the reality of corruption in Africa. The typical African politician grapples with financial pressure not only from family but also from kin, clan, hometown, and ethnic constituents. Indeed, the network of people that makes corruption possible and sometimes undetectable includes not just politicians and state bureaucrats but a whole circle of entities that includes ethically challenged financial and legal experts, and traditional institutions of restraint. In Africa as elsewhere, corruption is a group act.

Because of the absence of state welfare institutions in much of Africa, political constituents expect politicians representing them to cater to their quotidian and small-scale infrastructural needs. It is generally understood and quietly tolerated that a politician has to rely on his informal access to public funds to satisfy these informal requests for patronage and largesse. Many Africans euphemistically call this "patronage politics." They may tolerate and normalize it as African grassroots politics, a tolerable form of cash-backed populism. To Western observers, however, it is corruption at its crudest. Not only that, it is "African corruption." The relationship of Africans to public resources is complicated, and incomprehensible to many non-Africans. Many Africans seem to subscribe to two moral economies, one private and the other public. In their private, familial lives, Africans are uncompromising moral enforcers, teaching old traditional virtues to their children with a clarity that is informed by their different religious and cultural moral systems. But when it comes to state resources, the so-called national cake, many Africans subscribe to a moral tolerance that allows and forgives the public display of the same vices they condemn in private.

In this dualistic moral system, which was famously theorized by scholar Peter Ekeh several decades ago,[9] a fine, if labored, distinction is made between patronage politics that relies on illicit and unofficial access to the treasury and blatant theft of public resources. The problem is that it is never clear where patronage stops and where theft begins, where tolerable patronage terminates and where egregious abuse of public office in the name of patronage begins. And so, often, the narrative of socially beneficial patronage functions as an alibi for public officials and citizens alike to avoid having to account for illicit acts that benefit them.

One can argue that the normalization of access politics is a product of the nexus of over-centralized power, access to resources, and ethnic competition (which are all features of most African states), but this explanation hardly accounts for the multiethnic and socially diverse cast of actors in most corruption scandals in Africa. Nor for the fact that in much of the continent, corruption is often the reason why overly centrist, patrimonial, and illogical states endure, just as it is also a symptom of the excesses of these states. The tragedy of many African countries—and Nigeria particularly stands out—is that corruption and patronage politics are the recurring baselines of political compromise and consensus among self-interested but bitterly divided political elites. Antagonistic elites within postcolonial African nations often find expedient consensuses that preserve their fragile nations mostly because not doing so would threaten their access to nationally appropriated resources.

The causal intersection of dysfunctional states and corruption is almost beyond dispute. True as that may be, however, it is easy to overstate the argument about how the nature of the states inherited from colonial times sustains corruption in Africa. Such an overemphasis on state structure may elide more socially embedded, low-level, and less obvious platforms that support and legitimize corrupt acts—or at least make them seem normal. This pseudo-cultural normalization of corruption is one of the biggest obstacles in the way of entrenching transparency in government bureaucracies in Africa.

Nothing encapsulates this reality more than the pervasive Nigerian fad of traditional chieftaincy institutions doling out honorific titles to citizens whose source of wealth is questionable at best. What does one make of African universities that routinely give out honorary degrees to patently corrupt donors? Or churches and mosques that project demonstrably corrupt members as models of piety, accomplishment, and godly favor? What these practices do is to invest and implicate many Africans indirectly in the phenomenon of corruption. They are subtle and invidious, but they work to co-opt many Africans, even without their conscious consent, into the cultural and religious contexts in which corrupt acts and corrupt persons find rehabilitation and validation. The result is that many Africans, even while expressing outrage against corruption privately, are publicly indifferent to its manifestation, especially if they are situated in social networks that benefit from the patronage politics through which corruption thrives. Consequently, they may feel too culturally complicit to take a stand. This kind of complicity makes official policy against corruption difficult because it mitigates the public pressure necessary for official action against corruption.

But Africans also draw clear moral lines in their narratives on corruption. Their tolerance for patronage and its lubrication by state resources does not prevent them from sometimes condemning the abuse of this kind of politics by greedy politicians. Nor does it blind them to the political excess of treasury looting for purely personal enrichment. The distinction between patronage and brazen theft of state funds may not always be clear, and one may morph into the other (today's seemingly benevolent local political patron may be tomorrow's ministerial rogue with multiple Swiss bank accounts), but Africans recognize the destructive impact of the latter, and the moral evil that it represents. They make a distinction between the politician who practices vulgar populism with state funds and the one who stuffs his local and foreign bank accounts with budgeted funds meant for capital investments. The two forms of political behavior do not affect Africa's economies to the same degree. This is not a pedantic distinction. It is crucial for separating the hysteria of corruption from the reality of corruption.

This complex reality has sometimes been caricatured as mass African complicity in corruption, a kind of racial indictment on Africans, who are allegedly culturally predisposed to corruption. The more elegant variant of this thinking contends that corruption may be endemic in Africa and that this is because what Westerners call corruption is a historical, ever-present culture of patron–client relationships that are now lubricated, quite understandably, by postcolonial state resources. Some people go so far as to insinuate that Africans do not see corruption as corruption but as a proud, if atavistic, return to an African culture of the big man and his responsibilities. Like all stereotypical renderings of Africa, this argument exaggerates an African social reality for dramatic effect. Indeed, the dramatization and extrapolation of cultural norms that may or may not foster corruption is one of the bedrocks of conventional Western understandings of Africa.

One cannot deny that there is some cultural continuity between the African past and present, but much of the argument about Africa being a natural cultural habitat for corruption is cultural relativism taken too far. Some of it borders dangerously on intellectualized racism. Africans are more cognizant of corruption and its devastating effects than are other peoples precisely because corruption, especially in its postcolonial vulgarity, represents a perversion of familiar, largely harmless African practices of political patronage. It is precisely because this perversion is recent, and not historical, that Africans consistently express outrage, even if a largely impotent one, against state corruption. This outrage is sometimes hypocritical since Africans sometimes create the dynamic of expectation that sometimes fuels state corruption. Nonetheless it represents a moral disavowal of state corruption.

So pervasive is the narrative of mass complicity in corruption in Africa that many Africans themselves have appropriated it as a rhetorical device in their own discourses on corruption. There is a particularly Nigerian spin on this paradigm that must be discredited. It is very common to hear Nigerians argue that no Nigerian is free of the stigma or aura of corruption. The contention is that every Nigerian knows, is related to, or has benefited from someone who is corrupt. The argument is that it is impossible to exculpate oneself from the collective guilt of corruption when one functions in a corrupt system, with gradations and varieties of corrupt practices that implicate everyone.

But this narrative conflates a wide variety of corrupt practices, assigns them the same impact, and attributes to them the same moral outcomes. In analyses of the moral impact of corruption on Africa—which should be the focus of anticorruption anxieties—the distinction between an African politician who fritters away $5 million of his country's funds and a poorly paid policeman who collects a bribe of 50 cents from an erring motorist is a significant one. For it is not the low-level, quotidian acts of corruption—as bad as they are—that are responsible for the egregious effects of corruption in Africa. It may be hard to organically disentangle those two forms of corruption, but it would be analytically disingenuous to equate their impact on African people.

There is another problem with the rhetoric of the vicarious guilt of corruption. Humans are not unconscious automatons who must yield to the push and pull of the institutional and societal regimes in which they operate. They are able to maneuver in the crevices of even the most tainted of systems, and to project their ethical and moral convictions within the most impervious institutions. Most Africans are indeed people of strong moral convictions who would normally condemn corruption in unequivocal terms.

The mass guilt implied by this discourse of moral imprisonment to society's vices ostensibly disqualifies every potential critic of corruption from speaking or acting against the scourge. The rhetoric of mass complicity has the capacity to disarm the African critic of corruption, and to intimidate opponents of corrupt African institutions into a moral stupor. What is truly disturbing about it, however, is its reliance on the same rhetorical motif of a shared, ubiquitous, and generic culture of corruption in Africa. Lost in this argument are the individual African's free agency and ethical responsibilities. Those who make these claims imply erroneously that Africans are helpless captives of their distorted and corrupted institutions, incapable of exercising individual moral choices.

The Africanization of corruption proceeds from this mindset, but it is especially troubling to see Africans participating in this localization of a universal phenomenon.

ROOTS OF MISUNDERSTANDING

Many of the problematic assumptions about corruption in Africa stem from observations skewed in favor of the incidence, rather than the consequences of corruption. In a refreshing, if deeply problematic, departure from this way of thinking about corruption, one Nigerian cyber commentator once contended that we should perhaps make peace with the inevitability of some political corruption in Africa. Anticorruption crusaders should instead worry about the use to which the proceeds of corruption are put, and about the destination of corruptly acquired funds. According to this smugly pragmatic position, all political corruptions are not created equal and do not affect Africans in the same way.

This prognosis is of course problematic, but it is partly right to refocus attention on corruption's impact, and away from the controversial, charged debates about whether it is endemic or circumstantial in Africa. Focusing on the incidence and frequency of corruption in Africa misses the point of caring about corruption in the first place: its unsavory effect on peoples and societies. The Western obsession with corruption in Africa inspires many media headlines about the phenomenon. These headlines might tempt one to think that Africans are, by nature and nurture, more corrupt than other peoples. Many Westerners and some Africans actually believe this to be true, partly because every discussion of Africa's economic and political predicaments devolves lazily into a lamentation on corruption. But what is the statistical and evidentiary basis of this belief in Africa's preeminence in the dishonorable hierarchy of corruption? It is, for the most part, founded on the familiar Western quest for a different, exotic Africa governed by different ethical and moral impulses and concerns. The statistical truth is that, per capita, Africans are much less corrupt than Westerners.

The real problem of corruption in Africa is thus not "African corruption" per se; Africans do not steal more from their government treasuries or corporate entities than do other peoples. In terms of raw dollar figures and volume, Africa's corruption scandals pale in significance when compared to Western ones. The raw sum of Africa's yearly capital loss to corruption does not come close to that of Western countries. The main difference is that in the West the loss is internal while in Africa the loss is external, codified in the fiscal vocabulary of capital flight.

In the light of this, and contrary to what many in the West believe, the justifiable outrage against corruption in Africa cannot be founded on the prevalence of corruption on the continent, which is lower than in the Western World, but on the moral consequences of corruption, which are much greater in Africa than in the West. The emphasis should be on the effects and not on the prevalence or volume of corruption in Africa. This emphasis is the most politically neutral, least stereotypical, and most powerful way to inspire the necessary social angst against corruption in Africa.

This point deserves some elaboration. In the West, the impact of government and corporate corruption is absorbed by the sheer size of Western economies. The shock of corruption, state or private sector, is therefore hardly felt beyond the media frenzy that characterizes the prosecution of culprits and the lamentations of individuals who are directly affected. Such corruption hardly ever translates to infrastructural problems for society as a whole, much less causes the breakdown of political institutions. Despite widespread incidents of corporate and public corruption in Western countries, public utilities like electricity, water, and telecommunications, and social infrastructures such as roads, hospitals, and schools, are hardly ever disrupted.

In Africa, on the other hand, corruption kills, literally. The embezzlement, mismanagement, or misapplication of public funds often leads to a cessation of certain social services, or the abandonment of a road, school, or hospital project. The deterioration and scarcity of infrastructure and social services have worsened in direct proportion to the corruption problem on the continent. The loss of public funds to corruption translates inevitably to a lack of medicine in a rural hospital; a lack of access to education for millions of African children; lack of potable drinking water and electricity for millions of Africans; and a lack of good transportation infrastructure. All these can and do lead to millions of preventable deaths yearly.

The corruption is the same. The outcomes in Africa and the West are not. This should constitute the kernel of our outrage against corruption in Africa. Its devastating consequences occur because the small size of African economies magnifies the theft of government funds. African economies are so small that every corrupt act shows, and its impact is immediately visible and felt. The problem therefore is not corruption or its prevalence per se, but its morally reprehensible consequence.

This perspective should mitigate some of the hysterical pontifications on "African corruption" by Westerners. Columbia University economist Jeffery Sachs is one Westerner who refuses to participate in this feel-good hysteria and shuns the advancement of corruption as an alibi for doing nothing about poverty in Africa. He rejects the growing Western consensus that unless corruption is eradicated from Africa, no development can occur and no antipoverty intervention would work. His belief, which I share, is that corruption is largely a symptom of poverty in Africa, not its original cause. The continent's poverty, he argues, stems, among other things, from the environmental misfortune of poor soil, resource poverty, and uneven resource distribution. One does not have to believe that geography determines economic destiny (as does Jared Diamond, author of Guns, Germs, and Steel[10]) to recognize that these conditions produce poverty and that corruption—or, more appropriately, its impact and social toleration—are the outgrowth of poverty. Corruption, contrary to popular belief, is not the fundamental causative agent of poverty in Africa, although it has served to perpetuate and worsen it.

If a country is already poor, corruption can be a death sentence for its citizens. That is the reality of most African countries. But if a country is not poor, corruption has an insignificant impact on standard of living. This has been the reality in the West.

CONCLUDING THOUGHTS

There are two major forms of corruption in Africa—the official and the quotidian. Of these two, official corruption is the most consequential in terms of poverty and underdevelopment. Yet Western commentators routinely pretend that quotidian corruption is as harmful to Africa as official malfeasance, that the former begets the latter, and that this is illustrative of an African cultural inclination to corruption and disdain for accountability and the rule of law. This is reverse logic. The corruption of state officials perpetuates and exacerbates the poverty that nurtures quotidian citizen corruption—the corrupt practices of the African street—not the other way around. In other words, poverty is the mother of corruption. It is also, sadly, sometimes its devastating outcome.

Corruption is as integral to humanity as greed. It is in fact largely a byproduct of greed. If it would be unrealistic to expect Africans to break with humanity by completely ridding their continent of greed, it would be equally escapist to envision the elimination of corruption in Africa as a precondition for meaningful interventions and policymaking in the fight against poverty on the continent. For even if one were to devise a magical formula for eradicating corruption from Africa, in defiance of the human reality of greed, Africa would still be relatively poor. Such a feat would not obliterate the stubborn reality of Africa's resource poverty, the lingering legacies of historical injuries and handicaps inflicted on its people and landscape, the ecological bad fortune of poor soils in a predominantly agricultural continent, and the economic and trade hegemonies that continue to crush Africans' economic hopes.

The discourse of "African corruption," long advanced as an alibi by visionless African leaders and condescending Western commentators to foreclose developmental visions for the continent and to justify their inertia, incompetence, and aloofness, is thus largely a red herring. It continues to distract attention from the fundamental structural poverty of Africa and from the fundamental economic disadvantages into which history, geography, subaltern experiences, and bad leadership have thrust upon the continent.

The most potent weapon against corruption—and poverty—may therefore be the creation of wealth through sensible economic policies and partnerships and the deliberate democratization and redistribution of such created wealth. If poverty and economic insecurity, especially in countries without welfare systems and social safety nets, fuel corruption, wealth creation, provisions for basic human comforts, and post-work financial security and welfare benefits should minimize the incentive for bureaucratic larceny and reduce the corruption problem to the status of a residual, tolerable, insignificant social irritant—the product of an isolated but natural human predilection for greed. This is the social status of corruption in the West.

Simplistic understandings of corruption in Africa are a recipe for inaction and must, for all practical policy reasons, give way to a more nuanced understanding of the phenomenon.

CHAPTER 16

ABUJA MILLENNIUM TOWER AND THE PROBLEM OF EXPLAINING AFRICA

US-based African professors like me are often asked by Americans at academic gatherings, campus events, and informal social gatherings what we think of the never-ending civil war in the Democratic Republic of the Congo, the genocide in Rwanda, anarchy in Somalia, disastrous elections in Nigeria, the Kenyan political crisis, and other problems too numerous to list here. To volunteer information about your African identity, which your so-called accent and name advertise anyway, or to declare your academic expertise in African studies is to invite all manner of inquiries—both thoughtful and facile. You are subjected to a kind of anthropological and sociological inquisition: Why does this group of people in Africa do such and such? Are you from the "tribe" that's fighting with the so-and-so people? Did you see the documentary on the bizarre rituals of so and so ethnic group? The list is infinite.

Whether you like it not, Americans see you as knowledgeable about every political crisis torturing Africa and about all its countries—not just the one where you were born. You are, in a word, accountable for all of Africa, expected to explain its realities and defend its more visible deficits. And many Americans take liberties with African realities, generalizing recklessly and clinging to prejudiced preconceptions of a savage and seductively rustic continent. Intellectual dialogue about Africa and its travails is almost impossible with that kind of Westerner.

But what about genuinely curious Americans whose views on Africa and its peoples are not based on prejudice but are shaped by unflattering but ubiquitous popular images of Africa? As a scholar of Africa, I believe that I have an obligation to help these misinformed folks understand the nuances, complexities, multilayered culpabilities, Western complicities, and cultural underpinnings of the violence, famine, disease, poverty, waste, and bad government that are persistently presented as the essence of the continent. Without corrective interventions, the received imaged persist. And as an African, I feel that I am under assault each time my continent or my country, Nigeria, is stereotyped as a place of war, hunger, AIDS, and corruption. This stereotype calls for a sustained response, a thoughtful, committed fidelity to balance and intellectual rigor. To not respond when called upon to do so is a form of complicity, even though by responding one confers some credibility on perceptions that are jaundiced and sensationalize Africa.

That is one side of the moral dilemma that African academics in the West face. You feel that you have to teach Westerners about Africa. But the other side of it is that you do not want to rationalize, defend, or minimize the continent's many evils. As one of my colleagues put it, Africa's generous production of bad news complicates our commitment to a balanced explanation of its problems.

Sometimes I find myself in the unsettling position of trying to account for all that is wrong with Africa. In the process, I have gotten myself entangled in logical contradictions and pedantic distinctions. I have offered explanations that were so qualified and modified that they left my Western audiences confused, entrenched in their preconceptions, or convinced that I was more interested in defending the continent than in explaining the sources of its woes. At other times I was understood, on account of my occasionally obsessive accent on African failures, as being incapable of appreciating Africans' legendary resilience and allure. For someone who discusses Africa for a living, it is a constant struggle to balance the negative and the positive, the gloom and hope.

The most troubling occasions for me are when my American interlocutors think I am unwilling to acknowledge African complicity in Africa's underdevelopment. That misunderstanding unsettles me because I like to see myself as a harsh critic of bad African leaders, and as intolerant of corruption and bad government in Nigeria and the rest of Africa. I like to see myself not necessary as an Afro-pessimist but as a deliberate skeptic when it comes to Africa. My love for Africa expresses itself more in critique than in adulation, more as questions and demands than as satisfaction and empathy. Put simply, I am impatient with Africa.

126

Some of my compatriots and American colleagues have even upbraided me for focusing disproportionately on African culpability in the continent's economic and political problems, and for ignoring the role of predatory Western institutions and actors. Those critics accuse me of not giving enough weight to the lending practices of the International Monetary Fund, which have enabled and subsidized corruption while leaving African nations mired in debt, and of sidestepping the fact that Western countries routinely prop up incompetent, authoritarian, and corrupt leaders friendly to their interests. I plead guilty, for I may have sometimes gone overboard in my effort to stress the negative consequences of the bad choices that Africa's ruling elites routinely make.

I teach an undergraduate seminar on the history of poverty in Africa. Not surprisingly, my students come to class with preconceptions about the causes of African poverty and economic stagnation. Their favorite quest, regardless of precisely what topic and era we are discussing, is to pinpoint the cause of Africa's underdevelopment. They also want to know which side I agree with in the debate about the relative importance of Western actions, on one hand—including the historical injuries of colonialism and slavery as well as more-recent events, like the work of the IMF—and the disappointing and destructive choices of African leaders, on the other hand.

Often the students seek cut-and-dried answers, not nuanced, complicated ones. They want me to simply take a position and explain it to them, or persuade them to adopt it. But that is not my role as a teacher. I suspect that, while they enjoy my course, they are disappointed by my unwillingness to be conclusive. The notion that Africa's present conditions are caused by both external and internal factors does not satisfy all my students. The mushy middle in this case is unsatisfying. In my pedagogical engagement with Africa, I often dismiss my first instinctual reaction to any event on the continent because it is likely to be tainted by my emotional investment in it—by my quest for definitive judgment and for clear-cut culpability. Because I experience this internal struggle between explanation and judgment, I can relate to my students' appetite for judgmental precision.

Some of them believe that Africa's underdevelopment has been caused by Africans alone, and they do not hold the West's economic relationship with the continent, expressed through many institutions and practices, responsible. These students are adept at raising uncomfortable questions of responsibility, causality, and agency. The examples they cite, although carefully cherry-picked for hyperbolic effect, are hard to challenge. But they tend to do analysis backwards, beginning from a conclusion and then selecting evidence carefully from the abundant archive of African malfeasance as they work their way to that preconceived conclusion. Their evidence, again, illustrates the indefensible vignettes of Africa's poor postcolonial choices.

How, for instance, can I explain the decision of Felix Houphouët-Boigny, the late leader of the Ivory Coast, to build a Roman Catholic basilica in his hometown of Yamoussoukro for an amount roughly equivalent to his country's annual budget—an amount so large that it was almost certainly embezzled? I could point out that France, the former colonial power in the country, egged him on, but that is at best a feeble defense of his immoral behavior.

I love to cite as an example of the white elephant phenomenon of waste the $80 million Abuja National Stadium in Nigeria, which even the World Bank says could have been built for half that amount, and which, it must be said, is now a largely disused shell of a structure, requiring additional expenditures to make it usable again. Try explaining to an American undergraduate already stuffed on an evidentiary diet of Africa's dysfunction that building an exorbitant national stadium was more important than addressing other economic, social, and infrastructural problems.

In early 2001, just when I thought my task of educating Westerners about the complexity of Africa's problems, of redistributing the focus evenly between Africa's leadership and corruption problem and global structural constraints, could not get any more difficult, I read in the news that Nigeria's government would spend $350 million to build a Millennium Tower in Abuja, the Nigerian capital—a tower to belatedly commemorate the arrival of a new millennium and announce Abuja's position as a twenty-first-century city! I could see the headline in a Euro-American popular publication about this latest act of profligacy. I could see the sensational story of yet another misplaced priority feeding into the conceited prejudices of Westerners who reduce all of Africa's problems to a congenital African incompetence and economic irrationality. I could see new ammunition for Western (and African) scholars and commentators who peddle such inanities for a living. Yet I could not effectively debunk or deny the believability of the trope of waste and poor stewardship, seeing that empirical evidence for it oozed constantly out of Africa.

Then there are the billions of dollars that late Nigerian dictator General Sani Abacha and his family evidently embezzled from the Nigerian government when he was head of state. How can I convince a skeptical American student that Western banks and businesses have been complicit in such monumental corruption, and thus share the responsibility for it, without seeming to minimize Abacha's culpability or coming across as more concerned with alibis than with accountability? It may be unfair to expect Americans not to be seduced by the simplistic and surprisingly pervasive view that Africans are the only architects of their woes. We all love simple explanations; they cut to the chase of causality and culpability and ignore complexities that can sometimes morph into complicity. But Americans deserve to have a deeper understanding of Africa. That is why one should continue to try to explain the complexities of Africa to my students and to anyone else who is willing to listen without letting one's anxieties about being misunderstood get in the way.

CHAPTER 17

ARAB RACISM AGAINST BLACK AFRICANS: TOWARD AN UNDERSTANDING

In a contribution to a debate on Arab racist attitudes toward Africans and their causes posted on the popular and influential Toyin Falola–moderated USA/Africa dialogue Internet listserv, Professor Ilya Harik, a Lebanese professor emeritus of political science at Indiana University, posted the following, which I have edited for length and relevance without distorting its essence or context:

> I wish I could reassure everyone on the USA/Africa Dialogue forum that there are no racists in Arab countries any more than in any other part of the world. In general, antipathies in the Arab world tend to be cultural more than racial and I can say that racism is less in evidence there than in other countries of the world. I cannot agree...that Arabs are anti-African on a racial basis. They are not anti-African on any basis. For one thing, the largest ethnic component of the Arab world is African. Egypt, which is the most populous Arab country, is mixed of different races with a noticeably black African strain. I never noticed any markedly racial awareness or sense of difference associated with color there. The Sudan and Chad are mostly Arabic speaking, yet they are totally black African. Forget about what you hear and read in the media here that Arabs are killing Africans in Darfur. The people in Khartoum are no less black African than those in Darfur, as many of you well know. It is just that the government in Khartoum is oppressive in a way that affects all the population, but is mostly felt now in an ugly way in Darfur because the Darfurians dared stand up and speak.... Let me add that the populations of Libya, Tunisia, Algeria and Morocco are predominantly Arabic-speaking Berber, an Afri-

can race. You will find that there is a mixture of eastern Arabs and black Africans, too. Besides, Arabs and
sub-Saharan Africans have since independence been
together in the Non-Aligned Movement (that was
once dominated by Tito, Nkrumah, Sukarno, Toure,
Nasser, Keita and others) and its derivations.[11]

Professor Ilya Harik's piece is a commendable and bold attempt
by an Arab scholar to confront and discuss the sensitive issue of
tensions in Africa-Arab relations. There is need for an open, unfettered dialogue between Africans and Arabs on the fractured
state of relations between the two peoples, so Professor Harik's
contribution is a refreshing intervention.

Harik's perspective is, however, trapped in the language of
denial and obfuscation that has become a defining feature of
Arab responses to charges of racism against blacks in general
and Africans in particular. His response sounds eerily familiar;
I have heard many such feeble denials of Arab racism against
blacks. The tactic is simple enough: deracialize the racism and/
or emphasize the African roots of some North African Arabs as a
way to muddy and deflect the credible allegations of structural
and anecdotal Arab racism against Africans. One would normally
excuse such posturing, but it diverts us from the task of understanding the history of Afro–Arab relations, a history that preceded Africa's relations with the West.

Harik's rendering of the crisis in Darfur would be offensive to
many black people in that it is not only an intolerable simplifica-
tion and trivialization of a racist genocide being systematically
carried out by the self-described Arab government in Khartoum
but also an inexplicable attempt to dilute the fact that race, mediated by culture, is at the heart of the crisis in Darfur. For one to
subscribe to Harik's explanation, one would have to ignore the
rhetoric of Arab supremacy and Arab ancestral preordination
that has been oozing from Khartoum in its confrontations with
Darfur and, prior to the independence of South Sudan, the SPLM
secessionist movement in the South. To discount race and racial
narrative as a factor in the crisis one would have to set aside
the prevalent discourse of Arab racial manifest destiny and of
the inevitable triumph of Arab culture, a discourse on which the

state of Sudan anchors its responses to centrifugal challenges to its sovereignty.

At the heart of Sudanese nationalist identity is an exclusivist, rabidly policed claim to Arab ancestry for the elite and peoples of Northern Sudan. Variants of this claim alternately stress the power of Arab culture and the staying power of remote, tenuous, Arab–African racial miscegenation on the Red Sea and Nile corridors—part of the so-called Afro–Arab borderlands. To separate culture from race in this context is to be ahistorical, since both are conflated in Arab discourses of superiority in the Sudan. In this and several other Arab contexts, then, being "anti-African" on a cultural basis is the same as racial antipathy. The notion that identity is destiny, that Arab cultural and racial identity or claims to it confer the authority to pursue a manifest destiny that circumscribes the rights and freedoms of those designated as Africans or non-Arabs is at the core of fanatical North Sudanese proclamations of Arab identity.

All racial claims are, of course, constructed, and this is perhaps what Harik alludes to. But racial claims are also real, powerful, other-ing techniques. They authorize discrimination, ostracism, quarantine, exclusivity, dehumanization, and even genocide. And racial self-construction, like all self-constructed identities, is particularly powerful as a marker of the self and as a definition of those who do not belong, who are outside the favored, treasured community and who could therefore be poached for servitude and systematically excluded from commonly created patrimonies.

The racial registers that have come to define the relationship between Arab-speaking North Sudan and the African ethnic groups in Darfur—Fur, Zaghawa, Messalit, Birgit, and others who speak African languages and treasure their African culture—are the product of this original Arabization on the Afro–Arab frontier hundreds of years ago. They also flow from the politicization and lionization of Arab identity, culture, and ancestry by linguistically and culturally Arab elites in the North. To the extent that Northern Sudanese elites strategically authored this paradigmatic claim of Arab identity, put it to instrumental political use, and allowed it to define its Others, it was bound to produce an oppositional racial discourse, albeit one steeped in the rhetoric of noble victimhood, among the ethnic groups of Darfur. Skin pigmentation is of little consequence in this racial politics.

There is, to be sure, a problematic and facile understanding of the racial divide in the Darfur crisis, and this misunderstanding enjoys media currency. This perspective posits the dichotomy in essentialist terms and as a stand-in for immutable racial differences between Arabs and Africans. That characterization is, as Mahmood Mamdani has argued, simplistic, as essentialist racial categories are philosophically untenable and impossible to defend. Mamdani writes:

> The Save Darfur campaign's characterization of the violence as 'Arab' against 'African' obscured both the fact that the violence was not one-sided and the contest over the meaning of 'Arab' and 'African': a contest that was critical precisely because it was ultimately about who belonged and who did not in the political community called Sudan. The depoliticization, naturalization and, ultimately, demonization of the notion 'Arab' as against 'African' has been the deadliest effect, whether intended or not, of the Save Darfur campaign.[12]

What Mamdani is arguing against is not the racial arguments that the government in Khartoum uses to exclude and discriminate against the people of Darfur, whom it considers non-Arab black Africans, a label whose devaluing implications I will discuss shortly. What Mamdani is contesting is the tendency to reify the powerful racial claims at play and to ascribe permanence and naturalness to them. The meaning of "Arab" and "African" in the context of the Sudanese crisis is, as he argues, constructed politically. Nonetheless, elites and commoners alike on both sides have also appropriated these categories to mark identity, self-valuation, and self-distinction, as well as to establish a narrative of oppression and marginalization. Mamdani, in other words, does not deny that Northern Sudanese Arab racism is a driving force of the state-driven atrocities in Darfur or that the armed opposition and rebellion in Darfur casts itself in terms of racial resistance against Arabization and the erosion of "African" ways of life. He argues though, and correctly, that both racial narratives—one oppressive and aggressive, the other defensive—are political and socioeconomic constructs, as are all racial identities, especially hegemonic ones. Darfur is thus a racial conflict, fought on racial terms and with racial rhetoric, even if the contents of these racial constructions are contested and open to debate and deserve to be understood in their historical and shifting contexts—even if racial discourses are sometimes fronts for more substantive struggles over land, cattle, and economic privilege. As Kwame Anthony Appiah tells us in *In My Father's House*, race is powerful as a social and political object not because it is a primordial given but precisely because it is constructed and its meanings made visible and consequential by political and social acts.[13]

The racial terms of the conflict are traceable to the long, historical emergence of identity claims founded on Arab elite privilege and the historical prestige that Arab identity, especially Arab elite provenance, acquired in medieval Nubia and modern Sudan. These led to the consolidation of this Arab elite dominance through the construction of inferior "black African" Others on the margins of Sudanese society.

Professor Harik is only half right about the Arab-speaking Northern Sudanese. They are a dark-skinned people, although some of them are of mixed Arab and African ancestry. Most Northern Sudanese people—the cultural and linguistic Arabs of today—have only a scintilla of Arab biological attributes. This is because the racial mixture between Arab men and black African slave women that they celebrate as a seminal event of their identity affected a minority of the population, and occurred so long ago during the aggressive Arab migrations into Nubia (from the thirteenth century) that these black Arabs have, for all visible morphological considerations, been re-Africanized and stripped of any consequential Arab genetic signatures. Still, an early process of strategic assimilation and hegemonic marriages, the adoption of the Arabic language, and the subscription of many northern Nubians to many aspects of Arab culture have bestowed a cultural reality of Arab-ness on Northern Sudanese peoples. This cannot be denied. Hence North Sudanese peoples no longer perceive themselves as blacks, or African in any functional way. Indeed, for all functional political and social purposes, they have long become Arabized. So deep is this new sense of the Northern Sudanese Arab self that the region's metanarrative of origin and social evolution stresses the Arab imprint more than it does any other even though we know that the African racial element in that history is overwhelming.

This is construction of racial memory par excellence. A powerful Northern Sudanese elite has invested intellectual and political resources in not only preserving but propagating this constructed racial identity. The late John Garang captures the historical emergence of narratives of Arab superiority and dominance thus:

> In our country, the Sudan, the unprincipled elites who took over power after colonialism were not individual thugs like Idi Amin and Bokasa, but a social group which is collectively and popularly known in the Sudan as 'Jellaba.' But who are these Jellaba, where did they come from and how did they develop? The Jellaba (Afrabians) are a social group which has developed in the Sudan since the fifteenth century from elements of foreign and local traders including slave traders, and who have established themselves in trading centers which later became important urban centers and towns such as Dueim, Omdurman and Sennar. The Jellaba are a hybrid of different races and nationalities from the indigenous Africans, and the immigrant Arabs, Turks, Greeks, and Armenians, who have interacted and intermarried in the long historical process which took place mainly in Northern Sudan. The Jellaba are therefore part African and Sudanese, but they choose to identify themselves as Arabs although very many of them are blacker than myself. The Jellaba are thus the so-called Arabs of the Sudan.... I once asked a leading Northern Sudanese politician whether he considered himself as a Sudanese Arab or an Arab Sudanese, and he found the question puzzling! I have attempted to analyze the Sudanese situation objectively and dispassionately in order to correctly identify the

> problem of the Sudan, for unless a problem is cor-
> rectly diagnosed, a correct answer is difficult to find.
> I have argued here and established that the problem
> of the Sudan is the hegemony by the minority Jella-
> ba of Northern Sudan, and for lack of a better 'ism' I
> shall call the Sudanese problem the problem of 'Jella-
> baism.' How do we solve the problem of Jellabaism?[14]

Given the multiracial origins of the Jellaba Arab elite that is responsible for establishing and preserving Arab cultural, religious, and linguistic identity as the paradigmatic mode of belonging in the Sudan, the question should be posed as to how the Jellaba elite pioneers elected to self-identify as Arabs instead of embracing the plethora of identity options open to them. The answer suggests itself. At the time of the emergence of the Jellaba at the intersection of multiple racial interactions in medieval times Arab identity was already invested with significations of power, privilege, domination, and piety. Claims and constructed signifiers of Arab racial superiority preceded the Jellaba's embrace of Arab identity and in fact made it the preferred trajectory of identification. The historicity of Arab racial claims enabled the Arabization of the Jellaba and by extension North Sudanese identity. The long enunciation and enforcement of this identity in Nubia built on a wider, expanding frontier of what one might call an Arab racial superiority complex. The history of this larger rhetorical complex of Arab racial supremacy is easy to retell.

Arab and Arabized Muslims invading from the birthplace of Islam in the Arabian Peninsula had established themselves in North Africa and the Middle East as overlords in spiritual and secular affairs, Arabizing indigenous peoples in those locales. In the process they helped make Arab identity a coveted marker of privilege. The Afro–Arab borderlands of Nubia/Sudan partook in this long process of Arabization and Arab sociopolitical ascent. The Arabs had also developed forms of religious and secular literacy that they brought, along with Islam, to sub-Saharan Africa through the Sahara, the Nile, the Indian Ocean, and the Red Sea. Awed by the sophistication and the utilitarian applications of Islam and its accompaniments, many African peoples flocked to it and added it to their pantheon of beliefs. The resultant association of Arabs with the prestige and the epistemic culture of Islam further consolidated the aura of superiority that formed around Arab identity. All of these accouterments of Arab racial superiority pale in comparison to the impact of the Arab slave trade, which lasted from roughly the eighth century to the sixteenth century. The trade had two profound effects on the dialectics of Afro–Arab relations and on Arab claims of racial superiority vis-à-vis Africans.

The enslavement of Africans in the Arabized Maghreb and in the larger Arab world over many centuries devalued the humanity of Africans, constructing them as property at worst and servile members of society at best. Conversely, the ability to initiate, finance, and sustain the enslavement of Africans over a long period confirmed, like a self-fulfilling prophecy, the many circulating myths and narratives of Arab superiority. The slave trade, which I will return to shortly, sealed the claims of Arab superiority and the discourse of African racial and cultural deficit, making Arab identity attractive for many hybrid communities and even many Islamized African groups in the Afro–Arab borderlands, where claims of Arab identity had more plausibility than they did in other places in Africa. The Jellaba of Sudan emerged in this context as powerful human anchors for the claims of Arab identity articulated by the peoples of present-day North Sudan and for the related claims of the inferiority of non-Arab "Africans" in the rest of Nubia/Sudan.

For many parts of Africa, Arab culture came via military conquest and manifested itself as cultural and intellectual hegemony. Arabization in Nubia was particularly fraught with struggle and conflicts—conflicts that for the most part pitted self-identified Arab North Sudanese and their nomadic allies against the non-Arab Africans of South Sudan, Khordofan, and Darfur. North Sudanese territorial and cultural expansionism was the spark. The racial lines of antagonism were drawn in these early encounters, but the rhetoric of Arab manifest destiny lived on and intensified. Military and civilian leaders of Sudan since independence have pursued Islamization and Arabization in South Sudan and Arabization in Darfur, Khordofan, and other already Islamized parts of Sudan. General Ibrahim Abbud, who led a successful coup shortly after independence in 1958, set the tone with a brutal regime of Arabization and Islamization in the South. He sought to create a forced unity in the new nation by decreeing and pursuing cultural and religious homogeneity. He abolished missionary schools in the South, replaced them with Islamic schools, pursued mass conversions to Islam, changed the Sabbath from Sunday to Friday, and replaced English with Arabic as the language of instruction. In the West and other non-Arab parts of the state, where Islam was already established, the emphasis was on spreading Arab culture, promoting Arabic above the plethora of African languages that were spoken as first languages by the regions' ethnicities.

These early Arabization efforts targeted the mainly Sufi religious practices in the non-Arab sectors of West Sudan. North Sudanese ruling elites saw the Sufi orders of Darfur and other regions (which, like most domesticated Islamic forms in Africa, assimilates pre-Islamic African religious practices into its repertoire of rituals) as corrupted forms of Islam and sought to "purify" them. Subsequent governments in Sudan, notably that of General Gaafar Numayri (in power from 1969 to 1985), continued in this path of Arabization and Islamization, with the imposition of Sharia law across the country, including in the largely non-Muslim South, a policy that led to the third Sudanese Civil War. During the rule of General al-Bashir and under the spiritual guidance of Islamist cleric Hassan al-Turabi, the policy of Arabization and Islamization was no longer just a declared goal. It became a national priority. Turabi, the legal mastermind behind the Islamist bent of the al-Bashir regime until 1999 when the two fell out, was fond of declaring publicly the government's desire to Islamize non-Islamic sectors of Sudan and to Arabize the entire country. Kwesi Prah's characterization of the sectarian and cultural divide is instructive:

> For many Messalit, Fur, Birgit, and Zaghawa, the Islamic religion sits astride an older African religious system. There have therefore often been combinations of indigenous pre-Islamic traits, and, at other times, Africanized and nativized Islam. The popularity of these is what the Janjaweed see as a stumbling block to greater Arabization. [T]he Fur practice, in

effect, a religion, which is an eclectic mix of indigenous African pre-Islamic traditions and usages, and Islamic ones. But the injunction that "Arabic is the language of the God" has historically seduced many to bend to the sweep of Arabization and Arabism.[15]

Arab racism in the Sudan was intertwined with religious and cultural arrogance. It began from a baseline of claims that established Arab culture, language, and religious practice as superior and African languages, cultures, and religious practices as inferior forms that should be subordinated and if possible replaced by Arab cultural symbols. Arabization was real, calculated, and racist. Its legacies have included the erasure of the cultures, languages, and values of Nubian peoples characterized as backward, inferior Africans. Even more tragic, it has authorized a system of enslavement and subordination disguised as servitude that continues to this day.

SPECIFYING ARAB RACISM

Professor Harik claims that Arabs are not "anti-African on any basis." But this is a straw man. One would be hard pressed to find Africans who make such a sweeping characterization. The allegation, which Harik does not directly respond to, is that there is a disturbing pattern of anti-African racism in many Arab countries, and that, on a broader level, this attitude translates to a widespread Arab indifference (and sometimes hostility) to African struggles and sensibilities at a time when black African leaders are straining to accommodate and protect the interests of Arab nations on the international stage. In the interest of Afro-Arab political alliances and in order not to alienate their North African brothers, many Africans shy away from an open discussion of this issue. Arabs are not by nature prejudiced against Africans, and many Arabs, aside from buying into stereotypes about Africans, cannot be characterized as anti-African racists. But many others are overtly and covertly racist toward Africans, and there seems to be a tolerance of or indifference to the activities of these racists in the Arab world.

It is true that the population of most North African countries is mixed and that a few black Africans have participated in this racial and cultural diffusion throughout history, but it is not a secret that in these countries there is a gradation of human valuation that corresponds directly to skin color and racial ancestry, with the most privileged status accorded those perceived rightly or wrongly as being of "pure" Arab stock while those with the darkest skin and curliest hair are located on the lowest level of the social hierarchy. Pigmentation as destiny is alive and well in most Arab countries, with physiologically "African" groups living on the social, economic, and political margins of these societies despite long, traceable ancestries in these countries. The conditions of African voluntary migrants to these countries are even more deplorable. This is structural, entrenched, stifling racism, which is even more sinister than the experiential variety that Harik tries to muddle.

While it is true, as Harik argues, that Tunisia, Libya, Morocco, and Algeria all have significant autochthonous Berber populations, the rapid, forceful, and hegemonic Arabization of North Africa in demographic, political, and cultural terms in the last twelve hundred years has left the Berbers a minority in their own ancestral homelands. Their culture is systematically marginalized and their status as an economic underclass is one of the open sores of North African society, seen but shunned, detested but hardly discussed. Masters of the Sahara and the Sahel and middlemen in the exchanges between Africa and the Mediterranean world in pre-Islamic times, Berbers have for centuries, since the Islamo-Arab conquest of North Africa in the eighth and ninth centuries, been consigned to the status of a poor, neglected, and alienated minority. The Berber struggle for recognition in these Arabized countries of North Africa has metastasized into armed rebellion at several historical junctures. Berber subordination to Arab identity is brazen and brutal. Yet the plight of the Berber is infinitely better than that of black African transplants in Arab North Africa. The racial taxonomies of Arab countries are more inclusive of Berbers than they are of dark-skinned Africans.

The Arab conquest of North Africa and the subsequent conversion and marginalization of the original Berbers and Moors of

141

North Africa and parts of the Sahel were undergirded by a racist ethos. To this day, the descendants of the dark-skinned Moors, the Berbers, and other non-Arab peoples are confined to the fringes of North African and Northwest African society—in Morocco, Tunisia, Algeria, Egypt, and Mauritania. The plight of the descendants of blacks (some of whose ancestors inhabited the Maghreb prior to the Arab conquest as slaves, captives, and free migrants) is without parallel in that part of the world. In Morocco and Tunisia, and throughout much of the Arab world, the only ticket to social visibility for blacks is distinction in sports and other kinds of entertainment. Becoming a football star gives a black person access to coveted corridors of society and enables them to sometimes "marry up" the racial hierarchy. This is a sad commentary on the state of race relations in any society. So, while Harik is right that a uniquely complex racial classificatory system is at work in much of the Arab world, this reality hardly detracts from the presence of an unspoken, normalized, and stealthily institutionalized racism that casts black people as the dregs of society who must prove themselves worthy of social recognition and privileges.

Arab racial arrogance and the racial devaluation of black humanity were nurtured by several generations of Arab travelers and writers who constructed new racist images of the African world. These writers elaborated on existing racist fantasies that Arabs projected onto Africa, supplying pseudo-ethnological "evidence" for extant Arab and European speculations on black Africa. Ibn Battuta, renowned Moroccan Arab traveler and geographer of the medieval era, traveled extensively through West and coastal East Africa. His narratives on the African societies that he encountered were nuanced and sometimes complimentary by the standards of the time, but they also contain the stock racist tropes that were circulating in the Arab world about Africa. Ibn Khaldun was arguably the most respected Arab philosopher and scholar of the Middle Ages. Yet his characterization of African societies repeated the prevalent popular Arab descriptions of Africans as excitable, emotional, dirty, morally unclean, childlike, and "worse than dogs." He was a man of his time; his many racist views on Africans are distilled in this one excerpt from his *The Muqaddimah* or *Ibn Khaldun's Prolegomena/Introduction*:

We have seen that Negroes are in general characterized by levity, excitability, and great emotionalism.
They are found eager to dance whenever they hear
a melody. They are everywhere described as stupid....
Beyond [the Sahel] to the south there is no civiliza-
tion in the proper sense. There are only humans who
are closer to dumb animals than to rational beings.
They live in thickets and caves, and eat herbs and unprepared grain. They frequently eat each other. They
cannot be considered human beings.[16]

Ibn Khaldun saw the enslavement of Africans as a logical outgrowth of their childlike docility. Africans, he argued, were suited to slavery:

Therefore, the Negro nations are, as a rule, submis-
sive to slavery, because [Negroes] have little [that is
essentially] human and have attributes that are quite
similar to those of dumb animals, as we have stated.[17]

Other Arab and Persian writers with widespread intellectual
influence in the Arab world spewed racist characterizations of
Africans that mirrored the popularly held views in their own societies of Africans as savages and semi-human. Here are a few
samples from this menu of Arab racist intellection on Africa:

Of the neighbors of the Bujja, Maqdisi had heard that
"there is no marriage among them; the child does not
know his father, and they eat people—but God knows
best. As for the Zanj, they are people of black color,
flat noses, kinky hair, and little understanding or intelligence (Maqdisi, also known as Al-Muqaddasi (fl.
966 CE), Kitab al-Bad' wah-tarikh, vol. 4).

If (all types of men) are taken, from the first, and one
placed after another, like the Negro from Zanzibar,
in the southernmost countries, the Negro does not
differ from an animal in anything except the fact
that his hands have been lifted from the earth—in no
other peculiarity or property—except for what God
wished. Many have seen that the ape is more capable

of being trained than the Negro, and more intelligent
(Philosopher-theologian Nasir al-Din Tusi (1201–74),
Tasawwurat (Rawdat al-taslim)).

The notion that black Africans, defined in color, culture, and religious terms, are ordained by providence and predisposed by
natural attributes for slavery was conventional social wisdom
in the Arab world for centuries. This thinking is on its way out
of consequential, functional instrumentality. But it has been a
slow death; slow because discussions of the enslavement of Africans have focused over the last hundred years on Euro-American slavery in the so-called New World, and scholars, especially in Africa and the Arab world, have devoted a relatively small
space and time to analyzing the Indian Ocean and Saharan-Arab
slave trades in Africans. There is no conspiracy of silence with
regard to Arab slavery, as some people allege. There is, however,
reluctance, occasioned in my opinion by Afro–Arab and global
Southern solidarity, to broach, let alone scrutinize, the existing
narratives of Arab slavery.

Most discussions of Arab slavery lazily repeat a sanitized his-
toriography that claims that Arab slavery was integrative and
benign, and that, unlike chattel slavery in the Americas, it recognized the humanity, albeit an inferior one, of Africans. The basic
argument for this notion of benign and integrative Arab slavery
is the idea that, under Islam, the offspring of a slave is in most
cases free, and that Islam provides a pathway to eventual freedom through conversion to Islam.

The "conversion as freedom" argument is a claim that barely
holds up against the historical evidence and is even of disputed
theological foundation. Examples of conversion to Islam providing a pathway to freedom for African slaves are rare. The theological basis of the idea of conversion as a route to freedom is also
not settled; it depends on which school of exegesis one summons
to speak to the issue. The concept, which was largely ignored
and abused in practice across the Arab and Arabized Maghreb
worlds, has unfortunately continued to fuel the contentions of
Ali Mazrui and others seeking to attenuate the crime of Arab
slavery. They cite it, along with the canard of Arab slavery being
more benign and integrative than New World plantation slavery

(would this comparative footnote give comfort to the millions of Africans whom the Arabs enslaved and exploited?), as evidence that Islamic slavery, especially trans-Saharan and Indian Ocean enslavement of Africans, was less brutal and that Arabs are thus less (if at all) culpable than Euro-American slavers.

I respect Ali Mazrui's scholarship, but this aspect of his work seems to put ideology and identity before academic rigor and truth telling. Arguments that by design or effect provide undeserved comfort to Arab supremacists stifle honest scholarly accounting for a sad chapter in Afro–Arab history. It is common to hear subtle apologists for Arab slavery and racism argue that many Arab slave owners in North Africa and the Middle East willingly freed their slaves in obedience to the Qur'anic provision that one who frees his slave is entitled to a reward from God. As with the "conversion as freedom" concept in Islamic theology, the promise of reward for manumission did not translate to mass freedom for African slaves in the Arab and larger Islamic world.

Arab slave owners freed their slaves in trickles for a variety of strategic and self-interested reasons. And even when they freed their slaves in order to access the divine reward promised to emancipators, they often did so, as my friend Yacine Daddi Addoun's research has shown, in order to import other, presumably younger and stronger, Africans to replace the freed ones. In other words, freeing slaves according to the Islamic recommendation to do so actually fueled and sustained the Arab slave trade, for it necessitated the constant replacement of freed slaves with new African captives. Which is one of the reasons why the trade lasted as long as it did and the population of African slaves in the Arab world grew over centuries, despite (or because of) the fact that Arab owners freed some of their African slaves. The Arab slave owners were in fact not doing anything humane by freeing their slaves. They were, if one wanted to be cynical, being greedy, craving both the spiritual reward for freeing your slave and the earthly, economic reward that came with replacing your old, sickly, or tired African slave with a healthier, stronger, and more productive one.

HIDDEN SIGNS OF RACISM

Arab racism is so deep that it is inscribed in the fundamental semantic structure of the Arabic language. To this day, the generic word for a black person in the Arab-speaking world is the preface *abd*, which translates as "slave." Although *abd* is used in reverential contexts to denote devotion, as in *abd*-allah (slave or servant of God), its generic usage for blacks in the Arab world is a throwback to the slave status of the ancestors of black Arabs and is clearly pejorative. This linguistic norm, among many other racially charged ones, is an expressive constant that holds true for the entire Arab-speaking world regardless of dialect and orthography.

In the wake of the election of Barack Obama to the US presidency in 2008, a CNN.com story on the black population of Iraq (descendants of African slaves) and their struggle against racial discrimination chronicled the marginality of this black demographic in Iraqi society. The story is also an indictment of the persistence of the *abd* (slave) prefix-label and the racist attitudes that flow from it. All over the Arab world, stories of centuries-old oppressions and racist discrimination lay buried beneath pretenses of common Arab identity and shared culture. The black populations of the Middle East have largely been sucked into these performances of Arab cultural and racial unity, which pretend that shared cultural and religious values trump race. Arab nationalist discourse is a perfect foil for concealing a societal underbelly of anti-African racism in the Arab world.

Black Arabs have largely accepted their restricted places in Arab society because they lack the proverbial weight of numbers and because of a politically repressive culture that brooks no challenges to the official myths of common identity and history for black and "white" Arabs. Black Arabs are victims of deceptive official narratives of egalitarianism and equality rooted in a notional, historically impractical Islamic prescription for granting automatic freedom to the descendants of slaves. Many Arab and Islamic societies have largely skirted this prescription by merely substituting other equally dehumanizing genres of servitude, oppression, and dispossession for legal slavery. Ironically, then, many Arab states have sought rhetorical cover in the Islamic prescription on freeing descendants of slaves from legal enslave-ment. This has enabled them to oppress and exclude blacks from Arab social, economic, and political life while professing the mantra that since no new slaves are now being acquired from black Africa (except in Sudan and Mauritania, where residual Arab slavery is still practiced), black Arabs are free and equal. But the descendants of slaves and voluntary black migrants in the Arab world are seething with discontent even if they lack the numbers and the political freedom to transform their grievance into political and social action.

The case of the Sudan is perhaps the most vivid, poignant, and irrefutable example of Arab racism against black Africans. It should be noted that until the Janjaweed militia and their Su-danese government backers in Darfur gave a bad name to the art of hating, marginalizing, and murdering blacks, Arabs never quite saw the raiding of black villages for slaves and cattle, espe-cially in Southern and Western Sudan, as a crime. For centuries, Arab slave raids into African territories were normative acts of masculine distinction in parts of the Arab world contiguous with African societies—the borderlands between black Africa and the Arab world, like Sudan and Mauritania. Arabs on the Arab–Afri-can frontier saw frontier black African communities as one giant slave reservoir created by providence for their raiding pleasure.

Many Arabs still generally regard the Darfur genocide as a public relations disaster rather than a racist war against black people. We have yet to hear from Arab states unequivocal con-demnation of the Sudanese government's racist practices and declarations in its counterinsurgency in Darfur. To mouth con-demnation would, in any case, be hypocritical because some of these states themselves condone the racist practices of maver-icks or practice anti-black racism in their own official policies. For instance, black African immigrants were routinely killed or maimed, and their houses and properties destroyed, in Muam-mar Ghadaffi's Libya—the same Ghadaffi who wanted to be the leader of a politically united African super-state—with little or no official state protection and amelioration.

Another emerging side note to this story of Arab racism against black Africans is that the racist tropes that help trans-mit Arabs' racist thought towards blacks have circulated widely.

They have traveled to diasporic Arab communities in the United States, generating debate and controversy within Muslim communities on the elusive ideal of a color-blind, universal Muslim brotherhood. Long concealed beneath the rhetoric of Muslim racial ecumenism, this debate erupted into the open recently when Dawud Walid, an African American imam and the Executive Director of the Michigan chapter of the Council on American-Islamic Relations (CAIR), wrote a widely publicized op-ed calling on Arabs in America to stop referring to African Americans and other US black populations as *abed* (*abeed* in plural) because of the term's origins in Arab enslavement of Africans.[18] Abeed, Walid argues, is a "hurtful word" for black people, especially those who are Muslim and understand the etymology of the word in slavery and other practices of oppression, most of which had black victims. Responding to Arab Muslims who have sought to explain the word away as a generic term and prefix referring to servitude of man to God, and not man to man, Walid contends thus:

> 'Abed' is a term that, at one time, had a general meaning of slave, then became a specific term, referring to blacks, who were viewed as subservient. For instance, 'mamluk,' another term that is used for an enslaved person, came to specifically refer to a non-black slave, such as a Turk. Hence, 'abeed' became nomenclature, which strictly referred to people with darker skin, as it is continued to be used today. It is disingenuous to say that it is a good word, because excellent worshippers of God are 'abeed.' When people use that term, it is not because they are saying that black people are the best worshippers, nor do they call lighter skin persons, or their own pious family members, 'abeed.' The term has ugly roots and is derogatory; therefore, its usage should cease, instead of explaining it off to the offended and telling them not to be so sensitive, because it's a compliment.[19]

The servitude signaled by "abed" or "abd" is, Walid argues, not one rendered to God. It is also not a racially neutral servitude. Instead, the term enjoys a pan-Arab provenance as a signifier of black racial inferiority, a designation of inferiority with origins in Arab enslavement of millions of black Africans. The Arab diasporic manifestation of the term, and the ways in which its derogatory connotations are gradually becoming intelligible to discerning black American Muslims, confirm the insidiousness of Arab racist ideologies directed towards blacks. As Walid states, the term has become a part of the everyday descriptive vocabulary of many Arab Muslims, who have become "desensitized to its meaning," hence its acceptance as a benign term for marking what they regard as the strangely dark otherness of Africans.

In the wake of the publication of Walid's opinion, some Arabs supported his argument that the continued use of the term bespeaks the existence of anti-black racism among Arab Americans. Others lashed out at him with anonymous Internet vitriol. Yet others responded with an insistence that the term, whatever its origins, is an acceptable name with generic, even honorable connotations of servitude.[20] It is hard to divorce a term from its history, and the strategic effort on the part of some Arabs to disinfect "abed" and reclaim it for descriptive, racially specific use suggests that Arabs who challenge the term's rejection and insist on its usage are aware of its racist origins.

CONCLUSION

Afro–Arab political solidarity and alliances have survived not because of the absence of Arab racism toward black Africans—as Harik seems to suggest—but in spite of its painful existence. Kwame Nkrumah, Sekou Toure, Thabo Mbeki, Olusegun Obasanjo, and other African leaders have been aware of this racism but have been motivated by higher ideals and goals in their interaction with North Africa and the entire Arab world. This pursuit of South–South alliance and solidarity has cost Africa dearly in human and material terms. Sub-Saharan Africa has acquiesced in the lubrication of this relationship with the blood of Africans, the latest of such sacrifices being Darfur, where sub-Saharan African leaders have, to the disgust of their citizens, refrained from outright condemnation of the Darfur debacle as a racist genocide directed at black Africans.

The crucial question is: what price has the Arab world paid and what sacrifices and concessions has it made in the service of this alliance? My personal opinion is that we are approaching a watershed moment as Arab disregard toward the interest and person of the African intensifies and as African awareness of this historical problem grows apace. The emotional blackmail of accusing Africans of marginalizing Arab North Africa, or of engaging in reverse racism, which is often subtly deployed by North African members of the African Union (AU) to obscure the racist treatment of blacks in the Arab world, is no longer tenable.

CHAPTER 18

BOKO HARAM, AFRICAN ISLAM, AND FOREIGN ISLAMIC HETERODOXY

"There must be an enlightened religious discourse to protect society from alien ideas."

—Abdel Fattah al-Sisi, Egyptian President, criticizing the Islamist doctrine of the Muslim Brotherhood, and stressing the need for protecting the moderate, Sufi Islamic heritage of Egypt from foreign religious ideologies, such as Saudi Wahhabism and Salafism.

In the wake of the attempted terrorist attack by the al-Qaeda operative and Nigerian-born student, Umar Farouk Abdul Mutallab, on Christmas Day 2010, many commentators leaned temporarily toward theorizing Abdul Mutallab's terrorist adventure as a representation of Nigerian or African Islamic disposition toward the West.

Observers revived this contemplation on Islam, violence, and Africa in the wake of the Westgate Mall attack in September, 2013, a deadly attack in which the perpetrators, Islamic militants linked to Somalia's Al-Shabab, obviously planned and embraced the possibility of dying in action. Taken together with the suicidal bombing and shooting operations of Somali, Malian, and Nigerian Islamic militants, the suicidal bent of the Westgate attackers points to a chilling phenomenon: increasingly, African Islamic insurgents are relying on alien notions of martyrdom and suicide as a tactic of militancy.

This phenomenon of suicidal militancy is the culmination of a descent into violent heterodoxy by some African Muslim radicals. The phenomenon is not only relatively new, it vitiates a familiar, if occasionally violated, tradition of pacifism and reluctance for violent, suicidal militancy in African Islam. It is this African Sufi Islamic tradition of moderation, tolerance, and pacifism that Egyptian president al-Sisi was signaling in the quoted statement at the beginning of this chapter. In constructing his

Wahhabi and Salafist Islamist political opponents as beholden to "alien" doctrines, he sought to render them external and foreign to Egyptian history and culture. He also sought to call attention to the heritage of Egypt and Cairo as a historical haven of Sufism —the most prestigious and credible ideological wellspring for many of Sub-Saharan Africa's Sufi Islamic orders. For a country located at the intersection of Africa and the Middle East and within the enlightened Islamic cultures of both geopolitical entities, the implication of the statement is clear: we are Arabic speaking African Muslims with our own Islamic tradition and should therefore resist and reject the Islamic doctrines crafted in the deserts of Arabia, doctrines unsuited to our sociological conditions and political realities. Unfortunately, similar assertions of African or North African Islamic identity as a distinct corpus threatened by "alien" Islamic ideologies have been missing from discussions and debates on Islamic radicalization and Islamist violence in twenty first century Africa.

Commentators who tried to Africanize the behaviors of Abdul Mutallab, Malian Islamists, Boko Haram nihilists, and the Westgate attackers by locating them within an African Islamic matrix of suicidal violence should have read an obscure little essay written by Professor Ali Mazrui for the United Nations Foundation in 2004.[21] In it Mazrui contends that Africans—especially African Muslims—may have grievances against the West but they are, unlike Middle Easterners, more likely to favor reparation and peaceful redress than violent, jihadist retribution. He argues that for Africans, payback means reclamation, not nihilist revenge.

The difference in how African Muslims and their Middle Eastern co-religionists might express their anti-American sentiments is partly cultural, says Mazrui. Middle Eastern culture is steeped in what he calls a martyrdom complex. African culture, by contrast, abhors self-sacrifice as a tactic of political or ideological struggle. Moreover, we know from scattered oral and written evidence of African Islamic history that some African Muslim revolutionaries actively discouraged suicidal violence, even those calculated to achieve strategic ends in the context of war and the struggle between the *umma* and non-Muslim or nominal Muslim adversaries. The legend of Bakin Wake in pre-Islamic Hausaland is an allegory of a man who, determined to remove the tyranny of an oppressive prince, killed himself along with said oppressive prince, whom he was carrying on his back, by jumping into a furnace. This story indicates the pre-Islamic veneration of suicidal attacks in war and in militant acts designed to achieve a strategic goal in Hausaland. The term *Harin Bakin Wake* (suicidal attack or raid) is named for Bakin Wake, the legendary martyr of the suicidal mission in question. During the Islamic reform movement of the first decade of the nineteenth century, jihad leader, Othman bin Fodio banned *Harin Bakin Wake* as un-Islamic after it came to his attention that his fellow revolutionaries were using the tactic against the forces of their adversaries: pre-jihad Hausa rulers.

This African Islamic disapproval of violent suicidal mass killings and attacks was not restricted to Hausaland and would have traveled widely in the context of African Sufism and of widely circulating, paradigmatic orthodox Sunni theologies. This precolonial historical backdrop is germane to our understanding of the relative novelty of suicidal mass killings in the name of religion by today's African Islamic militants. There is hardly a tradition of this type of Islamic militancy in Sub-Saharan Africa. Self-sacrificial religious or secular violence is largely alien to Africa, as are violent approaches to ideological change.

Most Africans are largely socialized by their culture into a docile approach to politics and a gradualist response to political domination. This approach seeks compromise and peaceful resolution and disapproves violent, terror-spreading political acts. This docility has its drawbacks in the domestic political arena, of course: It is an enabler of political corruption, impunity, and incompetence and is an obstacle to transparency and leadership accountability. But in the realm of religious practice, it is an asset, a safeguard against violent, politicized religious extremism. Martyrdom, especially the one sought through suicidal acts of terror, is not glorified in African culture, even Islamized ones. Violent self-sacrifice holds no appeal in African notions of masculine honor. African Muslims exhibit this overbearing cultural signature of respect for one's life even in the context of struggle.

Mazrui would agree with this extrapolation. Simply put, Nigerians (as a subset of Africans) do not associate honor with killing oneself to achieve a political objective. The late Nigerian Afrobeat maestro, Fela Kuti, captured this reluctance of Nigerians to die for a political cause poignantly; *we no wan die* is the pidgin English mantra popularized by Fela's lyrical articulation of the phenomenon.

So, how did Abdul Mutallab journey from this cultural baseline to the world of suicidal anti-Western terrorism? Instead of starting and ending with externalizing Abdul Mutallab's radicalization, perhaps the search for origins and causation should start with the religious environment of Northern Nigeria, especially the strange connection that has recently developed between that environment and international circuits of Islamic extremism. To understand Abdul Mutallab and his ilk, one must start from the premise that he belongs to a recent tradition of African Islamism embodied by Nigeria's Boko Haram, Somalia's Al-Shabaab, and Al Qaeda in the Islamic Maghreb (AQIM), which are part of the global ideological complex of violent Salafist Islamism. In Northern Nigeria, this Salafist Islamist movement maps onto an earlier, Middle Eastern–inspired embrace of Wahhabi Islam. In the last four decades, there has been a slow, sneaky entry of Middle Eastern–originated Islamic doctrines into Northern Nigeria. Some of this has even been documented. Ousmane Kane's 2003 book, *Muslim Modernity in Postcolonial Nigeria*,[22] for instance, analyzes the well-funded arrival of Wahhabi Islam into Northern Nigeria in the 1980s and 1990s. Its most visible face was and still is the Izala sect.

The Jama't Izalat al Bid'a Wa Iqamat as Sunna (Society of Removal of Innovation and Reestablishment of the Sunna), popularly known as Izala, was founded in 1978 in Jos by a group of followers of the late Sheikh Abubakar Gumi. Sheikh Ismaila Idris was the leader of the group. Gumi was at the time studying and mastering the Wahhabi doctrinal canons in Saudi Arabia. He returned in the 1980s to take organizational and spiritual control of the anti-Sufi reform movement, leading the group through an explosion in its followership but also through internal fissures over leadership and doctrinal accents.

The group set up a network of Islamiyya (Islamic) schools, whose graduates where shepherded through multiple layers of Islamic instruction with a view to identifying future scholars.

The best products of these schools were then sent, on generous Saudi scholarships, to prominent Saudi universities for advanced study of Islam under a Wahhabi curriculum with a tinge of ultra-radical Salafism. The movement meanwhile grew and acquired many branches with followers in prominent perches in government, the bureaucracy, the armed forces, the professional class, and the private sector.

The sect was at first viewed with suspicion by most Northern Nigerian Muslims, especially after Sheikh Gumi declared the operative mantra of the group to be *iko ya fi ibada* (the attainment of political power is greater or more valuable than acts of worship). The slogan struck the Sufi and Sunni orthodox Muslims of Northern Nigeria as counterintuitive, and its seeming relegation of worship to the pursuit of Islamic political ascendance seemed at odds with orthodox Islamic teachings. But through careful, persistent explanation, Gumi enunciated the philosophy behind his advocacy of political Islam. For him the attainment of political power and clout by Muslims would create the conditions under which a higher, pure, and unimpeded worship could take place, conditions that would in addition help stem the spread of Judeo-Christian values understood to be threats to Islam and its propagation.

Once its seemingly heretical doctrinal bedrock was understood, the sect quickly gained mainstream appeal, especially among the Muslim masses because of its denunciation of expensive Muslim rituals and ceremonies and its recommendation of much cheaper alternatives to increasingly expensive rites. It parlayed support for these early sweeteners into its more explicitly political mantra that politics was more important than worship. For Northern Nigerian Muslims locked in tension and competition for resources and leverage with non-Muslim compatriots, Gumi's overtly political messages urging zero-sum confrontation with Christians was appealing. Gumi's combative sermons against the perceived conspiracies of Nigerian "infidels" against the fortunes of Islam and Muslims struck a chord with Northern Nigerian Muslims, who held longstanding anxieties about Southern Nigerian and Christian attitudes toward them. The Izala sect exploded with new members and today enjoys considerable mainstream adherence in Northern Nigeria.

Radical Shiite Islam came via the contagion of the Iranian revolution and is today represented by Sheikh El-Zakzaky and his sporadically belligerent followers. The sect's number is negligible and its acceptance in a predominantly Sunni Muslim culture has remained stunted by persecution and, at times, violence. Nonetheless, its radical religious politics, its advocacy of violent revolution as a method of social action, and its tradition of militant political protest have fed into the new environment of anger at the West and its perceived war on Islam.

The entry and spread of these Middle Eastern religious doctrines has caused two fundamental shifts in Northern Nigerian Islam that could give us a partial window into Abdul Mutallab's metamorphosis from a religiously curious boy to a radicalized, angry suicidal hater-of-America.

The two alien Islamic strains have undermined the African cultural disposition toward compromise and conciliation that Mazrui articulates in his 2004 essay. The second and perhaps more profound effect has been an over-politicization of religious practice and a corresponding conflation of anti-Western and anti-Christian angst and Islamic piety. Abdul Mutallab's quest for martyrdom may have started in this charged and fast-evolving religious environment.

These alien Islamic traditions were grafted haphazardly onto a preexisting form of Islam, which accommodated and gave rise to dissidence and doctrinal insurgence and embraced the realm of politics without the wholesale intolerance and overt political ambitions of the present wave of political Islam. Political Islam came to Nigeria with a splash, borne by the Wahhabi and Shiite strains. The combination of visions of puritanical, fundamental Islam opposed to Western modernity and an increasingly simplistic view of international relations as a violent clash of civilizations was combustible. Abdul Mutallab appears to be the long-feared spark that lit the cauldron.

Many frustrated and economically dispossessed Northern Muslim youths gravitated to these politicized Islamic systems because they presented a simplistic dichotomous interpretation of an increasingly complex, bleak, and unfriendly world. Even privileged Northern Nigerian Muslims were seduced by the ability of the two Middle Eastern religious strains to make an emotionally appealing sense of a seemingly intensifying clash of cultures on the international stage. Umar Abdul Mutallab would have been one of those privileged Northern Nigerian Muslims drawn to the hyperbolic, conspiratorial demonization of America and the West as the source of the troubles plaguing Muslims all over the world.

The condemnation of all things Western and the articulation of non-compromise between Muslims and the West is a staple of the kind of political Islam that made its way to Northern Nigeria from the Middle East. This new Islamic culture conflicts with African cultural orientation toward human and ideological hospitality. But as is characteristic of most African reactions to foreign ideologies, many Northern Nigerian Muslims embraced this new Islamic trend without scrutinizing its cultural origins and motives. Many were seduced by its pandering to notions of powerlessness and victimhood in the face of Western hegemony.

The politicization of Islamic practice in Northern Nigeria led many Muslims in the region to become intensely and emotionally invested in the political and cultural encounters between the West and the Muslim world. But as many pundits have noted, Northern Nigerian Islamic radicals were and are still more likely to channel their politicized interpretations into local political struggles that bear directly on their lives than into international acts of terror. Their religiously filtered opinions on international politics and diplomacy are likely to remain bottled up, expressed innocuously in private conversations and, occasionally, in the media. A small, growing minority has, however, crossed the line into the world of violent expressions of piety, a world in which jihad is a political and religious weapon, a failsafe path to paradise, and a tool of religious hegemony to enthrone Allah's just reign.

Further evidence of the recent radicalization of Islamic practice in Northern Nigeria is the fact that the Dariqa brand of Sunni Islam, which remains the paradigmatic brand of Islamic practice in the region (although its dominance is seriously being challenged by the now largely mainstreamed Wahhabi and Salafist strain), is a peaceful, largely apolitical, mystical order. Its texts and conventions are influenced by the teachings of the late Senegalese Islamic scholar Sheikh Ibrahim Nyas, whose teachings are hugely popular in Senegal, a predominantly Muslim coun-

try with a tradition of Sufi Islamic orders that coexist peacefully with an influential Christian minority. The African Sufi order
also accommodates a variety of Western modernist cultural and
economic innovations.

The distortion of this preexisting religious order is one
source of the growing radical trend—the radical, alien nihilist turn in African Islam. Once introduced, the foreign strains
gained ground and infected a religious mainstream moderated
and mediated by an African tradition of docility and hospitality.
Militant Islam acquired a powerful sway among young Northern
Nigerian Muslims such as Abdul Mutallab who gradually lost patience with the African Islam practiced through the overarching
authority of African cultural precepts of tolerance and passive
protest. The African Islamic traditions of their ancestors lost its
appeal to them.

In the last two and half decades, preaching in Northern Nigerian mosques and public arenas, conducted mostly in the Hausa
language, have become incrementally bellicose and edgy in its
endorsement of ideologies and methods of political protest that
are alien to African culture and African Islamic practice. The
Northern Nigerian Islamic mainstream began to resemble the
fringe doctrines brought from the Middle East and began to display overt sympathy for the latter's unsettling prescriptions.

One depressing indicator of the influence of these overly politicized Middle Eastern religious strains is the percentage of
Nigerian Muslims who sympathize with al-Qaeda's international jihad against the West and who, for good measure, endorse
suicide bombings as a justified weapon in confronting perceived
Western oppression. There may be a lot wrong with a CNN poll
(which shows 54 percent and 43 percent respectively for the two
categories), not the least of which is that international polling
is always problematic. But possible methodological flaws aside,
the numbers are disturbing on many levels. African Islamic heritages are not remotely compatible with what the poll, warts and
all, suggests. Those who came of age in the pre-Wahhabi Nigerian Islamic environment will find these numbers alarming. They
indicate the extent to which African identities have receded
from African religious practice and the corresponding influence
of foreign religious worldviews on African religious adherents.

Of course, most Nigerians who support suicide attacks—against the grain of their African cultural orientation—would balk at the chance to carry them out. But the line between sympathy for militant Islam and its romanticized activities and actual, direct involvement in these activities is blurry. It was only a matter of time before someone acted on their fantasy and crossed that line. Abdul Mutallab became that person because he had the means—financial and logistical—to pursue and put his admiration for militant Islam to practice. For the difference between an emotional al-Qaeda sympathizer and terrorist bomb carrier is a combination of opportunity, privilege, access, and money.

Abdul Mutallab possessed that combination. But he is by no means the only Northern Nigerian candidate who can be plucked and deployed by Middle Eastern Islamist terrorists. Too many young Northern Nigerian Muslims are still being exposed to a version of Islam that does violence to the moderating values that African Muslim forebears cultivated and nurtured as an integral part of their Islamic heritage.

It is clear from all the available evidence that Abdul Mutallab, like most radicalized Northern Nigerian Muslims, might not have made the fatal transition from romantic admirer of violent international jihad to a terror suspect if his Middle Eastern nihilist handlers had not planted the spiritual virtues of jihadist suicide in him. The idea of killing yourself to commit mass murder is un-African. But with a mind already introduced to the intolerant worldviews of Middle Eastern–borne Islamic strains, Abdul Mutallab's Yemeni indoctrinators had a relatively easy task turning him into a human agent of mass murder.

The roots of Abdul Mutallab's seduction by extremism lie in a history that can be reconstructed. But that history is fairly recent. Which is not to suggest that Northern Nigeria, or Africa for that matter, has no history of unorthodox and violent Islamic movements. As Murray Last demonstrates, Northern Nigeria has been a hotbed of many waves of Islamic reformist movements, some more violent and ideologically insular than others. Differences in intensity aside, all of them forcefully posited the fundamental arguments that (1) present rulers were corrupt and oppressive and "should be overthrown on religious grounds";[23] and (2) a strict adherence to the sayings and deeds of the prophet and the teachings of the Quran in every aspect of one's life was the only acceptable form of life for a Muslim. There were movements in the mold of *ahl alsunna wa'l-jama'a*, puritanical Islamic communities who argue that Muslims in any era ought to consciously "behave exactly as did the earliest Muslims (al-salaf),"[24] strictly emulating the details of the Prophet's life gathered from the Quran, the *hadith* (sayings of the prophet), and the *sunna* (deeds of the prophet), and rejecting the technologies and accouterments of modern life. Others preached unfamiliar heterodox doctrines outside the mainline interpretive schools in Islam.

In pre-colonial times, there were the Digawa, Salihawa, Isawa, and other sects with diverse doctrines considered contrary to mainstream Islamic tenets. In colonial times, some of the pre-colonial Islamic insurgent groups persisted, some coalescing into movements resistant to both the British and the emirate system of traditional and religious leadership. The Mahdist movement, the Satiru revolt, and several other Islamist insurgencies sporadically rattled colonial Northern Nigeria during and after the colonial conquest. In the colonial period, some of these movements began to articulate a clear message against Christians (Nasara), a category represented in their minds by the British colonialists, and against modernity, also represented by the British systems of rule, colonial technologies, Western education, and Muslims who adopted them. Murray Last argues that Muslims, confronted by a changing world marked by the erosion of traditional ways of life and by a dizzying cocktail of modern goods and practices that they associated with Christian British colonizers (Nasara), responded by adopting a new form of piety marked by a "general re-Islamization of the Muslim umma [which] would please Allah [so that] He would then get rid of the Christians (and their [Muslim] collaborators)."[25] Subsequent Islamist insurgent groups in Northern Nigeria have sustained this angst against modernity (or *zamani*), which is perceived as a threat to the vision of a just, moral Islamic society, against Christians who purportedly embody this modernity, and against Muslims who allegedly imitate it or allow it to infect their Muslim devotion.

This historical summary relies heavily on Murray Last's rich investigation of the history of Islamic dissent in Northern Nigeria, which he deploys to make the argument that there is a long precedent for homegrown Islamic dissidence in Northern Nigeria. Even postcolonial Islamic dissident groups such as the Yantatsine Islamic Ludites of the 1980s fit this mold of home-grown Islamist insurgency; the group emerged, as far as we know, from sociopolitical ferment in Northern Nigeria and Northern Cameroon, and sought, like other groups, to separate itself from modern society by constructing an alternative Islamic community (Tsangaya) on the fringes of mainstream Muslim societies in Northern Nigeria.[26]

In more recent times, however, a more virulent strain of Islamic insurgency has developed in Northern Nigeria, which, while partly indebted to prior Islamic insurgencies and their nostalgic strivings for a return to an "old-style Muslim unity" marked by political morality,[27] clearly draws inspiration from and exists in ideological symbiosis with global networks of intolerant and violent Islamist dissidence. Boko Haram, with its embrace of suicide bombings and other murderous acts of self-immolation, belongs in this new wave. It should thus be seen as something of a departure from a general reformist trend in Northern Nigerian Islam even though its leaders occasionally seek legitimacy by referencing the tradition of Islamic dissidence and reform in Northern Nigeria, most notably the Fulani jihad of the nineteenth century. Moreover, the organizational and inspirational connections of the new Islamic dissidence groups in Northern Nigeria to more established organs of global jihad and puritanical Islam are well known. This new insurgency, its methods, its targets, and its declared goals depart sharply in several respects from the history of Islamic insurgency in Northern Nigeria, although as Murray Last contends, there has never been a shortage of those who want to purify society through a return to some idealistic notion of Islamic piety and justice. The root of this novelty in Islamic radicalization and dissidence in Northern Nigeria needs to be understood both within and outside the history of Islamic dissent in the region.

Nihilist and puritanical religious ideologies seeping into or passing through Nigeria have not only radicalized individuals; they have become staples of discourse and practice in mainstream religious spheres. The legacy of the infiltration of Wahhabi and Salafist Islam into Northern Nigeria in the late 1980s and early 1990s has been manifesting itself in strains of puritanical Islamic practice that have endorsed violence as a way to both propagate and police its extreme doctrines. The latest, most visible embodiment of this wave of Wahhabi/Salafist resurgence is the group *amā'atu Ahlis Sunnah Lādda'awatih wal-Jihad*, popularly known as Boko Haram (Western education is forbidden).

The activities of Boko Haram are fairly well known. Much less known is the theological genealogy of the group and its doctrinal read-offs from obscure Wahhabi and Salafist corpuses. By all accounts, Boko Haram was founded by Muhammad Yusuf, who was killed in custody by the Nigerian police after being captured in a bloody confrontation with the sect in its Maiduguri base in 2009. Muhammad Yusuf's clerical biography and doctrinal trajectory are windows into the ways in which foreign strains of puritanical and political Islam get domesticated in Nigeria and become part of the fabric of Islamist challenges to the secular Nigerian state and a threat to non-Muslims and mainstream Muslims.

Muhammad Yusuf was a diligent student of Sheikh Ja'far Adam, a member of the first cohort of Northern Nigerian Muslim youths who went to Saudi Arabia for advanced study through Saudi-funded scholarships brokered by the Izala movement. Adam, along with other graduates, returned to Nigeria in the 1990s to find the Izala movement stunted by hierarchical strictures and by a leadership considered compromised by secular and existential pursuits outside the world of theology and propagation. The young Izala zealots returned with little appetite for pragmatism, insisting on a puritanical adherence to a doctrinal corpus faithful to the literalism and interpretive fundamentalism of the Wahhabi school of Islam. Their radical messages appealed to the youth wing of the movement.

Unable to find operative space in the Izala hierarchy, some of the more ambitious returnees stepped away and began assembling their own congregations with fiery sermons and a more political form of Islamic messaging. This is consistent with the nature of religious heterodoxy; those who desire to upend existing theologies or to draw in new followers from the fold of established religious orders must distinguish themselves from the familiar orthodoxies of their time by espousing radically contrarian doctrines. Adam was one of those who imagined and acted upon an alternative organizational path to fulfill the new theological goals their sojourn in Saudi Arabia socialized them to pursue. Like their inspiration, Sheikh Gumi, these returnee Wahhabi clerics laced their sermons with overt political critiques and messages, urging actions against the enemies of Islam at home and abroad. Some of their sermons focused on the familiar Wahhabi themes of railing against American and Jewish anti-Islamic conspiracies in the Middle East and in Nigeria. Others supplied incendiary theological and semi-theological justifications for resisting and defeating perceived persecution, blasphemy, and political domination by Christians in Nigeria.

Muhammad Yusuf, future leader of Boko Haram, was one of the youths drawn to Adam's puritanical Islamic messages, becoming, by some accounts, the cleric's favorite student. Under Adam, Yusuf, an eager learner with a nominal childhood Islamic education and some self-taught Western education, assembled an eclectic Islamic belief system that blends ultra-conservative Wahhabism, Salafi literalism, and extreme, sometimes contradictory, theologies culled naively from questionable and discredited Islamist sources. Yusuf was by all accounts a restless student of Islam, ever in search of doctrines claiming undisturbed faithfulness to the teachings and examples of the Prophet. He was likewise enamored with heterodox, minority, or disfavored doctrinal traditions. Emerging evidence suggests that Yusuf even flirted with Shi'a Islam in his theological and sectarian wanderings before quickly returning to the Sunni fold, albeit to its puritanical, largely discredited fringe.[28]

Yusuf cobbled together radical, ultra-conservative excerpts from the teachings of Ibn Taimiyya, a thirteenth-century Islamic scholar credited with developing the core outlines of Salafi doctrines. He combined these with the writings of Abu Zayd, a revered but controversial Saudi Wahhabi intellectual, academic, cleric, and legal author responsible for developing the rationale for rejecting Western educational, political, and social institutions as *haram* (harmful sacrilege), as well as for the anti-Western suspicions and conspiracy theories that characterize Wahhabi and Salafi theology today. Eventually, Yusuf's body of beliefs and prescriptions would prove too unorthodox even for his mentor, Adam, who sought unsuccessfully to set his protégé straight.

The late Sheikh Adam was not the only Wahhabi-oriented preacher who found Yusuf's teachings bizarre and unlearned. Sheikh Muhamman Auwal Albani Zaria, the late Salafi preacher and former leader of Islamic Salafiyya Movement, was equally scandalized by some of Yusuf's theological eccentricities and tried to persuade the late Boko Haram leader to abandon ideologies with questionable jurisprudential origins. Albani recalls his encounters with Yusuf thus:

> On some occasions, I sat with [Yusuf] and his students and in other occasions, only two of us sat. The essence was to convince him that Islam doesn't accept the ideology of Boko Haram. I tried to convince him that since he claimed to be the follower of Sunna, therefore Sunna has its teachings and principles, and the idea of Boko Haram is contrary to those teachings. All our efforts, because I know that other scholars like the late Sheikh Ja'afar also engaged him on such issues, fell on deaf ears. He proffered some defenses, which are not authentic in the jurisprudence of Islam.[29]

Among Yusuf's more extreme theological positions that Adam found unsound was his rather absolutist belief that employment in a secular governmental institution is *haram*, a position even more extreme than the one taken by many Wahhabi and Salafi scholars, who believe that government employment in the non-legal sphere is permissible. Adam and Yusuf fell out over this disagreement, and Yusuf founded Boko Haram in 2003 to disseminate his radical body of teachings. Adam was assassinated shortly afterward in circumstances that some speculate were connected to the split between mentor and mentee and their followers.

Once ensconced as an independent cleric, Yusuf commenced, through live sermons and recorded ones distributed across northeastern and northwestern Nigeria on CDs, DVDs, and cassettes, to establish the core messages of Boko Haram and its rejectionist philosophy. According to Ahmad Salkida, Yusuf was steered toward much of this early theological dissidence by one Mohammed Ali, the leader of the self-named "Nigerian Taliban" sect.[30] The group coalesced around Ali and the Indimi Mosque in Maiduguri between 2001 and 2002, drawing in radical-minded theology students that included the present leader of Boko Haram, Mohammed Yusuf's successor, Abubakar Shekau. According to some accounts, the group moved away from Maiduguri to Kanamma in Yobe State in 2002, in apparent symbolic imitation of Prophet Mohammed's *hijra* from Mecca to Medina.

It should be noted at this juncture that although the "Nigerian Taliban" attracted members who lacked formal Western education, many of those who gravitated to it were actually university graduates as well as undergraduates at the University of Maiduguri and other Northern universities, who, upon being convinced by the group's theological opposition to Western education, repudiated and discontinued their Western educational pursuits. These zealous converts to radical Islam once made a spectacular and widely reported public show of their new theological conviction by burning their educational certificates and denouncing their prior formal Western education. Also worthy of note is the fact that many of those who joined the "Nigerian Taliban" were from well-to-do homes, and included the son of the then-governor of Yobe State, Bukar Abba Ibrahim.[31] These foundational facts about the privileged background of many members of the initial nucleus of young, radical Muslims who pioneered the twenty-first-century wave of heterodox Islam in Northern Nigeria are important because they show that the genealogy of Boko Haram does not lend itself fully to an "economic and political disenfranchisement" explanation, and demonstrate instead that the movement began largely as a theological and ideological rebellion.

This is not to suggest that young men lacking Western education and who were thus shut out of the secular economic and political opportunities of modern Nigeria did not join the group—they did—or that members who had secular university education could not have experienced economic and political disenfranchisement. As with all insurgencies that rely on youthful energies, some educated but unemployed young men may have been attracted to the "Nigerian Taliban," the precursor of Boko Haram, on account of the paucity of opportunities elsewhere. Nonetheless, it should be noted that, more than anything else, the allure of the new theology of jihad, martyrdom, and rejection of orthodoxy was the decisive appeal, especially for young men who were already drawn to radical Islamist ideologies trickling into Northern Nigeria from Middle Eastern and Asian bastions of global jihad. It was the novelty of this contrarian doctrinal flourish that attracted Mohammed Yusuf, Abubakar Shekau, and other Muslim youth who possessed sound Islamic learning but found their radical inclinations in disfavor in Northern Nigeria's mainline Islamic mosques.

Although Yusuf did not embrace the full menu of Ali's unorthodox teachings, which included a blanket disavowal of democracy, a rejection of civil service employment, and a categorical denunciation of Western education, he did resign, perhaps at the urging of Ali, from his formal employment with the Yobe State government to go into full-time preaching, setting up base in Maiduguri and filling the vacuum left by the emigration of the "Nigerian Taliban" group. Salkida notes that in late 2003, when Ali's group, now based in Kanamma in Yobe State after the ritualized *hijra* flight from modern society, launched attacks on security forces in Yobe State and in Gwoza, Borno State, and was crushed by security agents who killed Ali, many of his surviving followers, including Abubakar Shekau, joined the Yusuf-led mainstream of a growing heterodox Islamic movement.[32] One can assume that these violent, nihilist Islamist survivors increased the pressure on Boko Haram to embrace the uncompromisingly narrow theological interpretations and ruthless violence that the group would come to be identified with.

Yusuf, for his part, became engrossed in the puritanical teachings of thirteenth-century Middle Eastern Islamic theologian Ibn Taimiyya, mentioned earlier. Ibn Taimiyya railed against innovations (or *bida'a*), such as visits to the tombs and shrines of Muslim saints, the celebration of Maulud (the Prophet's birthday), and the spiritual devotions of Sufism. He is also known for advocating against borrowings from Christianity and other non-Muslim traditions, for prescribing complete ideational separation between Muslims and non-Muslims, and for rejecting secularism, scientific ideas, and rationalist logic. Ibn Taimiyya was a proponent of a literalist devotion to the Sunna, and of a conscious, uncompromising imitation of the lifestyle of the Prophet that entailed the rejection of many forms of modernity and innovation. This was a dissident form of Islam that pitted latter-day practitioners against mainstream Sunni Islam. Muhammad Yusuf, already disillusioned with the supposed tameness of Wahabbism, was quite taken by Ibn Taimiyya's anti-modernism and his condemnation of both Christians and "syncretistic" Muslims. As an act of devotion to Ibn Taimiyya's body of teachings, Yusuf named his new mosque in Maiduguri Ibn Taimiyya Masjid.[33]

Boko Haram experienced rapid growth. A vast army of unemployed, poor, alienated, and desperate youth was drawn to Yusuf's charismatic and bombastic personality. They found his moral certainties reassuring in a world of confusing moral conflicts; they adored his antigovernment populism because they considered themselves victims of a failed, corrupt, and predatory secular system of modern governance; and many Muslim youths found in his puritanical early teachings an alternative vision of a just society. Many of Yusuf's new followers, Western-educated or not, connected emotionally to his obsessive condemnation of Western education and its methods because, in their interpretation, not only had decades of the growth of Western education not produced economic and social justice and opportunities, it was responsible for the moral and economic indifference of Western-educated political elites. What's more, whereas real life, especially secular life in Nigeria, tends to be complex, mushy, and unfathomable, Yusuf offered his followers simple—some might say simplistic—doctrines that divided the world neatly into digestible absolutes, into moral and ideological opposites.

Yusuf's acerbic teachings and advocacy of Islamist reform and his enunciation of the ideal Islamic lifestyle—a utopian escape from, and a revolutionary confrontation with, the existing, corrupt, secular, and Islamic establishment represented by both the Nigerian state and the mainstream Islamic clerical community—held a particular allure for Northern Nigeria's Muslim youth who detested the corrupt, secular book-based (or Boko) political and socioeconomic system and the oppressions that it purportedly sustains. An ideology justifying and glorifying vio-

lence against the state and against citizens it constructs as infidels and bad Muslims found a fertile ground in the minds of
young, impressionable men ignorantly incapable of enlightened
religious interpretation, or who were disillusioned with an ailing
society supposedly produced by an irreligious Boko or Western
education, and by modernity. These alienated youths, indoctri-
nated, angry, and eager to exact revenge for Allah and for themselves on an unjust, ungodly society, would later constitute the
foot soldiers in Boko Haram's murderous atrocities.

Having established the foundations of his insurgent Islamic
community, Yusuf began to veer even further toward bizarre beliefs with tenuous ties to the canons of Islam (the Quran, hadiths,
and Sunna). He fleshed out his theological rejection of Western
knowledge, arguing that, although Islam was not against knowledge, the content of Western knowledge disciplines—biology,
geology, chemistry, physics, etc.—contradicted the revealed
knowledge of the Quran and was thus *haram*. In debates with fellow clerics and in sermons to his followers, he cited evolution,
the scientific theory of precipitation as the source of rain, the
big bang theory, and the scientific estimation of the earth's age
as contradictory to the Quran. For him, since it was impossible
to strip Western education and science of these errant theories,
the entire edifice of Western knowledge was *haram* to Muslims,
who, in seeking secular, Western-mediated education, risked
subscribing to knowledge that contradicted revealed knowledge
in the Quran.

Yusuf preached the rejection of the authority of Nigeria's
government and, like all Wahhabis and Salafists, advocated its
replacement with an Islamic government governed by *sharia*,
hence his absolutist denunciation of government employment.
He even went so far as to reject the attenuating Islamic doctrine
of necessity, which many Salafis and Wahhabis subscribe to, and
which permits Muslims to obey and even participate in an un-Islamic government if this is a necessity whose alternative is anni-
hilation by the government. Yusuf endorsed instead a withdraw-
al from the Nigerian government and its violent replacement by
an Islamic state. Yusuf also echoed standard Salafi and Wahhabi
texts in forbidding Muslims to root for sports teams and ath-
letes because doing so might develop an unhealthy, un-Islamic

bond between the Muslim sports fan and a non-Muslim sports idol. Movies, especially Western movies that portrayed Western values and cultures favorably and Islamic ones in unflattering terms, were likewise *haram*. Yusuf also condemned participation in and consumption of many forms of music, dancing, and theatrical performance. A broad spectrum of African traditional and Western entertainment forms were, in this unfamiliar theology, branded haram.

The seeds of Boko Haram's uncompromising heterodoxy were sown in the sermons, recordings, and debates that circulated widely. Northern Nigeria's Muslim youths, many of them already disillusioned with the clerical and political establishments, gravitated toward Boko Haram's insurgent, radically fresh, Islamist spiritual escapism. Its rhetorical promise of a new societal order devoid of the symbols of Western neocolonial oppression and free of proximate local culprits of social inequality proved emotionally popular. The fantastical world envisaged by the extremist teachings of Muhammad Yusuf promised a society ruled by piety and justice, and uncorrupted by the stain of book knowledge and its sinful, un-Islamic seductions.

The thread connecting Sheikh Gumi, the Izala movement, Saudi Arabia, Wahhabism, and Boko Haram is clear from this retelling. The journey from the first entry of Wahhabism and Salafism into Northern Nigeria to this unrealizable absolutist religious society is even more convoluted than my summary here might suggest, but this is the essential trajectory of influence transfer. The supreme casualty of this Wahhabi and Salafi surge in Northern Nigerian Islam is the rich historical tradition of Sufism and Sufi Islamic brotherhoods with its ethos of pacifism, introspection, tolerance, discretion, restraint, and pragmatism. Boko Haram's willingness to use violence for defensive and offensive ends in both the Yusuf and post-Yusuf eras dramatizes the gradual embrace of combative action as a necessary accompaniment of the growth and reception of extremism theologies by Northern Nigerian Muslim youth looking for escape from a much-maligned society through an ethereal, if unrealistic, vision.

The long religious evolution that culminated in Boko Haram was a complex historical process. The uniting idiom in this process is the belief that society's economic, social, and political problems are reducible to and discernible as a moral crisis that can be solved only by a moral regeneration, a moral cleansing. This narrow perspective on societal ills is not to be dismissed, for not only did it anchor the seminal Fulani jihad of the nineteenth century, it also birthed extremist Islamic strains along the way as it persisted from the jihad to the present.

The Yantatsine (or Maitatsine) Islamic movement of the 1980s, with its mix of Luddite beliefs, antiestablishment populism, and strange, reclusive practices was a largely home-grown strain of violent extremism that drew on fringe apocalyptic Islamic doctrines to launch a bloody, widespread revolt against the state and society in general. The Maitatsine sect rejected the accouterments of Western technology and modernity, living insular lives under their leader and his appointees in compounds located in a few cities and towns in northeastern and northwestern Nigeria.

Boko Haram's rise occurred in a wider context of the rise of extremisms unleashed by the growing influence of Wahhabi and Salafi doctrines and clerics in Nigeria and Africa. In fact, during its growth phase Boko Haram had contemporaries that competed with it for the attention and affection of Muslim youth with appetite for the Wahhabi and Salafi strains of Islam. A small sect by the name of Kala Kato blossomed in Bauchi and a few northeastern towns at the time of Boko Haram's rise in 2007–2008. Led by Mallam Isiyaka Salisu, the group subscribes to the literalist fundamentalism of standard Salafi teachings. But, like Boko Haram, it goes further to develop its own unique body of beliefs, one of which is the rejection of hadiths as a guide. The group, like Boko Haram, rejects the authority and institutions of the Nigerian state and confronted Nigerian security agents in at least one reported showdown in Bauchi in 2008.

Yet another offspring of the Wahhabi invasion is the group Darul Islam, founded and led by Mallam Bashir Abdullahi Sulaiman. In addition to upholding the standard Wahhabi and Salafi puritanical beliefs, the group's members live lives of isolation, refusing to interact with a world they consider sinful. They, too, reject secular schools as corrupting and *haram* and refuse to enroll their children in them.

THEOLOGY OR POLITICAL ECONOMY?

The question of whether to emphasize the theological motivations and inspirations of Boko Haram over the economic and political realities that enable it to thrive and recruit members often dominates conversations about the movement among local interlocutors in Northern Nigeria and among scholars and intellectuals seeking a deeper understanding of the insurgency. Those who stress theological and ideological inspirations are often accused of ignoring the ways in which political and economic dysfunction has created an army of angry Muslim youth lacking empathy, compassion, and rationality. Conversely, those who emphasize the economic alienation motivation are often called upon to account for (1) the unmistakably theological and ideological grievances and demands repeatedly articulated and disseminated by the insurgents; and (2) the absence of violent extremism among other economically alienated Muslim youth elsewhere in Nigeria and Africa.

Among Northern Nigerians, there persists a feeling of disbelief and even denial: Boko Haram members cannot possibly be from us, and cannot possibly be Muslims like us. Then, there is the feeling—shared by many Northern Nigerian Muslims—that political and economic alienation accounts for Muslim youth in Northeastern Nigeria embracing a violent, extremist group and carrying out its gruesome mandates. Lastly, there is a small minority of Northern Nigerian Muslims who continue to subscribe to the conspiratorial belief that Boko Haram is a CIA plot to discredit Islam and to destabilize Nigeria or the Muslim-majority areas of Northern Nigeria. These are all distractions from the theological and ideological foundations of Boko Haram and other violent African Islamist groups.

In the early days of the insurgency, when the movement and its leaders were largely unknown, and when the shadowy atrocities of the group seemed rather distant, externalized conspiracy theories were fairly popular among Northern Nigerian Muslims in Internet forums and social media, and one regularly encountered them directly or indirectly in verbal conversations with Northern Nigerian Muslim interlocutors. Some conspiracies have sought to locate Boko Haram in local political plots against

Northern Nigeria. In a mark of how widespread escapist explanations have become in the effort to understand Boko Haram, one prominent Northern Nigerian Muslim leader, the governor of the Northeastern state of Adamawa, one of the states ravaged by Boko Haram, Murtala Nyako, lent authority to conspiracy insinuations when he suggested that Nigerian army commanders and defense officials may be complicit in Boko Haram's atrocities. In March 2014, he delivered a high-profile lecture in Washington, DC in a symposium on economic, social, and security challenges in Northern Nigeria, organized by the United States Institute for Peace in collaboration with the governments of Denmark and Norway.[34] In the speech, he advanced the possibility, long whispered by befuddled Northern Nigerian Muslims, that Boko Haram may be working in tandem with some politically connected individuals seeking to destabilize the Northeast or Northern Nigeria as a whole for their political gain.

Of course, no evidence, except conspiracy-affirming interpretations of puzzling circumstances and Boko Haram's murderous successes, exists to buttress these escapist theories. A region in the throes of a brutal Islamist insurgency naturally cultivates and is receptive to confirmation bias because it is simply inconceivable to many Muslims in this region of Nigeria that their co-religionists would embrace such a destructive path of utopian religious reform in disregard of the orthodox teachings of their faith, hence the proliferation of theories and speculations that externalize the Boko Haram problem. As of the time of writing this chapter, the conspiracy narratives divide into five broad categories:

(a) Boko Haram is a CIA plot to destabilize Nigeria and Northern Nigeria specifically.

(b) Boko Haram is a government-funded war on Northern Nigeria, a war designed to destabilize the region and make it a non-factor in the electoral calculus of future political contests.

(c) Boko Haram is the work of fifth columnists within the military apparatus or Niger Delta militants disguised as Muslim dissidents.

(d) Boko Haram is part of a Christian war on Muslims in Northern Nigeria.

(e) Boko Haram persists because the army works hand-in-hand with them in the Northeastern theater of the insurgency.

Other circulating conspiracy narratives are so absurd they do not merit a mention. Regardless of their gradation of plausibility or absurdity, what these narratives have in common is that they depend on and feed off Northern Nigerians' desperate search for explanations outside the unreliable official information loop and the independent media platforms that rely on information from the official stream. In this quest for alternative explanations for events whose horrors and persistence defy traditional and familiar explication, narratives that carry even a hint of plausibility or have even the flimsiest, most fortuitous circumstantial evidentiary support are elevated to the status of credible explanations. Otherwise rational people gravitate towards these explanations and sometimes eventually embrace them outright. Far-fetched conclusions and extrapolations are then spun around such "explanations," further inscribing them in the popular imagination and making it possible for them to travel through informal networks of information and rumor transmission.

These narratives travel far and are canonized in certain quarters as grand discoveries because, in a situation of war, suffering, curious happenings, and a glaring failure of the state to substantiate its dual claims of guarantor of citizens' security and omnipotent military behemoth, rumors become plausible and believable, and replace unsatisfying, truthfully grim reality. In this informational universe, it becomes quite possible, even understandable, to articulate the contention that these horrific things are happening to us because the government, the all-powerful, able-to-do-all-things government, must either be working in cahoots with the insurgents or is strategically withholding its military might from the fight in the hope of letting it fester and endure to achieve a sinister secretive political agenda. It also becomes possible to dignify and disseminate narratives and innuendoes that point to or exaggerate amorphously external, hidden sources of the ongoing travails.

As many Northern Nigerians peddled theories that all but sidestepped the internal ideological roots of Boko Haram's carnage, a counterpoint to these theories, itself just as conspiratorial and escapist, quickly developed among Christians and Southern Nigerians. It has become quite common for one to read on Nigerian Internet forums, letters to the editor, and online commentaries on Nigerian newspapers' websites that Northern Nigerian Muslim politicians who detest President Goodluck Jonathan, a Southern Christian, and want a Northern Muslim president, are out to make Nigeria ungovernable for the incumbent, register their political dissent, and blackmail the rest of the country into surrendering presidential power to them in future elections. There is also little or no evidence, save for far-fetched interpretations and extrapolations of curious circumstances, to suggest that this is what is fueling the Boko Haram insurgency.

There is, then, a curious convergence of multiple conspiracy theories, all of them intentionally or unwittingly avoiding the ideological and theological questions at the heart of the insurgency. Very few Northern Nigerian Muslims believe the external conspiracy explanation anymore. Instead, nowadays, it is fairly common to see online postings by Northern Nigerian Muslims scolding fellow Muslims who still invoke CIA conspiracy, and urging internal scrutiny within the Muslim umma in Northern Nigeria. Nonetheless, there remains a reluctance to take as a point of departure the ubiquitous visual, oral, and textual evidence from Boko Haram's history, evolution, and pronouncements, pointing to a poorly understood, admittedly confusing body of heterodox theologies and ideologies as the movement's motivation and ideological anchor.

More sophisticated analysts tend to exaggerate the economic angle. The factor of economic and political alienation is self-evident in any insurgency, especially since insurgencies need human recruits to fight and often target the most economically and political vulnerable groups in their recruitment drives. This is obvious and requires no debate. Acknowledging this reality, however, cannot substitute for a probing of the theological and ideological foundations of Boko Haram. Such an exploration is a first, important step in understanding the political and social goals—declared and undeclared—that flow from that ideological standpoint. Economic and political alienation is a safe explanation, a cop-out, if you will. Conversely, analyses that reference theologies and ideologies as sources of inspiration for groups doing despicable acts run the risk of being misunderstood as a critique of the larger religious and cultural community with which the groups claim affinity. As a result of this risk, most analysts, especially people who are concerned about protecting already maligned and misunderstood religious and cultural groups from smears and stereotyping, often stay away from ideological explanations, preferring economic ones, even if they fail to account for what is happening.

This problem is particularly acute for analysts on the political Left. We often prefer explanations and analytical trajectories that do not risk disturbing or being misread as critiquing whole cultural and religious narratives and practices. In an overly politically correct world, we seem to perceive every self-declared religious extremist movement as a fundamentally political and economic problem that can be cured by political and economic policymaking. We cling to this hackneyed analytical bromide even when it contradicts the declared positions and rhetoric of the extremist group in question. This is where those on the intellectual and political right do a better job than those on the left. Their motives may not be pure or sincere and their inquiries are often skewed by prejudice and bigotry, but they at least strive to locate the root of the "terror" they are trying to solve.

Whatever their beginning assumptions, and there are often several, right-wing analysts try to develop an ideological profile of the groups they understand to be terrorists as a prelude to making policy to grapple with their activities. They often go overboard and blur the line between inquiry on one hand and hysteria and demonizing generalization on the other, but the left will do well to start asking the same questions that many on the right privilege as a point of policy departure, which is to ask, when confronted with a murderous extremist group like Boko Haram, what the group believes, disseminates, and seeks as an end goal. In other words, what is the vision of the group and is that vision compatible with a negotiated settlement, and amenable to compromise and reason? There is no way you can unravel this without a systematic excursion into the ideological and theological positions that underpin the group's activities. Even the much-touted political exercise of separating the nihilist hardliners from the nominal members of Boko Haram would benefit from a profound knowledge of the internal theological debates and strands within the group.

Yet many analysts on the left shy away from these kinds of exploration, conveniently and sometimes lazily throwing around the well-worn explanation that poverty, corruption, and political positioning are responsible for producing Boko Haram and other religiously motivated insurgencies in Africa. At best, these analysts make it seem as though there is violent religious extremism everywhere you have these factors, or that violence and extremism follow mechanically from them, which is not the case. At worst, explanations that stress economic deprivation and dismiss theological and ideological motivation participate in, and reinforce, the racist image of Africa as a place where nothing but poverty and economic alienation exist, and the image of Africans as robots whose choices and behaviors are a function of economic stimuli occasioned by endemic poverty and corruption.

When the need for a foundational ideological understanding is posed in regard to Boko Haram, the stock response in several circles has been to deemphasize the religious and theological content of the group or to subordinate apparent ideological elements to the all-explaining fetish of economic deprivation and political exclusion. Another response is to point to the violent militancy of Niger's oil-producing Niger Delta, a false equivalence on several levels. Niger Delta militancy is not animated by any religious doctrine, does not seek religious goals or conditions purportedly consecrated in scripture, does not target victims on the basis of religion, and focuses for the most part on sabotaging state institutions and oil infrastructures. Because of these reasons, and as Murray Last has argued, they can be bought off with largesse and development while Boko Haram cannot be swayed by the type of political and economic amelioration that many analysts are recommending as a solution. If one does not understand the depth of the extremist problem confronting Nigeria and Africa, and the ideological roots of the Boko Haram challenge specifically, one runs the risk of proffering overly generic and thus ineffectual responses.

The most serious aspect of this inattention to ideological and theological factors is that it portrays a willingness to put prepackaged explanatory bromides ahead of realities in the regions affected by Islamist violence. Contrary to the obsessions with poverty, people on the ground in Northeastern Nigeria have discerned and expressed a more comprehensive set of explanations that includes robust attention to both theological and economic factors. In April 2004, the governor of Borno State, the epicenter of the Boko Haram insurgency, gave an interview to Nigerian daily, *Daily Trust*. On the spiritual and theological motivation of Boko Haram, the governor locates the movement within the same theological milieu as other Middle Eastern–originated violent Salafi jihadist movements:

> In life, the most inspiring force is a strong spiritual belief regardless of the rightness or wrongness of the action. As Blaise Pascal rightly captured it and I quote 'Men never do evil so completely and cheerfully as when they do it from religious conviction.' When you have spiritual belief in something, one might go to any extent to attain that goal. Though, to me, there can never be a belief that should lead a man into slicing the throats of fellow innocent humans for the simple reason that those humans share different ideology or faiths. For me, there are two major factors that drive the Boko Haram sect, which are spiritual belief and economic desires. Those with spiritual beliefs are led into believing that when they kill, they obtain rewards from Allah and the rewards translate into houses in paradise. When they are killed, they automatically die as martyrs and go to paradise straightaway. In other words, death is the beginning of their pleasure. Then, whoever they target to kill is an infidel and will go to hell. They mostly target security personnel, government officials and politicians. They also target residents who they assume support government and security agencies

or do not share their ideology of being opposed to western education. One dangerous thing about their ideology is their belief that when they attack a gathering or a community, any righteous person in the sight of God, who dies as a result of their attack, will go to paradise, which means they would have assisted the person to go to paradise in good time by their actions, and any infidel killed by their attack will go to hell, which to them is what he or she deserves and no regret for his death. This is the spiritual aspect that drives the sect, to the best of my understanding.[35]

The governor's detailed explication of the theological imperative of the Boko Haram insurgency could very well describe every other Islamist movement in Africa, whose members seek to kill their way to the purported rewards of a blissful afterlife, or to force their way through violence into the state so that they can implement their vision of a just, ideal Islamic society. The governor situates Boko Haram's motive in a second, more existential problem: "there is also the economic aspect that drives *some* of [the Boko Haram insurgents], particularly recruits who unfortunately are field operators."[36] The governor argues that these economically vulnerable young male field operatives of Boko Haram are essentially victims of the more consequential, more powerful ideological Islamists, who indoctrinate and mentor them to purse violent "jihad" while providing a financial lifeline for them and their families.[37]

AFRICA IN THE VORTEX OF ALIEN ISLAMISM

It is not only in Nigeria where a fortuitously combustible mix of unfamiliar heterodox ideologies and politico-economic problems has conduced to violent challenges to the state and atrocities against citizens. As political turmoil, economic ostracism, and poor leadership have decimated the economic prospects of Africa's Muslim youths, purveyors of foreign strains of extremist Islam have found a fertile recruiting ground for their nihilist doctrines. But the courtship has been mutual: African youths seeking alternative paths to recognition, and craving spiritual escape from their earthly worries, have flocked enthusiastically to foreign-inspired extremist brands.

In Somalia, Al-Shabaab, the militant ultra-radical extremist group, is popular among many Muslim youth as a haven for expressing religious anger at a largely secular set of challenges, a platform for pursuing fantastical religious solutions to intensifying socioeconomic and political challenges. So big is Al-Shabaab's appeal that it has aligned itself with Al-Qaeda, an affiliation that it flaunts proudly and that is demonstrated by the presence of foreign jihadist fighters in Somalia.

In coastal Kenya, as a result of both the growing Al-Shabaab contagion and the media-aided influx of intolerant Islamist ideas, extremist ideology and theologies of exclusivity have taken root. Extremism now threatens a coastal East African religious and social cosmopolitanism that has existed for several centuries. The growth of Wahhabi-inspired Islamic practice in this part of East Africa, meanwhile, stands as yet another inflammatory addition to the ethno-religious brew threatening the sovereignty and stability of Kenya in the aftermath of bitterly contested elections in 2007. Like Al-Shabaab, Al-Qaeda in the Islamic Maghreb (AQIM) has developed a franchise of jihad with tentacles and bases in Northern Mali, Mauritania, the deserts of Niger, and of course, in North Africa. In all these theaters, youths have been recruited in high numbers away from their traditional—and historical—Sunni and Sufi Islamic heritage into a brand of Islam that is overtly politically militant and revels in heinous acts packaged as noble jihad.

These brazen invasions of the African Islamic landscape by external Islamic cultures are decimating Sufi pacifist spiritualism across West Africa, East Africa, and other regions of the continent. The entry of these foreign Islamic traditions is threatening the fabric of African societal stability, undermining institutions and practices that have served for centuries to balance and moderate African societies' competing interests and heritages. Cardinal "African" concepts like hospitality, coexistence, religious ecumenism, cultural diffusion and syncretism, and respect for institutions and gerontocracy, long taken for granted as guarantors of peace, order, and restraint, now stand mortally challenged by the radical populism of exclusivist, puritanical forms of Islam.

Africans are, relatively speaking, disposed to pacifist accommodation and modes of redress and conflict resolution founded on compromise and pragmatism rather than on zero-sum violence and moral absolutes. Suicidal and homicidal trajectories of religious struggles have held little appeal for Africans throughout history. It is not naïve therefore to expect that their religious practice should conform to and be informed by that foundational identity, even if this proposition runs the risk of over-essentializing Africa and Africans.

Middle Eastern radicals can afford the cultural luxury of practicing an Islam that is steeped in a clash-of-civilizations, us-versus-them sensibility. Their history and social environment have cultured them into that mindset, and it is somewhat understandable that their Islamic traditions would follow that trajectory, assuming that Ali Mazrui is correct in ascribing to them a martyrdom complex. And given the relative religious homogeneity in many Middle Eastern states, it is understandable that sectarian struggles would take precedence over ecumenical instincts and throw up theological extremes more suited to medieval Bedouin societies than to a modern, interconnected world.

African Muslims need to go in a different direction. They need to return to the Islamic cultures that their forebears created as Islam made its way to the continent through the Sahara, the Indian Ocean, and the Red Sea corridor. Those cultures gave Islam distinctive African flavors that not only enabled it to thrive in an already saturated and pluralistic religious marketplace but also made it relevant and productive in the cultural constellation of African societies.

CONCLUSION

African Islamic pioneers dexterously managed the Islamic cultures that grew out of Africa's encounter with Islam. In this delicate but important historical task, they were able to preserve the religion's foundational truths, populate it with the distinct ideological positives nurtured in African societies, and denude it of puritanical absolutes that contradict the foundational, utilitarian religious promiscuity of African peoples. African Muslims would do well to find creative ways of curtailing the influence of alien Islamic orders and reinstituting the African brands of Islam that our history textbooks narrate gloriously.

Boko Haram, Al-Shabaab, and other visible Islamist groups are symptoms of a larger phenomenon: the gradual but discernible departure from Islamic traditions that served Islamic and mixed religious communities well in times past. To assert that violent Islamist insurgencies are alien to Africa's Islamic heritage is not to romanticize African Islamic history, or to suggest that violent ideological and political contest within African Islam and between African Islamic entities and secular authorities did not occur in the past. Rather, it is to underline the novelty of an uncompromising set of ideologies and theologies, ideological corpuses that seek to claim the entirety of the political and theological space rather than share it.

It is this all-or-nothing, zero-sum ideology that is un-African. Also un-African is the effort of Boko Haram, Al-Shabaab, AQIM, and other African Islamists to confront Western modernity and its increased globalization with violence-backed calls for parochial religious changes. African Muslim reformers of old found ingenious ways to manage incoming modernities and to accommodate the symbols of modernist change. A good example of this tendency is the ways in which the rulers of the defunct Sokoto Caliphate consciously and deftly sought to access, shape, and thus control the material and symbolic goods of British modernity, which were filtering into the caliphate and its outskirts in the mid nineteenth century. By contrast, today's African Islamist reformers favor violent rejection over strategic engagement with, and domestication of, Western forms of modernity.

It is only by unraveling and understanding this uncompromisingly Islamist ideology, its origins, development, appeal, and spread that one can discern the implacable ideological aspirations of groups like Boko Haram. This effort to understand and confront violent Islamism in Africa will be bogged down if we privilege well-worn explanations founded on the primacy of economic motivation while neglecting the equally consequential ideological and theological foundations and histories of these growing African Islamist insurgencies. Finally, although it is beyond the parameters of this chapter, a critique of the menace of foreign religious extremism also extends to new, imported forms of Christianity, which are not only incompatible with African religious and political traditions but are also polarizing African populations along absolutist us–them lines.

CHAPTER 19

AFRICAN PARTICIPATION IN THE ATLANTIC SLAVE TRADE: A DECONSTRUCTIONIST APPROACH

In April 2010, Harvard professor Henry Louis Gates, Jr., published an op-ed in the *New York Times* with the title "How to End the Slavery Blame Game." The article drew a flurry of critical rejoinders from respected scholars of slavery and the Atlantic slave trade. On African and African American–themed discussion forums, the motive, logic, and theses of Gates's commentary were scrutinized and debated.

The piece sparked ferocious exchanges on the USAfricadialogue discussion list, where I am a contributor. My overall impression of the ensuing debate was that most of those who responded harshly to the piece seemed to be critiquing the essay Gates did not write, the essay they suspected he meant to write. Much of this suspicion and rushed judgment stemmed from a residual—and legitimate—critique of Gates's previous pieces, which were also controversial. Accusations flew generously. They ranged from, "Gates didn't discuss European culpability," to, "He did not acknowledge African victimhood," to, "He is minimizing and excusing Euro-American culpability." We can forget about those who simply wanted to attack the author on the flimsy speculation that "he is doing his sponsors' bidding." There is nothing academic, intellectual, or insightful in such a critique. It is as pedestrian as it is distracting and does not deserve a serious response. We will examine the case of more serious critics both to challenge some of their assumptions and to use that as a touchstone to broach broader matters of African slavery that were left unacknowledged and thus un-discussed in the rush to beat down Gates.

Those who encase their critique in a lingering animus over Gates's documentary, *Wonders of the African World*, have a legitimate grouse, but they are a little unfair to the man. They claim that Gates's op-ed is a polemical continuation of an argument of white exculpation that began in *Wonders*. Context and precedents are important to any discussion, but they have to be contexts and precedents that actually exist. They don't in this case, so I consider this critique misplaced if not malicious for two reasons. First, to the extent that, even in *Wonders*, Gates never made a claim remotely excusing or minimizing European culpability, the polemical extension of the argument about "excusing or assuaging white guilt" to his op-ed is a stretch. Second, the op-ed in question does not in any way excuse or minimize white culpability in the slave trade. There is simply no evidence in either work that Gates excuses or denies Euro-American slave trade culpability unless the claim is that by paying attention to African agency one is exculpating white agency. Here is the offensive portion of Gates' op-ed:

While we are all familiar with the role played by the United States and the European colonial powers like Britain, France, Holland, Portugal and Spain, there is very little discussion of the role Africans themselves played. And that role, it turns out, was a considerable one, especially for the slave-trading kingdoms of western and central Africa. These included the Akan of the kingdom of Asante in what is now Ghana, the Fon of Dahomey (now Benin), the Mbundu of Ndongo in modern Angola and the Kongo of today's Congo, among several others.

Gates is precise in acknowledging the familiar culpability of white slave-trading entities. He is even more precise in his reference to culpable African entities, naming particular political actors instead of placing blame on Africa and Africans as a whole. Furthermore, it is clear from the above excerpt that the subject of white culpability is not his primary preoccupation in the op-ed, an assertion that is also true for his *Wonders of the African World* documentary series. Highlighting African involvement and possible culpability does not cancel out Euro-American culpability. This is not a zero-sum culpability game. And it is not, as some people allege, a "shifting of blame" from whites to Africans, either. Rather, Gates's intervention is an argument for full, evenhanded accountability. It is an insistence that African and European actors in the slave trade accept responsibility for their roles regardless of their economic and political position in the world today. In fact, even the semantic of culpability is ill suited to a critique of Gates's piece because Gates is concerned about participation and not culpability per se. Participation does not mechanically translate to culpability unless the terms of prior debates have already posited and calcified that conflation. I suspect that this understanding of participation as culpability is strategic and ideological, seeking to prevent a sneaky semantic iteration of African culpability under the guise of participatory agency. There is nothing wrong with this as an ideological project of intellectual vigilantism. Nonetheless, to the extent that Gates does not explicitly equate African participation with culpability, it would be an extraordinary extrapolation to insist that Gates posits participation as culpability or that this is the only possible reading. I realize that reading the unsaid is an important aspect of textual analysis, but if the author does not proclaim a point that *could* be deduced from his analysis, one view of the unsaid cannot be elevated into a metanarrative, or advanced as the only possibility for understanding the "unsaid-ness" in question.

Much of the anti-Gates critique therefore assaults a polemical straw man, an argument that Gates does not make, while conveniently ignoring or explaining away the one that he does make about African participation and *possible* culpability. Gates did not set out to write an op-ed about white culpability, either, so to critique him on an absence, on a project he didn't undertake, is unfair. If we are in doubt as to where he stands on white culpability and reparations, it would be more productive to prod him to disclose his views on white culpability (through another op-ed perhaps) than to take interpretive and extrapolative liberties with his piece. Slavery is a complex issue and we must entertain the possibility that Gates or anyone else could hold complex views that may appear contradictory to those used to judging the whole from a part or those accustomed to simplistic consistencies.

Gates set out to argue only one point in the op-ed, which is that African involvement in the slave trade deserves the same attention as the familiar narratives of European participation and culpability. He believes that this point has not been written adequately into histories of the slave trade. I don't agree with him entirely on this point. He makes it appear as though there is a conspiracy of silence, which there is not. Several recent studies of the Atlantic slave trade have accounted to varying degrees for African agency in the trade. I do, however, believe that there is an epistemological and methodological hesitation to highlight the full extent of African participation in the slave trade. This epistemic retreat is founded in part on concerns that an emphasis on African participation, even when it is offered as part of a broader effort of balanced historical reconstruction, could be misread as culpable agency. The one point that Gates set out to argue in the op-ed was argued brilliantly and persuasively. He relied in his argument on comprehensive, up-to-date databases on the slave trade—collations of a wide variety of sources on the trade—to make his central point that African participation in the trade was more extensive and documented than the current slave trade literature would suggest.

So, to advance a popular cliché in academe, let's not crucify Gates for the book he did not write (which we perhaps wish he had written). Let's wait until he writes that book before we pounce. The suspicion that Gates may harbor a broader anti-reparations agenda is not founded on anything he has published, although one recognizes the ideological anxiety that produces that instinctual fear. It is possible to argue for a full recognition of African agency (and even culpability) while making a claim for reparations, and while believing in greater white accountability. The two views may not perfectly align in the ideological universe of pan-Africanists, but they are not incompatible. Like Gates, I believe that African involvement in the trade deserves as much attention as white agency in it. But I also believe in reparations that are informed by fairly precise foundational distinctions and the accurate identification of culprit corporations and entities on one hand and victims and descendants of victims on the other. I have lingering concerns as to whether these necessary, preliminary distinctions are possible, given the murkiness of societal entanglements, the passage of time, and the problems of slave genealogical and commercial records.

This emphasis on complexity and coexistence of complex viewpoints brings us to the op-ed as a genre of journalistic writing. Those who fault Gates for not emphasizing Euro-American culpability and for not sufficiently delineating African victimhood should recognize that, as a polemical practice, the op-ed does not encourage nuance, self-negation, and complicated analytical flourish. For reasons of space and editorial conformity, it, instead, encourages punchy, forceful, and clearly articulated argumentation. Its stylistic encumbrances and protocols of expression demand that one does deliberate violence to nuance, caveats, analytical modesty, and tentativeness, while disavowing analytically useful modifiers and qualifiers. I write op-eds and I know the constraints under which an op-ed writer labors.

In fact, beyond the silences pointed out by critics (failure to account for African victimhood, failure to reinforce the familiar narrative of white culpability, etc.), I can point to another serious omission from Gates's piece: He does not give a visible analytical space to the many but often ignored documented instances of active African elite resistance to the slave trade (commoner resistance is a more familiar theme). In 2003, historian Sylviane Diouf edited and published a fantastic volume on the subject. Titled *Fighting the Slave Trade: West African Strategies*, the volume is a counterpoint to notions of generalized African complicity in the Atlantic slave trade, a reinforcement of the familiar reality that many African communities were resistant victims of the trade. Chapters of the book demonstrate the resilience of African communities in the face of rampant slave raids, the variety of reactive and proactive initiatives that many African communities devised to insulate themselves from the violence and inhumanity of the trade, and the remarkable variety of African relationships to the political economy of slavery and human commerce.[38] It is an established historical fact that some African kings even barred slave trading in their territories or turned abolitionist after initially profiting from the trade.

There are other nuances that are missing from Gates's piece. One could, among other complaints, fault Gates for not accounting for the ex-slaves from America, Britain, and the Caribbean who returned to Liberia and Sierra Leone and subjected African ethnic groups in the vicinity of their settlements to conditions analogous to slavery. But to heap these burdens of coverage and depth on Gates's brief op-ed is either to misunderstand the op-ed and its mission or to suggest that Gates should have written an academic article or book, in which a larger spatial latitude and a freer expressive convention would enable him to account for all the nuances, exceptions, and caveats of slave trade discourse. Perhaps Gates should do this—should have done this. But to use this standard to critique an 850-word op-ed is unfair and unhelpful. And to fault Gates for not accounting for all the important details of the slave trade is like asking a writer to substitute his footnotes for his text or like asking a webmaster to swap the sidebars of his website with its main pages. It is like ignoring the text and focusing on the existent and nonexistent footnotes of a piece of writing. It is rather disingenuous.

Also unfair is to use an absence (failure to indict white villainy) to connect the op-ed and *Wonders*. If there is any thread connecting *Wonders* to the op-ed, it is Gates's insistence on the imperative of shedding as much light on African participation as on Euro-American brutality. While some respondents have critiqued his equation of the two culpabilities, I haven't seen any persuasive, factually grounded argument refuting Gates's contention that African participants in the slave trade were as involved, as active and proactive agents, as Europeans in the trade. At any rate, *Wonders* had a more explicit accent on the theme of culpability than one could attribute to the op-ed in question, arguably because the audiovisual medium is a more emotive, melodramatic vehicle than the polemical genre of the written word.

Although I agree with Gates that African groups (with the emphasis on groups) *may* have been as culpable as European slavers, his error was not to further specify those groups or to at least make it clear that specific African groups took different positions during the trade, making it an analytical imperative to sift victims from raiders, and brokers from slavers. Here I sympathize with the argument that literary scholar Olabode Ibironke put forward on USAfricadialogue that Africa was the ground zero of the trade and was thus a primary victim, and that all areas of Africa affected by the trade and all Africans in those areas (slaver and enslaved, middlemen and merchant) *eventually* became victims—the notion of culpable victimhood—given that the demographic and socioeconomic aftermaths of the trade reverberated indiscriminately throughout the geopolitical space.

I have ideological sympathy for this argument, but I disagree slightly with it. Here is why. While West and Central Africa were indeed the epicenter of the trade and one could thus argue that its structural legacies made direct or vicarious victims of all African peoples in regions drawn to varying degrees into the socioeconomic and political vagaries spawned by the processes of commercialized enslavement, certain groups, kingdoms, and regions, and African slave traders, brokers, and merchants cannot partake in this victimhood and have to be theorized out of it. To the extent that many of these African profiteers of the slave trade were able to parlay the profits and statuses derived from the trade into political and socioeconomic investments in the subsequent periods of Legitimate Trade, colonialism, and the current postcolonial moment, it would be problematic to describe them as *eventual* victims. Not only did the profiteers leverage their loot to escape the negative conditions created by the trade, some of their descendants have used their connection to the profits and domination of that destructive era to immunize themselves against the ravages and negative structural continuities of the trade's legacies on the continent. Structural conditioning should not supplant individual and group culpability and profiteering.

As I indicated before, my contention would complicate and perhaps delay reparations, as extensive research has to be done to make multilayered distinctions between Africans who suffered and continue to suffer the consequences of the trade and those who were empowered by it. And this should not, of course, follow from a mere dichotomy between those who enslaved and those who were raided for slaves, although that would be a good starting point. There were in-between communities—neither slavers nor enslaved—who nonetheless were burdened by the trade because they had to take in refugees and runaways, lost trading opportunities and economic outlets, and had to wrestle with the vicarious economic costs of instability. There are, I am sure, other variables and parameters to consider.

There is one other argument that relates to the one on "structural victimhood": the "European guns" argument, which is advanced as a mitigating variable in claims about African participation. I am indifferent to the gun–slave cycle argument as an attenuation of African participatory agency because guns were extremely valuable political and economic instruments in pre-colonial Africa. They created as much wealth as they destroyed, if not more. They killed, maimed, and captured Africans, but they were also instruments for protecting accumulated licit and illicit wealth, trade, and economic opportunity. They also helped in conquests. Conquests brought territories, which meant booty in the short run and tribute in the long run. Guns intensified warfare, but they were also instruments of wealth creation. And African chiefs and merchants with political leverage during the trade used guns effectively to preserve and expand their personal and state economies. This strategic agency of demanding and deploying European guns for self-interested pursuits has to be recognized, for to not do so would portray African chiefs and big men and their citizens and followers as helpless victims of European gun exports, which they were not. For me, this historical reality offsets the exculpatory effect of the gun–slave cycle argument.

Another argument that emerged on the USAfricadialogue list in discussions of Gates's op-ed is the one on slavery in pre-colonial Africa. The argument that there was no slavery in pre-colonial Africa is so ahistorical and escapist it should be denied the dignity of a response. The more serious claim that powerful African polities sold only convicts, outlaws, and war prisoners flies in the face of evidence of organized slave raids and, later, of wars launched solely for the purpose of producing captives for European slave ships. Even during the trans-Saharan slave trade, which was slower, less intense, and less probably disruptive, not all captives were outlaws, criminals, and war prisoners. Some were snatched from their livelihoods and families and sold into bondage.

Understandably, today's inheritors of the power and prestige of old, slave-trading polities claim to have been exporting only outlaws and criminals. No kingdom or people wants to be inscribed in history as one of the villains of the notorious Atlantic slave trade or smeared with the stigma of slave raiding. For this reason, the public oral scripts of powerful, previously slave-raiding African kingdoms in the post-slave-trade era denies deliberate slave raiding or deliberate warmongering for the purpose of slave production. A culture of strategic silence is at work among peoples whose ancestors raided vulnerable communities for, or mediated the trade in, captives. As the eminent historian, Sylviane Diouf, observes in regard to African narratives on the slave trade, "not surprisingly, it appears that the people whose areas were most closely associated with the trade as providers...are less loquacious."[39] The testimonies and accounts of these slave-trading polities are often tainted by today's antislavery climate and by our evolving knowledge of the brutality of slavery as an institution. But if you listen hard, you will discover, depressingly, that some of these kingdoms' esoteric narratives and oral traditions of past glories include heroic accounts of successful slave raids and slave-producing warfare. It takes methodological innovation and ethical sincerity to unearth and highlight these internal scripts. Only when the public and internal scripts are harmonized can we get at the true picture of African slavery and African participation in the Atlantic slave trade.

There is then a need to refuse to be seduced by the revisionist, morally conscious, and politically scripted oral testimonies of the descendants of African slavers. There is a concurrent need to extend our inquiry to African polities and peoples who were raided for slaves—those treated as slave reservoirs and vulnerable Others deserving of enslavement and tribute exaction. The oral narratives and memories of these communities on slavery and the slave trade can depart dramatically from those of their former raiders—the powerful slave-raiding polities. We need to ask the victims of slave raids if the raiders made a distinction between criminals, convicts, and outlaws when carting away men, women, and children. Did the raiders demand and inspect judicial records and memories in the passion of the raids? What about those who were plucked from farms and other productive activities, those who were respectable members of their societies—were they, too, outlaws, and did the raiders stop to check their criminal records?

Let us document the experiences of the victim societies and refuse to have our accounts of slavery and the slave trade skewed in favor of the self-serving narratives of powerful African slave-trading polities. A little bit of "history from below" will clarify the shortcomings of listening exclusively to the archives and traditions of those African groups and state entities that dealt with the Europeans—the active African participants.

Of course, we should also scrutinize the narratives of the victims, for there is now political capital (in many parts of Africa) in claims of victimhood, resulting in a tendency for exaggeration and melodramatic discursive reenactments in the testimonies of former slave-raid victim societies. Because such narratives perform instrumental roles in claims of self-determination and sometimes anchor identity formation and assertion, we must be vigilant. Nonetheless, the narratives of raided polities and peoples would only enrich our repertoire of knowledge on slavery and the two slave trades—Saharan and Atlantic.

Another strain of the anti-Gates's critique devolves rather predictably into a balance sheet analysis that seeks to posit Euro-American slave trade actors as bigger culprits based on their bigger share of slave trade profits. There are, however, two important points working against this argument. First, it is wrong and misleading to use absolute numbers in the profiteering calculus. You have to adjust for the size of the economy, the importance of slavery and the slave trade to the overall economy of the state, and then use the statistical outcome of this exercise to determine the percentage of the economy and overall productivity represented by or dependent on slavery and the slave trade. To put it quite simply, absolutes are misleading indicators of profiteering and economic benefits and are thus poor guides to culpability and accountability. Absolute profit numbers have to be explained in the context of the overall economy. For several African slave-trading states and kingdoms, slavery and the slave trade was an integral part of their economy for 150–250 years. When one compares the centrality of the slave trade to the economies of these states and its centrality to Euro-American economies, one can begin to sketch a fairly accurate comparison of benefits and benefits-based culpability. In this comparison, one should note that the bigger size and capital diversification of the Euro-American economy meant that, apart from the case of some areas (such as the Southern United States, perhaps), the slave trade, despite yielding much more profits in Euro-America, may actually have constituted a smaller element in the overall economy than it did in the economies of individual African slave-trading states and kingdoms. The second reason why the raw comparison of profit figures is a misleading indicator of culpability is that profit figures alone do not always account for the depth and reach of participation, as profitability could correlate negatively with the extent of participation.

Culpability, to the extent that is a worthy analytical endpoint to establish, should thus follow rightly from the extent of participation. And on that score, I agree with Gates that African actors in the trade were as involved as their Euro-American counterparts.

The genealogy of "black on black" crime in certain corners of Africa is worth looking into, especially as we are today struggling to understand the brutality and rapacity that define the relationship of African political elites to their compatriots and their countries' resources. Racial patriotism should not hinder a reasoned acknowledgement of intra-racial evils. What's more, at the time of the slave trade, the category of "Africa" and its associated meanings and practices of solidarity did not exist, so the idea that some communities raided and enslaved others and even made slavery a fulcrum of their economies for decades should be understood within the historically prevalent norm of competition, tensions, and zero-sum conflicts between contiguous states and peoples. This is the simple answer to the absurd notion that Africans sold other Africans, an inane formulation that I suspect is the source of the reluctance on the part of many to acknowledge the participation and complicities of specific African groups in the slave trade. There is no shame in such an acknowledgement. Asians, Europeans, Amerindians, and Arabs also enslaved their kind. Africa's story is only a fairly localized subset of the human story, which is a story of both evil and good.

CHAPTER 20

WHY DO AFRICANS MIGRATE TO THE WEST?

I participated in a discussion about the motivations for African emigration to the West at a conference a few years ago. Because I scoff at pedestrian, commonplace explanations I found the contribution of one participant, a professor, particularly interesting. He challenged the dominant perception of African emigration as a function of economic hardship.

He was responding to another participant who was essentially rehashing, albeit in a sophisticated manner, the classic African migration tale of economic push and pull, advancing it as the major causal factor in the growing phenomenon of African professionals migrating to the West—what some lamentingly call "brain drain." The professor's argument was interesting and refreshing. First he debunked the notion that African emigration was a novel phenomenon, a modern problem threatening the demographic and economic fates of both Europe and Africa. Voluntary emigration to areas within and outside the continent of Africa has always been a defining social characteristic of African societies, he argued. Secondly, and more important for our purpose here, he posited the thesis that such emigrations were not always for economic reasons, but that throughout African history, individuals and groups also migrated for psychosocial comforts. To put it crudely, Africans emigrated for the psychological and social benefits that adventure, discovery, travel, and sojourning provide.

He didn't quite make this point, but let me make it for him. The logical destination of his argument is simple: Africans are not very different from other peoples in the world. They, like Europeans, Asians, and others, do not migrate only because of economic opportunity, or out of poverty, hardship, destitution, and helplessness. They also migrate because migration sometimes makes you feel better about yourself. Sometimes migration is, to put it quite simply, its own justification—its own reward. It satisfies an innate human psychosocial desire to explore the unfamiliar, the Other, the distant, and the different.

I make this small addition to the professor's thesis because I suspect that, like me, he sees that the excessive focus on the economic motivation for African migration, the concept of the African immigrant as an economic refugee, satisfies and reifies the patronizing rhetoric of African helplessness, as well as the discourse of African deviation from the West. Let me briefly outline this rhetoric and its implications. Africans are said to be different from Westerners because they purportedly act on basic human instincts such as hunger, lack, and desperation, while Europeans act out of the spirit of curiosity, scientific inquiry, and a quest for knowledge. Africans are sentimental and reactive respecters of bodily instincts while Europeans are proactive pursuers of knowledge and scientific illumination. Africans do not explore; they exploit—or so it is alleged. Differential migratory impulses therefore contribute to, and express, the Europe–Africa divide. It is argued that the aforementioned attitudinal divide explains the supposedly different motivations for European and African migrations. The differences in the motivations of Africans and Europeans who emigrate from home, so goes thinking, therefore underline once again the fact that Africans are fundamentally different from—and inferior to—Europeans.

To advance an alternate thesis of African emigration, especially one that veers from the well-worn narrative of economic motivation and embraces the "European" motivation for migration (the psychosocial factors) is therefore to make a larger argument against racial essentialism and against the notion that biological and genetic signatures confer innate, inescapable socio-behavioral propensities that differentiate Africans from Europeans in a fundamental way.

With this insight in mind, let me posit a thesis of my own regarding African migration to the West. My thesis will attempt to synthesize the popular economic explanation of push and pull and the refreshingly illuminating thesis of psychosocial relief. If we must account for the range of motivations for African migration to the West, we have to embrace an explanatory hybrid that recognizes the obvious economic motivations as well as the increasingly significant matter of convenient relocation. One does not have to discount one factor in order to stress the other. For that reason, I do not believe that the psychosocial factors that influence migratory decisions are too removed from issues of poverty and economic (and political) alienation. In fact, I think that one could formulate a thesis that unites the two explanations, one that sees psychosocial longings as coextensive with poverty, albeit a different kind of poverty.

We all know that poverty and economic desperation make people want to move to places of perceived economic opportunity. This is so straightforward that it should not be diluted by any psychosocial invocations. But if we define poverty and hardship not only in starkly economic terms but also in terms of what one may call the quality of life quotient, then it is possible to see how a successful African professional in Africa, although not poor or desperate in the economic sense, could be poor and desperate in terms of the quality of his or her life. For analytical convenience, let me call this kind of poverty *existential poverty*. This kind of poverty is also an impetus for emigration out of Africa. What I am positing here is what one may also call vicarious poverty, in which poverty is experienced not by the self but indirectly through the trauma of living in the midst of grinding poverty and of being assaulted daily by reminders and images of poverty, economic collapse, infrastructural deficits, and so forth. The psychological torture and burden of such an environment is sometimes as depressing as personal poverty.

There are two aspects of this phenomenon. The first one revolves around the fact that no matter how wealthy or successful one is in Africa, one still has to depend, to various degrees, on state-provided social services—among them, electricity, water, roads, and security. As we all know, these services are either poor or nonexistent, so you are forced to participate in the broader experience of poverty and underdevelopment. Your economic success cannot insulate you from this. Your quality of life will therefore be poor and may motivate you to migrate to the West, where social services are delivered more efficiently. In other words, there is a limit to the amount of comfort wealth and material success can bestow on you in Africa.

The second aspect has to do with the ironical psychosocial trauma of being rich or successful in Africa. Being rich in Africa is not the same as being rich in the West. In Africa, more so than in the West, the successful professional is confronted daily by sights, sounds, and smells of acute poverty. He is surrounded and tortured by poverty. He sees it in his employees, junior colleagues, neighbors, relatives, friends, co-religionists, and kinsmen. On his daily commute to work, his sense of accomplishment is diluted and deflated by disturbing and haunting images of destitution and economic hopelessness. These images nibble at his edifice of success, filling him at once with guilt and anxieties about what might have been (or what might still be). The images erode the joys of economic success and make lofty economic and professional perches seem less secure than they actually are. Insecurities, anxieties, guilt, alienation, dissatisfaction, and depression take a toll on the quality of one's life.

I have often wondered if rich and successful people in my country, Nigeria, can enjoy their successes fully in the midst of such mind-numbing poverty. What does it feel like to be the big man of the neighborhood even as you behold images of misery around you daily? The intuitive answer is that it must feel great to be one of the few who made it—who "got out." But I think that this is only one side of the coin. There must be a psychosocial ambivalence that comes with being a rare economic success in a place where people work so hard and still live in unspeakable poverty. Surely it must place some moral burdens on one's conscience, a constant reminder that one is an aberration. There is, I believe, an unspoken existential turmoil that haunts the successful professional in Africa.

On top of this emotional torture you have to deal with the envy, jealousy, and resentment of economically unsuccessful neighbors, junior colleagues, employees, and even relatives. The not-so-veiled insinuations, snide remarks, misplaced acts of provocation, mischievous speculation about the source of one's wealth, and other kinds of social ostracism from the majority of one's countrymen make one's materially rich life socially barren.

You can take refuge in social circles populated by other successful professionals, but this is at best an escape, not a natural social support system. The mutual validation and incestuous interactions of Africa's small professional elites hardly substitute for unconditional social acceptance in one's own society. It cannot make up for the inner peace that comes with knowing that you are not the stand-out object of misplaced anger in your poverty-ridden neighborhood. And it certainly cannot insulate you from the pain of being held wrongly accountable for the misery of others, whose real victimizers are the succession of incompetent and corrupt governments that African countries have been saddled with throughout their postcolonial lives.

It must therefore be tough and emotionally painful to be rich and successful in Africa, and this is the paradox that I am getting at. It is a different kind of poverty, which is both experiential (at the psychosocial level) and vicarious. It can be summarized as the quality of life dilemma. The quality of your life has little or nothing to do with your economic success; it is essentially a psychosocial effect. In this case, a poor quality of life and its psychosocial effects follow ironically from economic success. In other words, you are poor by being rich. And the quality of your life does not necessarily rise in tandem with your material success. Such a condition of economic success and low quality of life could motivate the economically successful African to emigrate to the West, not for further economic success, but in order to obtain some physical and mental distance from the rot back home. In the process, the immigrant hopes to improve the quality of his life, become happier in the psychosocial sense, and relieve himself of the sights, sounds, and experiences that frustrate him in Africa, despite his economic success. African migrants rarely acknowledge let alone appreciate the satisfaction that physical removal brings, but it is a reality.

What we are dealing with is therefore a migratory flow caused by psychosocial alienation and yearning as well as systemic poverty and infrastructural collapse, which are so ubiquitous that you cannot escape them no matter how materially successful you are. This migratory phenomenon departs from the popular notion of Africans migrating to the West to seek economic opportunities that have eluded them at home. It is an aspect of the immigrant tale that has been marginalized and deserves to be told.

If the African immigrant's journey to the West is a manifestation of his effort to take control of his life and destiny while escaping the conditions that diminish the quality of his life, the processes that make the journey possible are shaped by forces and narratives beyond his control even if they are available to him to manipulate. Furthermore, once he is situated in the West, the immigrant's life and choices are no longer his own; rather, they are shaped by the circumstances and ideological positions produced by the dynamics of politics and self-fashioning in Western societies.

Both the migratory process and the way the migrant narrates his experiences are constrained by preexisting discursive regimes in the West, which perhaps explains why, in spite of the increase in professional migrations from Africa to the West, the migration-as-economic-escape paradigm continues to color the dominant perspectives on African emigration. This dissonance should be explained. How does this narrative formula impose itself? How does it work?

The paternalistic racial attitudes of Western liberals construct and legitimize certain migratory stereotypes, privilege and silence certain migration narratives, and cause African immigrants to become active participants in this process of silencing and myth making. Liberal appetite for pathetic and dramatic African immigrant stories of escape, heroism, and exile confers validity on immigrant narratives, true or false, that satisfy that demand. In this process, other narratives of migration and other migratory experiences and trajectories are marginalized. Exile is a particularly powerful and revered trope that has come to define how Western liberal discourse communities, suffused in a benign humanitarian racist ethos, skew and shape what qualifies as a worthy, interesting African immigrant story. The power of this idiom of exile and escape has in turn shaped how African immigrants themselves narrate and sift their own experiences for the consumption of Western interlocutors.

Ismael Beah's *A Long Way Gone*, a melodramatic book in which several implausible plots and outlandish claims flourish side by side, and writer Chris Abani's disputed and implausible claims about persecution in and escape from "death row" in Nigeria are illustrations of this intersection of African immigrants' need to tell their stories and Western pressures to tell these stories in certain preferred templates. Sometimes the narrative pressures placed on African immigrant autobiographers by Western audiences' hunger for dramatic and evocative African stories cause the migrant storytellers to even make up events and scenarios to fit a certain prepackaged Western sensibility. The itinerary being narrated has to reinforce existing tropes to be valued and canonized. Foundational Western perceptions of Africa as the quintessential arena of the exotic where all evils and oppressions are not only plausible but common have created a discursive tyranny in which exile is caused exclusively by bizarre and dramatic events, and where migration is always a product of economic and social helplessness.

The resulting stories of exile penned by African sojourners in the West mirror these hegemonic pressures, stressing the exotic over the banal and familiar; difference over sameness; and the melodramatic over the usual. These African immigrant tales, then, reinforce, reproduce, and perpetuate the very stereotypes that they pander to, that they satiate. They become active participants in a particular Western pathology of validating and rewarding personal narratives of African exotica. More crucially, they help intellectualize and legitimize the political economy of representing and narrating Africa through the idioms of suffering, helplessness, political excess, and endemic, violent "tribal" convulsions.

Prolific Nigerian novelist, Chimamanda Ngozi Adichie, has eloquently signaled the perils inherent in the normalization and perpetuation of a one-dimensional image of Africa in the Western mind and media. In her much publicized TED talk, "The Danger of a Single Story," Adichie decries the insidious and seemingly innocuous mechanisms by which the single story of Africa as a habitat of sundry tragedies and deprivations gets seared in the consciousness of Euro-Americans and Africans alike.[40] Many people understand her argument to center around Western tropes and practices that make Africa the object of exotic Western fantasies. That is one side of her contention. The other side, less explicitly stated, concerns the African participants in propagating the single story. It is not a big leap from a view of the single story as a self-comforting Euro-American creation to one that suggests that Africans who move within Western circuits and are influenced by the ambience of hegemonic Western understandings and stereotypes sometimes repeat these stories back to Euro-America in conscious and unconscious social and literary enactments.

There is also a profound Western conservative appetite for exotic and helpless Africa, and this also constrains the experiential discourses of African immigrants in the West. This conservative understanding of Africa converges with a liberal do-good humanitarian gaze to authorize and finance African immigrant tales of escape and redemption. This powerful intersection of Western conservative and liberal palates makes African immigrant storytelling a charged arena of self-representation. What does the conservative engagement with Africa and Africa-originated migration look like? Simply and crudely put, Western religious and political conservatives regard the African immigrant, regardless of his circumstance, as a humanitarian case waiting to be mediated by material charity or other forms of ameliorative intervention. The African immigrant is indexed, in this narrative, as a predictable statistical and humanitarian outcome of congenital African dysfunction. The refugee is a favorite trope of the conservative Western view of African immigration, and migrant stories and realities that depart from it are unintelligible to Western conservative sensibilities; for why would any African leave their countries other than for the reason of being pushed out or displaced by Africa's myriad social and political conflicts? And would they migrate to the West if not for the purpose of accessing its "generous" receptiveness to refugees? The template seems clear in its sound-bite simplicity: Africa is a land that perennially produces refugees and the West is a unit of the world that takes them in and nurses them back to socioeconomic stability. This becomes the standard protocol for validating African immigrant stories and for determining which stories qualify for the attention of the religious conservative humanitarian and asylum lobby industry. It also works in reverse to devalue immigrant stories and journeys that do not fit the refugee model. Africans who go to the West to study, work, and better themselves as a voluntary process of self-improvement or adventure get neither sympathy nor attention from the Western conservative humanitarian obsession with the typology of the African refugee immigrant.

CONCLUSION

Together with white liberal paternalism, conservative human-itarian gestures toward African immigrants define the bodies, choices, experiences, and narratives of many immigrants, con-stituting an undifferentiated framework for perceiving and re-telling African immigrant lives. This homogenizing gaze is cen-sorious in that it blunts the kind of immigrant stories that the first part of this essay privileges. That is not all it does, though. It also burdens the African immigrant with unrealistic and simplis-tic responsibilities. Under the weight of the broader narrative of African experiential homogeneity, the African immigrant be-comes not just a spokesperson for all of Africa; he also becomes, willy-nilly, Africa's ambassador to the Western institutions in which he functions or circulates. He is responsible for all of Afri-ca, expected to explain Africa in a template imposed on him by preexisting hegemonic Western narratives on Africa.

CHAPTER 21

IMMIGRANTS, UPRISING, AND THE REVENGE OF HISTORY

In 2005, African immigrants rioted in Paris and other cities in France, protesting their systematic exclusion from the economic and social opportunities of the country. The French had for years pursued a lofty sounding but insidious policy of multiculturalism. French multicultural obsession was a foil for preserving the socioeconomic chasm between native-born and immigrant French people, for keeping everyone in their proverbial place and pretending that this was a recipe for order and stability. The protests laid bare the drawbacks of multicultural pretensions.

The French should have learned from Hurricane Katrina that the ghettoization of poverty and similar acts of concealment are not a long-term or effective solution to the problem of social and structural inequities. The ghetto is, after all, only a natural disaster or a riot away from blowing up in everyone's face, shattering the myth of accomplished integration and the self-congratulatory escapism of dominant power structures. But the French have always been poor students of history. The immigrant protests were nothing short of history's revenge for years of pretending that the African immigrants in France do not exist or are little more than uncomfortable visual reminders of French colonialism in Africa.

The French empire struck back, and the children of empire, long hidden away in the dingy slums of Paris and Marseille under a peculiarly French variety of segregation misnamed multiculturalism, revolted openly, demanding the substance and recognitions that French republicanism proclaimed. France had ignored the inexorable human legacies of its imperial adventures in Africa too long, and at last, its hens came home to roost. The French thought that they could wish away their colonial past by ignoring the visible human artifacts of that inglorious history, and by pretending to have a doctrine of post-imperial inclusion and homogeneity without actually living up to its more practical, financially demanding aspects. France has failed to learn from its own imperial history of advancing empty rhetoric and escapism as alternatives to actual problem solving and social integration.

France has always been a sanctimonious imperial power, playing the imperial game by refusing to match lofty rhetoric drawn from the French Revolution with actions that bear out that rhetoric. It inaugurated its imperial history in Africa by enacting an empty administrative policy ostensibly aimed at making African colonial subjects into Frenchmen. The Africans would only have to acquire some Francophone trappings, defined in strictly Euro-modernist terms. The policy was aptly called *assimilation*. As we now know, when assimilation was abandoned for a French version of indirect colonial rule called *association* after World War I, fewer than 50,000 African colonial subjects had actually become French citizens. The disparity between seemingly revolutionary proclamations and tokenist window dressing was palpable. The French moved away from assimilation as quickly as they had embraced it because the potential social, economic, and political cost of sustained implementation was high. It was an eloquent testament to French imperial ambivalence.

But the French never learned. They would repeat the same mistake of offering the hope of universal French citizenship only to dash it once again. In 1947 France extended citizenship to all of its African colonial subjects as a strategy to avoid having to meet the actual economic demands of a growing African labor and nationalist movement. This escapist solution appeared lofty but it was counterproductive; it only increased the intensity and frequency of African agitations as African laborers in the colonies began to covet the rewards of citizenship: the wages paid to French workers in France.[41] Africans also began to migrate to France throughout the 1950s by invoking their imperial citizenship rights to emigration. Much of the African immigrant population in France originates from this postwar, pre-independence migration.

Once again, the French retreat was swift. They moved quickly to grant independence to their African colonies, a move that was designed to invalidate the notion of imperial citizenship, which was helping, for good or ill, to populate the ports, docks, and cities of France with an unwelcome, potentially disruptive African and Muslim presence. Hence, the recent revolt of this discontented African community in France must therefore be understood partly as the inevitable but unintended consequence of the idealistic and half-hearted solution of 1947.

The absence of pragmatism and sincerity in French policy toward colonized peoples has characterized the French treatment of the African immigrant community in France. Plagued by unemployment, poverty, discrimination, and ostracism, this community has lived in economic and political abeyance for much of its existence. The French have refused to confront the African presence realistically with a view to integrating it into the sociopolitical and economic fabric of French society. Instead, there has been a subtle effort to write the African community off of French patrimony through a combination of willful ignorance and tokenist, half-hearted, and illusory acts.

Tokenism, denial, the multiplication of slum shelters, and a policy of pretending that if a situation or problem is ignored it will cease to exist have all failed France. Likewise, the selective assimilation of skillful French soccer players of African ancestry has not done enough to articulate the message that the French desperately want to convey: that all is well between France and its African immigrant community. The uprising was the price of pretense and the illusion of French unity, a tragic reminder that the carefully nurtured myth of homogeneity is just that: a myth. For a long time, France convinced itself that if it promoted the illusion of oneness, the economic and social concerns of the immigrant underclass did not need to be addressed as a separate problem. Nothing could be more wrong, or self-deluding. The French paid the price for shunning the path of pragmatism and embracing pretentious idealism. What happened in France was a tragic but inexorable consequence of a history of French refusal to truly integrate the African immigrant community, a living legacy of French imperialism in Africa. What happened was historical recompense, of sorts.

There are two possible solutions to the problem. The French should pursue real integration by investing in the educational and economic uplift of the African immigrants as a prelude to political integration. Or they should allow the immigrants to enjoy real social autonomy as an un-integrated community, and stop compelling them to assimilate into a largely mythical homogeneous French identity. The French need to make a choice instead of waffling between two trajectories.

CHAPTER 22

OF AFRICAN IMMIGRANTS AND AFRICAN AMERICANS

Relations between native-born blacks and migrant black communities tend to generate tensions, controversies, and silences in abundance. In America, sporadic tensions between African Americans and African immigrants occasionally bubble to the surface of intra-racial conversations—conversations that are fraught with cultural misunderstanding, historical misrepresentations, and the legacies of racial registers imposed by dominant Euro-American power structures. Sometimes these conversations are triggered by events, other times by relations between the two groups as both try to navigate the racially charged landscape of America. One such conversation occurred in March 2012 on the Toyin Falola–moderated USAfricadialogue listserv.

As an illustration of how quickly a conversation with remote intra-racial implications can snowball into familiar discursive fisticuffs between the two groups in question, a reported incident of alleged police harassment of an African American professor at Delaware State University (DSU) morphed quickly into a discussion of African and African American disposition to the antiracism struggle in America. The ensuing debate, in which I participated, is a window into the unresolved and largely undiscussed fissures of global African solidarity, which have intensified as black mobility has increased in the last half century.

The triggering incident was simple enough. A member of the list posted a story on the alleged police harassment, a story with the obvious racial element of a white police establishment allegedly harassing a black faculty member. The story also suggested that the school administration and faculty members did not seem particularly sympathetic to the accuser's claim and protest. An African American member of the list, an academic whom I will not name as a courtesy, opened a flood of commentary on the story with a provocative, four-part suggestion. First was that the lukewarm reaction to the incident by faculty was the result of the university, a historically black college, having so few African American faculty members. Second was that African immigrant professors who constitute the majority of the institution's black faculty were, like other African immigrants, less sensitive to racism and thus less likely to react to it than African Americans; third, that a larger contingent of African American faculty would have fought on the side of the professor who was allegedly harassed; and finally, that African immigrants in general tend to show little or no interest in African American affairs, as opposed to the latter, who invest time and resources in exploring the lands, peoples, and cultures of their ancestors' continent of origin. The member then advanced a fairly strong case for increasing African American faculty (and student) recruitment, not at the expense of African immigrant or other black immigrant recruitment, but as part of a holistic effort to give native-born blacks a more visible stake and footprint in historically black colleges and universities (HBCUs).

If it is true that the ratio of African American faculty and students at HBCUs is declining, that is indeed a serious problem which needs to be addressed as a way of restoring the historical mission of these schools, although legitimate questions remain about whether that foundational mission is still relevant today. Regardless of where one stands on the debate on the continued relevance of HBCUs to black educational advancement and to the important matter of black access to higher education, one has to accept the basic premise that these institutions serve a purpose, a niche that is unlikely to be filled or appreciated by mainstream, white-dominated institutions, and that they have glorious educational and community service histories and legacies that are worth preserving. If that is a settled, less controversial premise, then the question of raising African American faculty and student recruitment should be an uncontroversial vision.

DIFFERING REACTIONS TO RACISM?

The other contention, about African immigrant reactions to racism in America and the implied suggestion of antipathy to African American freedom struggles, is less settled and deserves some discussion. The assertion that Africans in America are *less likely* to oppose white racism may be true, as long as the emphasis remains on "less likely" and the statement is not allowed to slide into an absolutist terrain where African immigrants are constructed or construed as being indifferent or hostile to the issues and grievances animating African American political protests. As is often the case with conclusions founded on observation and conjecture rather than on systematic study based on carefully collected evidence, they can easily be appropriated or co-opted to support unedifying ideological positions far removed from the nuanced, qualified observations that produced them. That is a concern.

Which brings us to another problem with the argument on African immigrants' alleged insensitivity to the insidious power of race in America. There are several variants of the argument, but most of them are founded on the weight of anecdotal evidence. Anecdotal evidence can swing both ways, however; in this case it can validate the opposite contention, since there is also evidence, anecdotal and conjectural, that points to African immigrant participation in both large-scale African American freedom struggles and more localized incidents of the type that allegedly occurred at DSU.

The basic premise of arguments about African immigrants' lesser disposition to challenge racism is fairly sound, but even seemingly logical observations need to be put through the crucible of rigorous evidentiary standards for them to anchor important arguments about group behavior. It is true and commonsensical that, because African immigrants migrated from all-black or black majority societies in which race is not an intelligible or visible factor of difference, there is bound to be a divergence on how they perceive America's race-infused social relations vis-à-vis African Americans. The fact that race is the primary idiom of identity and politics for African Americans and it is not for Africans is thus a foundational condition that should be acknowledged. For African immigrants (especially of the first generation), like Africans in the homeland, other identity markers such as ethnicity and culture tend to trump race as the primary organ of primordial solidarity. But to the extent that this can condition social behavior, it renders them indifferent not to race in particular but to all forms of solidarity that are in competition with ethnic and cultural idioms, including national identity and pan-African gestures of continental solidarity.

This variable might explain a disproportional African participation in antiracism movements, if such a disproportional participation can be taken as a foundational baseline of argumentation. However, even the argument about the de-racializing effect of African upbringing constituting a hindrance on African immigrants' participation in racial struggles in America is a tad simplistic and exaggerates for effect. It is an argument steeped in definitional narrowness. It defines the term "African American" in terms that close off the possibility that African immigrants or their children could become, by association, racial self-education, or experiential socialization, African American in their political sensibilities. The idea that an African immigrant of the second generation might be considered a native-born black or an African American, part of the variegated demographic we call African American, does not seem to feature in this argument about Africans and African Americans cultivating separate relationships to racism. For at what point does the African immigrant's life, when subjected to the same structural impediments as the lives of African Americans, begin to mirror the familiar struggles of African Americans in the orbit of American racial politics? African immigrants do eventually assimilate into some facet of the African American racial experience, a development that disturbs the intra-racial dichotomy implicit in the claim that Africans and African Americans see and hear racism differently.

This point bears explaining. When Africans migrate to the US their self-perception shifts and race consciousness develops as a natural process of grappling with race in a milieu in which the most visible marker of your status as a minority is your color, a context in which racial identification is a bureaucratic and statistical staple of how service-providing state and private institutions relate with citizens. The moment African immigrants settle into their new lives in America and begin to insert themselves into the statistical apparatuses of an increasingly documentary state, they realize that their blackness is central to how the state sees and records them, how in fact the state conditions them for their life in America.

This original ritual of racial definition is not to be dismissed as a simple statistical exercise, for it is the moment in which the African immigrant is forced to choose a race, to become documented in discourse and in bureaucratic practices as black—with all the baggage and burdens that come with blackness in America. The African immigrant, in short, becomes, at least in the written artifacts of American social relations, a subject in the debate over the prevalence of institutional and everyday racism of America. The African immigrant is aware of this. To suggest otherwise is to deny the obvious fact that immigrants tend to quickly come to grips with the identity politics and conflicts of their host societies, especially aspects of that politics that disturb their aspirational idealism.

For African immigrants, the process of racial (re)education is often swift and jarring, given their coming of age in non-racial societies, where their only encounter with race was in the context of their relationship to a white colonial state. Consider the case of temporary educational migrants like Kwame Nkrumah and Nnamdi Azikiwe, or of African musical tourists like Afrobeat maestro, Fela Anikulapo Kuti. A few years of residing in America as educational immigrants were instrumental in profoundly impacting Nkrumah's racial self-awareness and the politics that grew from it. Nkrumah encountered the ideals of racial equality, anti-colonialism, black liberation, and egalitarian struggle by consciously circulating within black American activist circles and by interacting with black activists while devouring the intellectual works of influential black American and Caribbean thinkers.[42] Similarly, Nnamdi Azikiwe, pan-Africanist and first president of independent Nigeria, acquired an active racial and anti-colonial imagination that was forged, as he himself wrote, during his years as a student at Lincoln University between 1925 and 1935.[43] Also, Fela Kuti, mentioned above, spent just one year in America between 1969 and 1970 but used his associations in the black American community to reeducate himself racially and on the American struggle for equality, civil rights, racial justice, and pan-African solidarity.[44]

There are two takeaway insights from the lives of these three pan-Africanists. First, they consciously sought racial education from their more racially aware African American interlocutors.

In other words, they were quick to assimilate into America's black struggle for equality, as well as into a globalized struggle for black liberation. Second, the experiences of these individuals illustrate the fact that immigrants can and do learn the vocabulary and praxis of the anti-racism struggle in America; for if these individuals who stayed in America only temporarily could acquire such a profound level of racial awareness and become iconic referents for those fighting racism across Africa and its diasporas, it is safe to assume that permanent, resident African immigrants with a growing stake in the American social fabric would embrace the struggles and vernaculars of anti-racism in their new home country.

A FLAWED PREMISE?

There is yet another reason why the argument about black immigrant indifference to racial protest in America should be made with utmost circumspection and moderation. The premise of the argument is problematic in that it defines protest, dissent, and struggle narrowly. This narrow definition is, I suspect, colored by the familiar templates of civil rights activism in America (the primary referent)—pickets, marches, street demonstrations, confrontations with the police, sit-ins, and so forth. These were and are heroic tactics in the struggle against racism in America. But protest and opposition can take many other forms, as historians know all too well, forms that may be unrecognizable and unintelligible to someone schooled and socialized into a distinctly American (or civil rights) tradition of protest. That Africans in America are not always marching or organizing sit-ins does not mean that they do not protest or challenge institutional or experiential racisms when these forces manifest themselves. African immigrants may be subtle, more selective, and less effusive in their confrontations with racism in America than African Americans might be. But the methodology of protest is not necessarily an indication of how opposed or accommodating one is to racism. Method does not always betray intensity.

The other thing is this: While all blacks may be victims of the burden of blackness in America, there are genres of racism

that peculiarly victimize African Americans and African immigrants separately. In addition to the general struggle in America
against anti-black racism, African immigrants also have to contend with—and challenge—another kind of racism that equates
having a so-called accent with dumbness and cognitive deficiency. Added to this are the familiar psychological and sociocultural adjustments that African immigrants have to make—adjustments that require huge investments of time, effort, and anxiety.
Because they are fighting multiple battles in their own corner of
American blackness, Africans may at times seem uninterested or
less involved in the mainstream struggles of African Americans.
But appearances can be deceptive, and conclusions derived from
these appearances of detachment and docility are problematic
in their failure to account for the many struggles that African
immigrants fight out every day on the streets of America, struggles that may constrain the ways they grapple with the signs and
sounds of racism around them.

Activism and protest come in many forms. Some are visible,
audible, and demonstrative; others quiet and reflective. Activism against the injustices and institutional racism of American
society need not be advertised with fanfare and ceremony to be
acknowledged as a part of the fabric of the black struggle for recognition and patronage in America. Whether that activism is the
loud, vociferous, and seemingly implacable type or the subtle,
quietly effective type, it serves to ameliorate the egregious injuries of racism on the individual black person and on the broader
black community. Both kinds of activism are important, and devaluing one type because one is not trained or socialized to value
it is not helpful.

There are two other factors to consider as attenuations of a
generalized statement of African immigrant racial illiteracy and
detachment. The first is that because African immigrants constitute a relatively small proportion of the US black population,
their challenges to white racism or the statistical incidence of
it will be naturally less visible and smaller than the challenges
of African Americans, whatever form those may take. This is a
statistical reality that the arguments outlined at the beginning
of this essay ignore.

The more important question, much more important than the question of whether African immigrants are capable of perceiving and reacting to racism, is whether as a proportion of the US black population African immigrants are actually less likely to challenge racism than African Americans or whether they are invisible and thus absent from narratives of the black struggle in contemporary America on account of their status as a minority within a minority. In other words, is their participation proportional to their numerical strength in the US black population? How does this proportional participation compare to the proportional participation of African Americans in these struggles? As long as this remains unaddressed, the argument about black immigrants being less likely to challenge racism falls flat, although it is important as an expression of aspirations toward greater black solidarity in the fight against racism.

The implied conclusion that African Americans are more likely to protest white racism does not tell us anything particularly insightful or new. It merely points out a statistical logic, which is that African Americans constitute a much larger percentage of the US black population have a more intimate historical relationship with the trauma of racism and have more roots in society, and that perhaps as a result their activism is more visible and their methods of challenging racism paradigmatic. This greater visibility due to the weight of numbers and history is not indicative of a more "natural" disposition to antiracist activism. Conversely, the fact that Africans may be less visible in protest, again a function of their number, is not an indication that they are less inclined by nature or nurture to protest and self-assert—or that they are more inclined to docility than their African American cousins.

THE VALUE OF EXPLAINING

All told, the argument about African immigrants' disinclination to racial and political solidarity with African Americans is often asserted as folk wisdom instead of explained or explored. Even if we begin from the reasonable baseline that African immigrants are "less likely" to protest racism in America than African Americans, the more productive question to pose, it seems to me, is why this is the case. In answering this question a little empathetic understanding of the plight of the African immigrant is necessary. I am not sure that it is fair to expect folks who are trying to situate themselves (and their families) and put down roots in a foreign country, with all that that struggle entails, to participate in mainstream civic movements to the same degree as native-born blacks. Black immigrants have many anxieties to wrestle with. They participate in their own struggle to overcome the bureaucratic and socioeconomic challenges that white-dominated America places on their path to the vaunted American dream. These struggles are no less courageous, and no less challenging of institutionalized and bureaucratized racism, than the mainstream black struggle against wider societal racism.

The other aspect is that, in these days of homeland security obsession, African immigrants, like other immigrant groups, have become the targets of surveillance. They can legitimately be branded troublemakers and summarily deported. As national security anxiety has intensified, even naturalized citizens are now being deported on mere suspicion of participating in "subversive" activity—subversion being vaguely and elastically defined to capture activities that used to be regarded as legitimate forms of protest and self-assertion. Participating in public, loud, visible protest movements poses quite literally an existential threat to African immigrants. African Americans do not have to worry about this. They do not have to worry about being deported and separated from their families, or about being labeled an ungrateful immigrant. African immigrants do have to consider these unsavory possibilities in deciding whether or how to protest against racism in America. One of the big unspoken rules of contemporary American society is that African immigrants, like many other immigrant groups, are informally required to perform their immigrant gratitude publicly, especially in these days of heightened xenophobia, while engaging in more subtle, less confrontational modes of struggle against racist institutions and practices. It is a delicate balance, a burden to be managed carefully, away from the traditional theaters of protest.

At any rate, some African immigrants do participate in the struggles initiated by African Americans and play active roles in them, disregarding the risks. Others fight more quietly. Some work within the system to bring about change. Others take advantage of the system to invert it for their own self-interest and ultimately for the interest of other black folk. Protest is a variegated phenomenon; one should not reduce it to its most recognizable symbols. To not consider all these nuances and to then proceed to the conclusion that African immigrants are less predisposed to antiracist protest is to be reductive.

There is an additional danger. The argument about African immigrant indifference to racism can quickly become an argument about their denial of their political and social blackness, and their attempt to assimilate into honorary whiteness, or the whiteness marked by privilege and certain forms of self-carriage. Already, there are self-appointed guardians and gatekeepers of black authenticity who accuse not just African immigrants but also upper class African Americans of refusing to identify with the realities and revolutionary struggles of the African American underclass—the "authentic" black culture of the ghetto, if you will. These guardians of appropriate black political behavior chalk up this alleged self-quarantine on the part of African immigrants to a desire to validate the expectations of and curry approval with white society.

EXTERNAL DISCOURSES OF DIVISION

Some of these more accusatory discourses arise from the anguish caused by the manipulative and divisive notion that seeks to project African immigrants and other immigrant groups as models of success and hard work to African Americans, a deeply flawed thesis that some African Americans themselves have bought into, either in opposition or in naïve adulation. The idea of African immigrants as a model minority group that validates long held racist views of African Americans as congenitally lazy, dependent, and underachieving is a source of some of the resentment that characterizes relations between uninformed groups of African immigrants and African Americans. The former may internalize and act upon the idea of African immigrants as exemplary blacks (a new incarnation of the old, discredited idea of representative black men and women) to haughtily devalue African Americans. The latter may act on it by resenting African immigrants as arrogant, white-acting snobs. The stage for tension and conflict may then be set on this false and dangerous premise.

The problem of the model minority narrative is of course that it conveniently ignores the fact that the immigrant groups recommended as models of hard work, thrift, and achievement are, unlike African Americans, preselected collections of people who for the most part were already set apart and privileged to varying degrees in their home countries prior to their migration to America—people who do not represent the general populations of their countries. America does not hand out immigrant visas like cookies to random Africans or Asians. Rather, it screens them for the possession of minimum standards of education, aptitude, and prior success—all of which, when transplanted to America, give the African immigrant a head start against not just African Americans but also, in some cases, whites.

Amy Chua and Jed Rubenfeld's recent book, *The Triple Package: How Three Unlikely Traits Explain the Rise and Fall of Cultural Groups in America*, has rekindled the debate on model minorities in America.[45] Of particular relevance to this essay is the fact that the book features Nigerian immigrants alongside Lebanese, Chinese, and other immigrant groups deemed to possess the three traits the authors argue help explain economic ascendance in American society. The authors highlight insecurity, superiority, and thrift—what they fancifully renamed "impulse control"—as the three qualities that have enabled Nigerian and other African immigrants to outperform African Americans and other native-born groups. Much of this argument is already familiar as staples of informal discussions on immigrant success in America. In fact, the trope of immigrant thrift, or impulse control, has been a part of the menu of explanations for immigrant economic ascendancy in America for decades. But the authors, like the aforementioned informal commentaries, oversimplify a complex matter. For me, the bigger, more productive question is, what is driving the African immigrant's thrift, his catalytic sense of insecurity, refusal to fail, and his paradoxical belief that he is better and more capable than others?

This question leads to what for me is the biggest deficit in the authors' thesis, which is its lack of understanding of immigrant pre-selection and, more crucially, its inattention to what one might call a culture of remittance, a powerful catalyst for the success of immigrants from non-Western, traditionally marginalized parts of the world. This catalyst is also, ironically, a burden that pushes the immigrant in directions which promise the biggest and most tangible return on work, not the most happiness. Thankfully, the authors, careful analysts that they are, acknowledge that their definition of success and ascendance in starkly materialist terms leaves out the damage that such success can do to the exemplary immigrant's quest for happiness.

Socialized in the trope of Western individualism, the authors clearly could not comprehend how the culture of expectation, itself rooted in the African communal ethos of collective success (*Ubuntu*), determines and constrains the choices and freedoms of the individual African migrant. It is not as though the migrant is completely free to choose what he does in America. That choice, in many cases, is or has already been made for him by family and kinsmen back in Nigeria, Ghana, Kenya, and Zambia.

Certain career and educational choices are incompatible with the expectational pressures hovering over the immigrant—the expectation that he remit some of the material and symbolic rewards of his American sojourn to relatives in Africa. In crude terms, certain careers and professions, no matter how desirable, will disappoint kinsmen and women back home in Africa in both symbolic and material terms, producing scorn and mockery for the immigrant. Without the approval, acceptance, and satisfaction of those who have "sent" you to America to prosper and share that prosperity with them, your happiness as an immigrant will never be complete; it will remain hollow. Most African immigrants know this, and live within this unspoken culture of remittance, which forces them to get into lucrative professions and toil harder than normal so that they can export the prestige and rewards of these professions to their expectant families and kinsmen in Africa. The visible signs of African immigrant success can thus be misleading, concealing more salient causal social factors.

African immigrants know that a consideration of how their choices in America might resonate materially in their home countries is a crucial factor in their decisions. This cultural variable, ignored by the authors and by many discourses on Nigerian and African immigrant distinction, shapes the immigrant's choices in America. It underpins the choice of what to do, how to do it, and how hard to work in America. Without this powerful stimulus, it is likely that African immigrants would make more mainstream choices and work at a pace similar to that of native-born groups, including African Americans.

Amy Chua, Jed Rubenfeld, and other scholars who espouse or explicate the model minority paradigm are clearly oblivious to this cultural variable largely because it is invisible to them in America. This culture is the unconsidered factor in any discussion of immigrant success in America. It is clearly implicated in the now ubiquitous story of Nigerian-American socioeconomic ascendancy. It is the reason that many Nigerian immigrants, the most visible segment of the African immigrant community in America, seek advanced degrees and/or become doctors, engineers, and nurses. Chua and Rubenfeld chalk this up to abstract psychological factors and ignore the cultural push factors emanating from the immigrant's home country and culture. This unseen cultural hand in African immigrant success in America ought to moderate expressions of the model minority sentiment.

Furthermore, immigrants tend to reconstitute their prior class identities and affiliations in America. First generation immigrants who were doctors, professors, accountants, and lawyers in their home countries may not be able to realize their dreams of transferring their skills and status to America due to certification disparities and other existential hurdles. Because of this, it may sometimes take the second or third generation to complete this recreation of prior class and status identities. But these identities tend to eventually emerge and persist among immigrant groups in America, thus perpetuating the socioeconomic gap between African immigrants and African Americans. A foundation of socioeconomic ascendance may be interrupted, but it often reemerges, again underscoring the importance of traditions, precedence, and foundations.

Yet African Americans are right to discern a pattern of interracial accommodation between African migrants and white Americans, which is not replicated between African Americans and whites. The limits of this reality need to be recognized, and it should be acknowledged that, without exposure to and familiarity with the heritage of an African immigrant through the clues left by the immigrant's name, speech, mannerisms, and dress, a white American is likely to relate to an African immigrant as they would to an African American. Nonetheless, given the many institutional and personal avenues through which such a familiarity can be acquired, it is often the case that the African immigrant gets identified quickly and then separated from African Americans in the perception and gestures of the white community. These perceptions, gestures, and accommodations are hardly extended to native-born blacks.

These tangible and intangible relational benefits are what one might call the privileges of difference. These privileges enjoyed by the African immigrant are analogous to those that might be accorded an African American visitor in Africa upon locals discovering that he is American and not a citizen of the country he is visiting. This special treatment can be the radical opposite of the ways that competing African ethnic groups within the country in question treat one another. Such privileges conferred by foreignness may differ in degree but they are fairly common across the world because they are products of the fairly universal truism that locals in a given society tend to feel less threatened and more comfortable around foreigners than they do around adversarial local Others. Whether the opportunities and privileges conferred by foreignness and difference are sufficient to erase or compensate for the burdens and pains of exile and outsider status in a host community is another question altogether, requiring a cost–benefit analysis.

A NEGATIVELY MEDIATED RELATIONSHIP

The relationship between African immigrants and African Americans is not a direct one of voluntary interactions that have the capacity to produce their own logics and discursive undertones.

Rather, it is mediated by racist media images and political and cultural narratives that alternately cast Africans as jungle-dwelling, foul-smelling savages, and African Americans as lazy, shiftless, welfare artists. Relations between the two communities are not stand-alone interactions propelled by their own intra-racial momentums. They are shaped, rather, by the invisible mediatory hands of racist images, ideas, and tropes long applied to—and internalized by—Africans and African Americans. This internalization, repetition, and behavioral perpetuation of the tropes supplied by white America ensures the continuity and potency of mutual denigration between black immigrants and African Americans. A slew of dueling perceptions has grown around these externally produced discursive baselines.

The uninformed African American's perception is two-pronged. One perception is of Africans as dirty, uncivilized refugees from the jungle continent. The other is of African immigrants as stuck-up, even arrogant achievers who look down on African Africans and engage in the same derogatory stereotyping of native blacks as white Americans.

On the African side, the pre-selection and self-selection that goes into the immigrant's journey and that shapes his self-perception can become a relational burden, conditioning him to see himself as special, unique, and better than his African American cousin. The other related factor is that the black immigrant in America often becomes aware of the structural and discursive—not to mention racist—elevation of him to the status of a model, exemplary minority, a construction that requires the simultaneous portrayal of African Americans as lazy underachievers. Some African immigrants internalize these narratives as a way of self-fortification and self-definition in a society in which they are struggling for recognition and respect. The consequence of this internalization of inaccurate and demeaning stereotypes for their relations with African Americans is grave, as their attitudes and gestures toward native blacks may be conditioned by these internalized social codes. This in turn produces the proverbial self-fulfilling prophecy of hostile arrogance, prejudicial suspicions, and skittishness on the part of African immigrants in relation to African American interlocutors.

TERMINOLOGIES AND CONTEMPT

In this climate of recriminatory exchanges, mutual appellative put-downs emerge and ossify. African immigrants are known to use the term *akata* to refer to African Americans in both descriptive and derogatory contexts, with the derogatory connotations seemingly eclipsing the descriptive appellative function of the word among both African immigrants and African Americans. As research by Georgia State University professor of communication, Farooq Kperogi reveals, African American popular culture semiotics have since come to associate the term with "slave," "cotton picker" and even "nigger."[46] These are obviously false semiotic extrapolations, but as most linguists argue, the socially constructed meanings of words often outpace their denotative meanings in both usage and social function. The actual provenance of the term is in dispute. It is supposedly a Yoruba term for "wild cat." This explanation holds that Yoruba migrants to the US in the 1960s and '70s applied the term to African Americans they encountered, who, in their behaviors and mannerisms, seemed to them to be wild, unfettered, and aggressively expressive.

Whether this explanation for the origin of akata is true is a matter of debate. For one thing, contemporary Yoruba speakers do not recognize the term in their conversational, formal, or sacred vocabularies. Moreover, there are other theories of the term's origins, such as the suggestion by Ghanaian economist George Ayittey that akata is a corruption of "I gotta," a coinage by African immigrants that emanates from their exposure to a frequently used expression that seemed to be a conversational staple among African Americans. Then there is also the fact that Akata is the name of a small village outside the town of Katsina Ala in Benue State, Nigeria, which hosts a lake with the same name. Lake Akata is the venue of an annual fishing festival officially known as Akata Fishing and Cultural Festival, which features fishing contests and cultural displays by the Tiv and Etulo ethnic communities of Katsina Ala.[47] The festival has grown in recent years, helped by funding and logistical support from the government of Benue State. In the last few years, a beauty pageant has been added to the festival. Occurring concurrently with the festival, the pageant, which takes place at Benue State University, Makurdi, chooses a "Miss Akata," who is rewarded with a tiara and a car branded to announce her status (see photo).

"Miss Akata" 2012 pageant prize car. Photo taken by author in Makurdi, Benue State, Nigeria.

Akata is thus a more complex term than its implication in African immigrant versus African American relationships might suggest. There is an additional etymological possibility for the term. K. A. Familoni, Professor Emeritus of Economics at the University of Lagos, Nigeria, claims that the term originates with his uncle, a Nigerian college student in the United States in the 1950s. In a post on a widely read pan-African online forum, ChatAfrik.com, Familoni tells the story thus:

> As we celebrate this historic fiftieth anniversary of our MARCH ON WASHINGTON for jobs and freedom led by Rev. (Dr.) Martin Luther King on August 28, 1963. I feel obliged to make the following information available: Frederick Jaiyeola Falodun, an immediate brother of my mum, coined the name *AKATA* for Negro, probably because he did not like the 'N' word, when he was a student of statistics at the University of Chicago in the early 1950s. He left for Nigeria after obtaining his MS in statistics to become the first Fed-

eral Director of Statistics in Lagos, Nigeria. Although
he had gone back home before the historic MARCH
ON WASHINGTON for jobs and freedom in 1963, he
had identified with the struggle of blacks for whom
he had coined the name AKATAs.[48]

The spirit of this retelling rehabilitates the term, rescuing it
from its contemporary negative uses. If Familoni is right, and
there is no way to independently verify his claim, it suggests
that akata has its origins in the effort of a politically conscious
African immigrant to show affection for, cultivate solidarity with,
and endear himself to African Americans in a racially segregat-
ed 1950s America. Such a positive history clearly belies akata's
sociolinguistic status today. Whatever its benign origins, akata
has become a carrier of pejorative associations that may or may
not be products of recent relational histories. The larger and
relevant point then is that, etymologies and historical contexts
aside, akata today bespeaks the depth of the growing acrimony
between the two black communities that a term of such variegated and disputed provenance has become a stand-in for the
mutual resentments that characterize the fraught relationship
between American blacks and immigrant black communities in
America.

On the African American end of the spectrum of denigrating
appellations, terms such as "jungle bunny" gained currency as
a referent for African immigrants. The term is a clear read-off
from the racist motif of Africa as an untamed jungle peopled by
animalistic savages, a racial trope given audiovisual popularity
by the Tarzan movies and comics begun in second decade of the
twentieth century. More recently, the term "booty scratcher"
has entered into the vocabulary of derogatory terms reserved
for Africans by African Americans. The term, Professor Kperogi's
findings indicate, is derived from the benignly racist portrayals
of starving, emaciated African children in so-called feed the
children commercials on American television. The children are
sometimes shown to be scratching their dry, itchy, and diseased
bodies and behinds, hence "booty scratcher." How the term traveled from that narrow world of benign white paternal racism to

an arena where it now functions as a metonymic symbol for all African and African immigrant identities remains unknown.

More recently, as more of the African immigrant population reflects the demographic displacements produced by wars and from centers of conflict in Africa, contemptuous labels identifying African immigrants with destitution, famine, poverty, helplessness, and degeneracy have gained more currency in both white and black America. The implosion of Somalia and fratricidal wars in the Sudan have further complicated the African immigrant demographic landscape, adding a religious element that in a post–September 11 America stokes fear, suspicion, and xenophobia. Many of these refugee-immigrants happen to be Muslims, who practice the sartorial and devotional rituals of their religion and culture in American public spaces socialized since September 11, 2001 to regard public expressions of Islam as threatening, uncomfortably foreign, and incompatible with the American body politic. There are no statistical numbers to express how this convergence of Islamophobia and xenophobia breaks down along racial lines. Nonetheless it is safe to assume that in states like Minnesota and Tennessee, where Somali, Sudanese, and Eritrean Muslim populations have grown and caused tensions with native born populations, black American Christians are also partakers in new forms of anti-African expressions.

A TINDERBOX OF TENSIONS

Such is the depth of the repertoire of intra-racial slurs and putdowns that irrational suspicions have morphed into a thick cloud of tensions that hovers over every discussion of black immigrant relations with African Americans. This tense climate engenders the imputation of sinister intentions to the most benign intra-racial conversational or exploratory act. Even academic inquiries offered only as explanatory backdrops to the politics of race in the larger American society become fodder for further mutual recriminations between immigrant blacks and African Americans.

Take the case of the controversy that trailed the publication of an article titled "Ivy League Fooled: How America's Top Colleges

Avoid Real Diversity" in 2011.[49] The article's aim, its needlessly provocative title notwithstanding, is to expose how the use of racial representational taxonomies by elite institutions in the US masks their perpetuation of elitism through the conscious recruitment of black students from affluent, and thus mostly immigrant, black families. A fairly straightforward, statistically driven narrative about black enrollment in Ivy League universities and its implication for class and race dynamics and for the maintenance of class-based privilege quickly became a lightening rod of intra-racial controversy.

Within the American black community and in online forums, opinions sprang in support of and opposition to the most sensationally simplistic reading of the piece: that it laments the disproportionate presence of African and African immigrant students in Ivy League institutions and suggests that the elite institutions recruit more African Americans to balance the book and fulfill "real diversity" as envisioned by the policy of affirmative action. The piece in question was in truth more concerned about the ways in which Ivy League institutions actively seek out black candidates among the nation's most successful black families, many of them likely to be immigrant black families driven to success by their pre-selection and prior preparation, the peculiar pressures of home and exile, and their relative insulation from historical and structural processes that curtail the upward social mobility of native-born blacks and or limit their capacity to aspire and strive for the highest goals in America.

The article was a data-driven analysis of class more than anything else, a commentary on how Ivy League institutions reinforce their elitist status while performing the perfunctory observance of commitment to diversity. They do this by shunning lower-class blacks (most of them African Americans), and recruiting "ready-made" students requiring little institutional maintenance in order to fulfill the ritualistic obligation of including blacks—of *performing* diversity. In other words, Ivy League schools are able to use this practice to avoid the dirty business of actually including and nurturing black talents from spaces and experiences that do not fit into their intellectually elitist identities—demographic and experiential elements that may not enhance those identities. This, again, is a class analysis, not an argument about immigrant blacks taking the place of native-born blacks. But that is precisely the interpretation that was accorded it in several quarters. A flawed interpretation became the premise of a less than productive conversation. The backlash was instant, and an article that could have opened up productive conversations about pretentious commitments to diversity and about elitist practices that abuse the true meaning of diversity became a site of renewed intra-racial confrontations.

CONCLUDING THOUGHTS

A problematic thesis of black immigrant exceptionalism is a poor foundation for constructing intra-racial relations and perceptions. So is a blackmailing narrative of African immigrant inferiority or arrogance. When he encounters African migrants, the African American should perhaps see beyond the simplistic trope of ungrateful Africans who come to America and appropriate benefits and set-asides produced by African American struggles. Conversely, perhaps the black immigrant needs to gesture in the direction of solidarity, for we, as newcomers to the racial jungle of America, need to submit ourselves to reeducation by those seasoned by oppression and battle.

If I have not encountered the acrimony and conflicts that are common in African immigrant–African American relations it is perhaps because I have sought understanding and reeducation from African Americans in matters of race and social mobility in America rather than seek to extrapolate explanatory insights from my own experiences. It is perhaps because I decided to approach African American acquaintances with an open mind, a listening ear, and an empathetic disposition. Perhaps a deeper appreciation for historical African American sacrifices and struggles that paved the way for many African immigrants was ingrained in me by the great mentoring of Professors Kevin Gaines and Julius Scott, equipping me with a more nuanced perception of African Americans as far from monolithic and as a people in perpetual struggle. Both mentors taught me to appreciate the interconnectedness and divergences between African and African American history without falling into the trap of naïve intra-racial xenophilia or xenophobia. This type of engagement may be the way forward for African immigrants and African Americans as they try to understand and negotiate their precarious locations in American society.

CHAPTER 23

DEBT CANCELLATION, AID, AND AFRICA:
A MORAL RESPONSE TO CRITICS

Since the announcement of debt cancellation to a select group of highly indebted African countries who are said to have met some of the conditions for such a gesture, the initiative itself has been criticized by a motley intellectual crowd of African and non-African commentators. These critics of the Tony Blair initiative, if I may conveniently call it that, argue that Africa neither deserves what is commonly called debt relief/debt forgiveness nor has it proven itself worthy of increased aid. Extending debt cancellation and increasing aid to African countries, the critics argue, would simply be rewarding bad debtor behavior and would also be providing money to corrupt African governments that they claim mismanaged aid money in the past. What is needed in Africa, these critics contend, is not debt cancellation but a thorough reform of African states with the aim of eliminating waste and avenues of corruption.

Some critics have gone so far as to ask that increased aid be conditional upon the completion of, so far, largely elusive political reforms, or that aid be channeled outside governmental control directly to what they call the civil society, a supposedly autonomous domain of mobilization and civic action that is free of the problems that plague the state in Africa. In their effort to focus attention squarely on the internal dimension of the African predicament, some of these critics also seek to minimize the impact on African economies of unfair and hypocritical Western trade practices and of so-called free market stipulations, which are often attached to Western aid and/or written into reform recommendations of Bretton Woods organs and debt negotiators. Finally, the critics denigrate the efforts of Western antipoverty groups, especially Bob Geldof's Live Aid, which is critiqued as a feel-good, self-justifying jamboree of naïve Western entertainers and their equally naïve fans.

In this essay, I take on some of these criticisms, outlining their faulty premises, commenting on their weaknesses, and suggesting alternative methods of evaluating both governmental and nongovernmental Western efforts to tackle Africa's poverty problem. Let me start by deconstructing the idea of "debt relief" or "debt forgiveness," two innocuous but ideologically weighty and suggestive concepts that have come to dominate discussions on the debt cancellation package agreed upon at the 2005 G-8 summit in Scotland. The two concepts betray the extent to which notions of Western magnanimity have converged in the current analyses of Africa's problems. Even African scholars and intellectuals have allowed themselves to be seduced by the faulty foundational assumption that the West is altruistically lifting a burden off Africa. We should reject such misleading assumptions. Instead of the concept of "debt forgiveness," I subscribe to the more appropriate and neutral concept of debt cancellation.

To people unschooled in the politically powerful art of using words and concepts to shape political discussions and reality, this distinction may seem like a pedantic semantic obsession. Far from being so, it is a distinction upon which the current discussion of Africa's debt problem revolves; it may even help determine what African negotiators are able to exact from ongoing negotiations on debt. Concepts deployed in international political discussions are hardly neutral; they are often carefully and strategically crafted to shape perceptions and discussions that emanate from such perceptions.

In fact, in this particular case, the medium is the message, to use a mass communication terminology. The concepts of debt relief and debt forgiveness suggest that Africans do not deserve the gesture and that it is a magnanimous act of minimal or no self-interest on the part of the West. The two concepts also efface the nature and archaeology of these debts, which, as we know, emanate from dubious loans knowingly provided to African governments that, it was known, would, with the active assistance of rapacious Western businessmen, economic hit men, and financial institutions, embezzle them to benefit themselves and their Western collaborators. You do not forgive bad loans. You write them off or cancel them. The gesture of debt cancellation (as opposed to debt relief) connotes, more than anything

else, an important willingness on the part of Western governments to be self-critical and to admit a certain degree of culpability on their own part and on behalf of Western actors in
the aid–corruption–Swiss bank accounts racket. The concept of
debt cancellation, then, speaks to both a present imperative and
a need for analytical, historical accuracy in the matter of African foreign debt. The concept of debt forgiveness, on the other
hand, re-inscribes the same obdurate insistence on the part of
the industrialized world that it is merely coming to the rescue of
a self-destructive Africa—an Africa wracked by a crisis devoid of
Western culpability.

THE BLAIR PLAN AND ITS CRITICS

Most critics have argued that the Blair plan simply endorses
throwing money at a bad situation. This is a gross disservice
to and a crude mischaracterization of the Blair plan; it reduces
the plan to yet another attempt to raise money and throw it at
Africa's myriad problems. It is an unfair caricature of a three-
pronged, nuanced proposal, of which aid is only one aspect. Debt
cancellation, which the plan calls debt relief, is another aspect.
The most important aspect of that proposal—and this is what
makes it radical in an unprecedented way—is its courage in calling for the abolishing of many anti-Africa Western trade practices, not the least of which are the agricultural subsidies that not
only close Western markets to African producers but also belie
the West's rhetoric of free trade and globalization. The failure of
the G-8 to reach an agreement on the issue is not an indictment
of Blair's proposal regarding it; it is an indictment of the unre-
lenting Western commitment to its global economic hegemony.

Critics such as Professor George Ayittey of American University argue that Africa has already received and absorbed the
equivalent of several Marshall Plans, and argue that this inval-
idates calls for an African Marshall Plan. Comparing Western
aid to Africa to the Marshall Plan of post–World War II Europe
is however misleading. The $450 billion purportedly "pumped"
into Africa between 1960 and 1997 was not free money but a
plethora of soft loans, with conditions that are anything but soft.

The Marshall Plan, on the other hand, was direct, free American aid, the only condition being that the nations of Europe had to form a collective and devise a comprehensive plan on how to spend the money. One could say the world has changed and that the political threats and goals that made the case for the Marshall Plan no longer exist today. That may be so, but who is to say that hunger, disease, destitution, and anger in Africa pose a lesser threat to the United States than did the advancing wave of Soviet socialism?

It is also argued that no African government has been made to account for how it expended past aid money. This is a fair statement, for state accountability is indispensable to any transparent regime of aid disbursement. I have no doubt in my mind that the day of reckoning is coming for all the leaders who mortgaged Africans' collective patrimony and destiny by taking and squandering foreign loans and aid on behalf of expectant and needy compatriots. But I have no illusions that the West will be the champion of such a project of accountability. The West will not demand such an accounting, not because of their anxieties and guilt over historical injuries inflicted on Africans; as anyone can see, the West has since shrugged off the guilt of the slave trade and colonialism, and mainstream revisionist histories that exonerate and assuage the West's conscience now proliferate in academic and nonacademic circles. Rather, the West will not pursue such a project because a full accounting will inevitably indict Western actors and complicit financial institutions, not to mention some respectable Western figures who do business with African leaders and who either are in power in Western countries or have politicians in these countries who are beholden to them. Such a process of accounting will open Pandora's box and reveal the underbelly of the fraudulent, two-sided, corrupt, poverty-producing machine. This is why the West will not demand full public accounting on these debts. They will not investigate their own institutions and practices.

Analyses that harp only on the misdeeds and corruption of African governments are, at best, one-sided. If African kleptocrats have yet to be held accountable for collecting and misusing dubious aid, no Western contractors and economic hit men (apologies to John Perkins), who callously pushed dubious waste-pipe projects on greedy African bureaucrats and politicians, have been called to account for their destructive adventures on the continent. They, too, must not get off scot-free.

Perhaps the most contentious argument offered so far against increased aid and debt cancellation is the claim that until Africa "cleans its house," Western gestures will be meaningless to the continent's peoples. On the surface, this appears to be a reasonable claim, and it would be a noble assertion were it not for the fallacy that inheres in it. How can Africa not be better off, even with all the corruption and waste, if it no longer has to pay the billions of dollars that it pays annually to service debts that were dubiously incurred, debts that ended up for the most part in the West with the active collaboration of Western institutions and persons? Take Nigeria for an example. The country had spent more than four times the amount of the original loan amount in servicing, penalty, and interest payments and still had to pay a $12 Billion lump sum to the Paris Club of debtors to settle Nigeria's foreign debt with that group. Given this reality of overpayment and predatory lending, repayments of foreign debts and the withholding of so-called debt relief are immoral. And this is just a microcosm of the African debt situation. If only the critics would temper their economics with some morality and humanity, it would be easier for them to lend a sympathetic understanding to the clamor for debt cancellation.

I do not subscribe to the notion of aid as *aid*. These aids—which need to be shorn of their soft loan character and the imprisoning strings that make them tools of hegemonic control—should also be seen as token restitutive and compensatory payments *deserved* by Africa and Africans as a negligible material compensation for past and ongoing devastations of the continent. Such devastations result from the wanton extraction of the continent's resources by environmentally nonchalant Western companies, and the resultant destruction of African ecologies and agricultural traditions, livelihoods, and lifestyles, not to mention Western mavericks' instigation and exacerbation of armed conflict and their repatriation of tax-evading profits to Western capitals. No amount of Western aid will adequately compensate Africans for these Western schemes or their devastating aftermaths.

It sounds good to call for complete reform of African states and institutions as a prelude to increased aid and debt cancellation. Without discounting the need for transparency, is this complete cleansing feasible or possible—not only in Africa but anywhere in the world? Is this insistence on cleansing as a condition for aid in the interest of the suffering (and innocent) mass of Africans, some of whom depend solely on foreign aid handouts for survival? Is this not tantamount to withholding food and medicine from a child until its parents "clean up their acts" and start being financially responsible? Some critics call for outright stoppage of aid because they contend that it creates dependencies that cannot be sustained indefinitely—a valid, compelling argument—but neglect to say how *already existing* dependencies, created, to be sure, by Western donors for self-interested ideological and economic purposes, would be ameliorated or eliminated without causing economic disruptions that would defeat the very purpose of the proposed aid stoppage.

There may be some phase-out mechanism that gradually removes the dependencies and their long-term economic debilities without being disproportionately counterproductive, but one is yet to see such a proposal from the stop-the-aid advocates. Yet other critics pose the question of whether Africa's future lies in aid or trade, a false scenario that, beyond its catchy, rhyming play on "aid" and "trade" has little analytical or illuminating value. The question is advanced as though development is ever an either/or proposition of making a simple choice between two paths. Nor does the framing of the question consider the possibility that, if properly applied and managed, targeted aid could in fact spur trade and with it the benefits that exchange and markets confer.

It is a good thing that the critics of increased aid and debt relief offer some alternatives. The most bandied-about of such alternatives is what the *New York Times* calls "smart aid." Smart aid, it is argued, would bypass the predatory African state and deliver help directly to the Africans in the traditional and informal sectors through civil society organizations. This is a sensible alternative, one that does not punish innocent Africans for the sins of their leaders and does not insist on elusive governmental cleansing as a condition for helping Africa's needy populations.

But this alternative makes a naïve and crucial assumption: It fetishizes civil society and ignores the organic connections and appendages that unite the governmental sector and the so-called informal sector. The idea that civil society organizations and the informal sector are corruption-free and could thus serve as an accountable, efficient, and effective channel for aid distribution and implementation reveals a mindset that is hopelessly out of touch with realities on the ground. It is a fiction of self-congratulatory Western development experts symbiotically linked to careerist Western NGO personnel, whose organizations mentor local NGOs and need to justify their relevance in order to have access to a steady flow of funds. The redundant bureaucracies, inefficiencies, and waste that have resulted from this bureaucratic detachment from African grassroots problems, and from the veneration of civil society for its own sake, are now part of the problem of the failure of aid to improve situations in Africa.

Moreover, since the power of the African state is so ubiquitous, the smart aid proposal may not work, because state officials may resist or undermine this usurpation of what they consider their jurisdictional prerogative. It is illusory to expect that state bureaucrats will not invade or interfere with the implementation of such a smart aid package.

There is also a tendency for those who criticize Western aid in Africa to extend that critique to private aid and charity initiatives, especially those glamorized and spearheaded by Western celebrities and marked by musical concerts and other glitzy events of show business. Let's examine this critique of Western "help Africa" movements and its claims.

CRITICISM OF LIVE AID AS A DISTRACTION

I disagree with certain hypercritical views on the Live Aid movement in the West, which compare the latter to the Berlin Conference or the Scramble for Africa that crystallized in it. The analogy is a little farfetched. The Scramble was animated by a different set of historical forces and was characterized by a more brazenly explicit social Darwinist and racist ethos than the present global initiatives on Africa. What's more, it endorsed and formalized a process of physical conquest and rule, while the present movement, condescending as it is, portends no such scheme.

Certainly, one can sense some rhetorical congruence between the grandiose redemptive proclamations of the G-8 summit and the "save Africa" rhetoric of mid- to late-nineteenth-century Europe. The spectacle of a self-righteous and arrogant Europe (this time joined by Japan, Canada, and the US), pontificating on the failings and supposedly intractable problems of Africa is disturbing and reminiscent of similar proclamations in the past. It does conjure up images from a not-so-distant history of Africa's interaction with Europe. And, of course, no self-respecting African would find palatable the television and radio sound bites about do-gooder white men and women once again raising money to help Africa's needy and hungry. One would wish not to encounter such images. In short, I have serious problems with the occasional cacophonous proclamations of the G-8 regarding Africa's problems, declarations that are not usually accompanied by sincere and comprehensive plans for redress, recompense, and amelioration. Indeed the forum is more a gathering for Africa-bashing and the repetition of an almost pathologized notion of Africa's hopelessness and dependence than it is a meeting for an honest quest for comprehensive solutions to the African predicament.

While I remain very critical of—among other things—the G-8's unacceptable failure to make a deal on fair trade and Africa-friendly trade practices, I do not extend my criticism of the G-8 summit of political leaders to the Live Aid initiative. The Live Aid initiative is different in that it casts itself as a purely humanitarian and pressure-generating intervention. That such humanitarian interventions are always targeted at Africa is a cause for concern. The ways in which these initiatives are packaged and the rhetoric deployed to publicize them can be disturbing, paternalistic, and patronizing toward Africa and Africans. They are sometimes the stuff of media sensationalism. But these images are also the unfortunate products of the reality of the African situation. The truth is that certain parts of the continent are in dire need of urgent humanitarian interventions. It is sad but true that Africa is still the world's poorest continent and thus the poster face of global poverty. Let me hasten to add that my definition of poverty here rests purely on macro- and micro-economic indices and not on the presence or absence of resources and wealth-generating capacity.

This reality of poverty is not the fault of Bob Geldof, Bono, or Madonna. It is the fault of a multitude of actors and circumstances ranging from corrupt African leaderships, to lethargic and indifferent African civil societies, to Western corporations and governments that participate in and tolerate shady schemes and policies that worsen the continent's economic fate. Western musicians and actors at the vanguard of the antipoverty movement have no moral culpability in the ruination of Africa. One could very tenuously argue that they are culpable on a certain level, being vicarious and unwitting beneficiaries of some of the historical and contemporary Western practices that have contributed to Africa's present plight; but this would be a weak and ultimately untenable argument.

These antipoverty activists have, for the most part, earned their livings honestly from creative expression. They do not have to care about poverty in Africa. They do not have to do anything. After all, they are not the Western politicians, bureaucrats, bankers, and businessmen who contribute to the impoverishing of the continent through dubious schemes, intolerable environmental and ethical practices, the fueling of conflicts, and hypocritical trade practices. These musicians are not the Western politicians and corporations who will benefit from a prosperous and stable Africa or suffer the adverse but logical consequences of a poor, unstable, and badly governed Africa. They are not the ones invested in the emergence of an Africa made safe for Western investment by a revitalization of civil society and restive rural and urban underclass sectors. In spite of this mental, moral, and material distance from the African predicament, these privileged men and women in the Western antipoverty movement have the humanity, sense of compassion, and conscience to craft a humanitarian initiative that could bring immediate relief to the hungry, the diseased, and the needy in many parts of Africa—people who do not care about the nuances or contradictions of the Live Aid initiative or the matters of culpability, causality, and racialized imagery associated with current discussions of the African situation; people who just need immediate humanitarian help. In the interest of their own existentialist preoccupations, these Africans are willing to look past the unpalatable suggestions and connotations associated with Live Aid and similar initiatives.

I don't think Africans gain anything for themselves or for their struggle for basic human comforts and dignities by mocking or trivializing the efforts of the antipoverty movement in the West. It is, at best, a distraction from the challenge of awakening major stakeholders in the African situation to their obligations and responsibilities. We can point out the near-revolutionary naïveté and utopian idealism that inevitably color Western antipoverty movements. But in the end, the Bonos and the Geldofs deserve praise and commendation for their extraordinary humanity, and for using a private antipoverty initiative to put pressure on Western officialdom, which lags behind Oxfam, Bono, Geldof, and others in appreciating the dire need for action and change on the continent and for a departure from faulty premises of problem solving.

There is room in Africa for both the grandiose, bureaucratic (elusive and pretentious) plans of the G-8 and the humanitarian gesture of Live Aid. The former, if it ever materializes, is a long-term systemic initiative aimed, at least in rhetoric, at generating economic growth, curbing corruption and bad governance, and increasing responsible social spending. The latter is aimed at providing immediate relief for Africans whose lives may depend on such help and who cannot afford to wait for the elusive international Marshall Plan for Africa to materialize, if ever it will. Small, ad hoc, and target-specific steps like Live Aid should not be derided; they go a long way, and fill niches that often get forgotten in esoteric international discussions on African problems. Live Aid does not remove from the table the need to devise feasible developmental plans for Africa; it does not obliterate the need to encourage and fight for democratic reforms or the need to curb corruption and its internal and external props. In fact Live Aid complements these goals and draws a popular, show-biz attention to them. For good or ill, entertainment has proven to be a great tool of activism and awareness in our world. Caring, if self-righteous, Westerners who recognize this convergence of entertainment and social consciousness and are willing to put their celebrity status at the disposal of the movement to fight poverty in Africa deserve a lower critical standard than the Western politicians who have so far refused to do the right thing regarding Africa because of a plethora of economic and political pressures from their countries.

In fact, it would be nice to see Africans become Bonos and Geldofs, sidestepping the endless political analysis, discussions, and complex and long-term "salvation plans" for Africa to save lives, feed hungry stomachs, and deliver medicines to those who need them on the continent. I recognize that initiatives like Live Aid have their own red tape and don't always translate smoothly or mechanically to relief and comfort for needy Africans. But one gets tired of hearing endless, trite, repetitive analyses of familiar African problems and of reading countless developmental models for Africa calling for elusive political, economic, and social actions which may take decades to happen, and most of which mean nothing to the needy in Africa. Their imperfections aside, Western antipoverty initiatives of the nongovernmental variety are rarely hamstrung by the pressures of domestic politics in Western countries, a problem long established as the bane of most Western-originated governmental initiatives for Africa.

What is particularly impressive about the latest Live Aid movement is that, while raising money for humanitarian actions on the continent, it is also focusing attention on the major dimensions of the African crisis, namely, debt cancellation; increased, more responsible, but unconditional aid; fair trade; and political and economic transparency in Africa. For all these laudable efforts I am willing to overlook the problem of image and rhetoric, which also plagued the first Live Aid movement in the 1980s and 1990s and which admittedly is hurtful to African pride. But pride is valuable and worth protecting only in a context in which one's existence is not threatened and is thus not an issue. That is not the case in many African regions and for many African peoples, and so I am willing to subordinate my African pride to the imperative of saving and nurturing a few African lives where possible. Africa is not a concept whose honor should be preserved at the expense of its human inhabitants.

CHAPTER 24

RACE, RACISM, AND THE IMMIGRANT
BLACK EXPERIENCE IN EURO-AMERICA

A few years ago, an African American colleague and friend engaged me in a conversation about the name of my then unborn daughter. I told him that my wife and I had decided to name her Agbenu. I knew which question he would ask after learning how to properly say the name, especially "gb" part, a knotty syllable for many non-Africans trying to pronounce African names that contain it. My friend got the name down fairly quickly, and I was right about his next question: he asked what the name meant. I told him it meant treasure in the Idoma language.

My interlocutor then posed a question that challenged me to reexamine a fairly familiar subject in America: the connection between one's name and one's access to opportunities. Was I not concerned that giving my daughter an obviously African name might mark her out as black, immigrant, and African and thus make it easier for her to be targeted by structural and relational xenophobia and racism, my friend asked. He went on to reiterate the point, proven in many studies and experiments, that so-called African American names are barriers to economic and professional opportunities in American society.

I was, of course, familiar with that factual addendum to American racism, the correlation between naming and getting. My friend's question and commentary were, as he articulated them, much deeper, however. Many African American families from the middle and upper classes now give their children quintessentially American or "mainstream" American names as a small gesture toward freeing these children from nomenclatural racism—from the sneaky, preemptive racism of those intent on closing the door to people whose names offer clues to their racial and cultural Otherness.

Given this apparent aspirational backdrop of upwardly mobile African American families trying to throw off the yoke of an "ethnic" name by embracing "white," Anglo-Saxon and Christian names, why was I doing the opposite? Why was I willing to burden my child with the off-handed rejections that might come with bearing an "exotic" name? Why, in short, was I potentially complicating my child's future as a black child of immigrant parents in America, as if the poor kid did not already have enough obstacles waiting to stop her ascent in America? I was bucking the trend, but my friend was not sure why or to what end I was doing so.

It became clear as we continued the conversation that he had speculated that I was trying to make a statement about my child's identity and African heritage. But his questions suggested that he wasn't convinced that making a point about heritage and cultural continuities in a second generation immigrant experience was worth the price my daughter might pay for bearing a name that was sure to be a magnate for all the familiar racial and cultural resentments of white America, a name on which racists and xenophobes might unload their anxieties and fears. By marking my daughter with identifiers that may enhance her marginality in American society, was I, in a way, enabling these racists and xenophobes, daring them to target my daughter?

My responses at the time were rather instinctive and simple. Only later did I realize the deeper import of this conversation. I told my friend that it did cross my mind that a girl named "Agbenu Ochonu" might attract both unwanted attention as the "exotic African kid" in the class and also consequential discrimination on account of being marked as foreign or foreign-descended. I certainly didn't want her to experience the strange fascination with the African exotic that names like Dikembe Mutombo and Akeem Olajuwon conjure in Americans, black and white. Nor did I want her to answer for her name when trying to access opportunities for which she is qualified as an American.

However, I reckoned that since my unborn daughter already carried a last name that was obviously foreign and African, giving her an American or Christian first name might not insulate her from xenophobia and racism, where she to be confronted by both. It might save her from the mocking, malicious butchering of "Agbenu" in Middle and High School, but with a last name like "Ochonu," such ephemeral respite might only provide false protection, an unhelpful sense of insulation, from the negative attention that foreignness and blackness tend to attract.

Facing up to xenophobic bullies in middle school and acquiring toughness and defensive confidence in herself and in her heritage was preferable to offering her temporary protection only for her to confront the burdens of the "exotic" last name, unprepared, later in life. I further reasoned that those who would discriminate against a candidate named "Agbenu Ochonu" would do the same against a candidate named "Stephanie Ochonu." It was not really a simple choice between saving my daughter from future racial and xenophobic discrimination and surrendering her to it, I pointed out to my friend.

I also made the point that, given the widespread, if misleading, association of Nigerian—and African—immigrants with extraordinary intelligence, excellent work ethic, and disciplined professional drive, Agbenu might actually catch a few breaks along the way on account of her name—on account of the xenophilic dimensions and unintended outcomes of American racial and cultural obsessions. In this scenario, the net effect of Agbenu's "exotic" name on her American dream might be insignificant. It would all, in the final analysis, be a wash, I argued, and my daughter would come out ahead with her African heritage, signaled by her name, intact and with her pursuit of the American dream largely undisturbed.

If my assumption is true that the discrimination and xenophobia that might come with an African name can be offset by America's strange fascination with and veneration of certain ethnicities and cultures, then securing for Agbenu the ethnic and cultural baseline of a grounded identity may produce a net gain. Certain forms of psychological security can become assets in a hypercompetitive Twenty First Century America. Whether this security comes from the values and solidarities cultivated by the family, from an appreciation of culture, ethnic identity, and ancestry, or from both, it can be a platform for overcoming the incidental and structural racisms that plague black Americans who bear certain stereotyped names and African immigrants with so-called exotic or foreign names. This security can cancel out the burdens of difference while conferring other advantages that endure for a lifetime. I argued that, though intangible, the benefit and certainty of self knowledge and of proceeding from a set of cultural values rooted in a cherished African ancestry can only boost Agbenu as she negotiates her way through the socioeconomic maze of America.

In other Western spaces where blacks have settled and built communities, whether as recent immigrants or as part of old diasporas, the burden of blackness in particular and of difference in general is the subject of individual and group struggles. In the United Kingdom, the term "Black Britain" has become a familiar referent in discussions of several waves black immigration from different geographical origins and with different migratory itineraries. It is also the title of Paul Gilroy's book that visually documents the lives of blacks in Britain over the last two and half centuries.[50] This poor, working class black population of Britain was profiled in Samuel Selvon's classic novel, *The Lonely Londoners*.[51] Black people, mainly Africans and Caribbeans, have been passing through, settling in, and helping to remake Britain even before the big colonial wave documented by Hakim Adi in his book, *West Africans in Britain*.[52]

The so-called old diaspora consists of black people from Africa, the Caribbean, and the Americas and predated the era of colonization in Africa. The colonial encounter that began in the mid nineteenth century unleashed a human exchange that saw the beginning of several tranches of black migration to Britain. Paul Zeleza identifies three main waves of this migration during and after the seminal moment of colonization, namely "the diaspora of colonization, decolonization, and the era of structural adjustment, which emerged out of the disruptions of dispositions of colonial conquest, the struggles for independence, and structural adjustment programs (SAPs), respectively."[53] The latest group of Africans to migrate to Britain are refugees from Africa's wars and political crises, mainly Somalis but also Zimbabweans. Given this historical backdrop, it is safe to state that African and Caribbean immigrants have, at least demographically, been part of British society for centuries. Have these African and Caribbean peoples been able to access the rights of citizenship or find a niche commensurate with their contribution to British society? This is the question to which this essay now turns in comparison to America.

I returned from a research trip to the United Kingdom in May 2014, where I stayed in the metropolitan bastion of the defunct British Empire, London. The United Kingdom for me is a fascinating place, demonstrably cosmopolitan but insidiously restrictive for people who embody difference, being outside the white British archetype. The country is a laboratory for the peculiar problems and anxieties of post-imperial and post-World War II migration from the colonial peripheries of the world. The immigrant experience in the United Kingdom also brings into sharp relief differences between the American black immigrant story and the experiences of immigrant black Britons. These differences should make us pause and rethink narratives about a homogeneous trans-national black immigrant experience.

To be sure, the experiences of African immigrants in Britain mirror some of the features on display in my personal anecdote above. During my latest trip, I sought out a relation of mine, who, with a UK Masters Degree in hand, continues to toil away in the grind of minimum wage home care drudgery, with no chance of ever escaping to a job on which he could live and build a career and family. In discussing with him the institutional racism that holds African immigrants down in Britain, rewarding white mediocrity and ignoring black competence, he told the story of a friend of his who submitted his actual resume to a company under a made-up white British name and also under his actual African name. He did it only to confirm what everyone already knew, what similar experiments, big and small, in Euro-America have long proven: that "white sounding" names get a fairer shake than "black" ones, given the same conditions and objective facts.

The company promptly called his white persona in for an interview and ignored the resume under his real name, only to discover that he was black, an African with an "accent," when he showed up. The joke was on them as the applicant amused himself at the confusion into which his prank had thrown the organization and the interview crew. Satisfied that he had the xenophobic profilers where he wanted them, he proceeded to lambast their attitude and walked away with a bitter confirmation of Britain's endemic structural racism, a racism which coexists quite comfortably with performances of post-imperial

ecumenism—a racism for which the deceptive façade of cosmopolitanism is a poor mask.

If America is, in many ways, a pretentious, escapist society,
where the national self is fashioned and expressed as a post-racial site of color blind opportunity, Britain is even more so. It deploys the de facto presence of the so-called children of empire as
a foil for proclaiming itself welcoming, cosmopolitan, a land of
equal opportunities for descendants both of colonizers and the
colonized. Americans themselves recognize their own uneasy
interventions in racial matters and their country's struggle with
the presence of new immigrants of color. In that sense, there
is an open, ongoing engagement with immigrants, foreignness,
and Americanness, and their philosophical and political riders.

Americans may not be comfortable discussing how names
and color determine or affect one's destiny, but they will hardly
deny their country's racial past and present. In fact they tend to
overcorrect the discourse sometimes by chalking up every instance of racism to the country's racist past and by exaggerating
their country's undeniable racial progress. But this is not denial,
nor is it a proactive self-declaration of post-racial modeling. If
anything, it is unacknowledged defensive recognition of America's problem with race and race-based exclusion.

Britain offers something a little different. It rejects accusations that non-Whites, especially blacks, have been left behind in
British society as loudly as it proclaims itself a model of post-imperial and postmodern integration. This rebranding combines
defensiveness with an audacious narrative of denial and boast:
look how many of our former imperial subjects and former inferiors we have magnanimously brought into our country, integrated, and shared our prosperity and modernity with. In his
many essays, Caribbean-born British scholar and activist, Stuart Hall, called out this two-faced British devotion to promoting
symbolic inclusiveness while preserving a socioeconomic status
quo that retains the old order of a color-coded gradation of Britishness.

This culture of pretense, denial, and concealment seeps into
many arenas of Britain's post-imperial engagement. Everyone is
getting in on the act, it seems, including the managers of the
Rhodes Foundation and Rhodes House, Oxford University; the

same Rhodes of "Africa from Cape to Cairo" infamy—the Rhodes of Rhodes scholarship. Cecil Rhodes, empire builder on behalf of the British Crown. In 2000, as a graduate student at the University of Michigan, Ann Arbor, I was at the Rhodes House library and archive in Oxford to conduct research. It was still firmly named for the man who killed, maimed, and stole and thereafter endowed the foundation with money made from his brutal African adventures.

When I returned eight years later, it bore a new name: The Rhodes Mandela Foundation. It still bears this strange, pretentious name. The Mandelization of Rhodes' legacy extends to the interior décor of the House. A portrait of Mr. Mandela adorns the wall a few meters from that of President Bill Clinton, a former Rhodes Scholar. For added symbolic import, Madiba took the portrait next to the bust of Rhodes. To complete the ensemble, there are two banners on the interior back wall of the main auditorium—one with a digital, artistic portrait of a young Cecil Rhodes captioned by one of his platitudes about freedom and justice, the familiar type that was a staple of colonialists' rhetorical justification of their bloody conquests in Africa.

In these juxtaposed images, Mr. Mandela's stature is subtly but persuasively appropriated to sanctify the contested legacy of Cecil Rhodes. The recency of this image sanitization project may point to the unwelcome effects of a recent surge in awareness about Mr. Rhodes' atrocities in Southern Africa. What better way to deflect critique, assuage raw emotions, and proclaim and prolong the post-Apartheid, postcolonial reconciliation momentum than to call upon the image of the very embodiment of postcolonial forgiveness and reconciliation, the very epitome of racial harmony.

So, out with Rhodes Foundation, and in with Rhodes Mandela Foundation. Mandela's moral credential as a post-Apartheid reconciler forecloses discussion on past wrongs, on the silences of history, and on disturbing memories of Cecil Rhodes' genocidal campaigns. To the obsessive critics of empire and its architects like Rhodes, the display seems to say, take a look at the new, rebranded Rhodes-Mandela Foundation and its representation of Africa and Africans and reconsider your stance. Let's all get on board with the program of post-oppression reconciliation and racial harmony, these images seem to announce in their own way. Perhaps some analysts of colonialism are right that the distinction between colonizer and colonized is passé, meaningless, and that the drama of the colonial situation required the cooperation, constrained or not, of colonizer and colonized. Perhaps this spirit of cooperation—displayed in full glory by the Mandela-Rhodes symbolic rapprochement—is needed as colonizers and the colonized struggle to comprehend and navigate colonialism's unsavory aftermath.

I wonder, though, if this is what Rhodes would want. Mandela was an avatar of all that is noble, but he was also a feisty revolutionary, fighting against all that Rhodes stood and fought for. So, I am not sure that lending Mandela's brand to the Rhodes legacy necessarily ennobles the vision of its founder and financier. Perhaps in the reckoning of the foundation's current trustees, this incongruity is a small price to pay, a small insult to bear for a fumigated, sanitized institution. More poignantly, this new image of post-imperial equality between former colonizers and colonized is part of an elaborate British façade that masks the marginality of blacks in British society, as well as their systemic exclusion from the coveted privileges and opportunities of modern Britain. What little privileges immigrant Britons have snatched through their own tenacious striving now stands threatened by the rise of the racist and xenophobic UKIP in British politics, a political party which rails against the resources that immigrants purportedly take from Britain without acknowledging the ones that the immigrants bring to or produce in Britain.

The empire is alive and well. It continues to normalize and rehabilitate itself, transferring the responsibilities of redemption and reconciliation to the colonized. The Rhodes-Mandela Foundation is a telling example of how Britain papers over its racist past as a way to deny and gloss over the neo-imperial racial practices of the present. The idea that an economically disenfranchised black immigrant underclass exists on the margins of British society disturbs Britain's insistence that the empire is over and that both its proponents and victims now live free to pursue their dreams side-by-side in a British metropolitan melting pot.

Against the personal and group claims of a neatly disguised color line and of discrimination on account of origin, ethnicity, culture, and color, Britain, through its spokespersons, often goes on the offensive to claim a cosmopolitan high ground and to tout its diversity. But diversity without equality and in the midst of a racialized social hierarchy is meaningless. Diversity is not simply about presence or demography, a presence that, to be sure, is a product of the migratory initiative of the formerly colonized and not of a generous British post-imperial state. Americans may sometimes shoot down talk about racism, but its official-dom and respected historians do not advertise their country as a race-neutral society showing the world how to invent a post-imperial and post-racist national community. Only Britain displays this chutzpah, and it comes from its culture of telling itself that neo-imperial racial hangovers are inventions of malicious critics and not descriptive facts about modern Britain.

When it comes to matters of racism and xenophobia, Britain thrives on aggressive, boldface pretense as much as America thrives on defensive acknowledgment and blame shifting. Such is the depth of this British culture of denial that when Labour Party leader, Ed Miliband, was asked to assess a comment made by UKIP leader Nigel Farage that he would be concerned if a group of Romanian immigrants moved next door, he could not even bring himself to call the comments racist or xenophobic. [54]

In British society, much more than in the less pretentious expressive cultures of America, cultural denigration and concerns about immigrants' morality and habits have replaced the old, franker forms of racism. This shift has in turn foreclosed the possibility of Britain coming to terms with the plight of its black immigrant underclass and enabled white Britons to preserve the status quo while projecting their society as a racially egalitarian society.

This phenomenon of advancing cultural denunciation as a stand-in for color prejudice and its social narratives is not exclusive to Britain, as Eduardo Bonilla-Silva shows in his book, *Racism without Racists: Color-Blind Racism and the Persistence of Inequality in America*.[55] However, in Britain, color-blindness is part of a narrative of officialdom about the British cultural self in that it is imbricated in a strategy to fend off the escalating problems of a restive, excluded black immigrant underclass while nurturing the myth that Britain is an exemplar of racial integration, a cosmopolitan, equal opportunity society. Britain, in this narrative, shows the rest of Euro-America how to manage the social fallouts of post-imperial African and Caribbean migration. The depth of this myth is indicative of a subtle but systemic British acceptance of the existing outlines and hierarchies of rights, opportunities, and privileges, and their visible correspondence to race, national origin, and cultural heritage. In this universe of national mythmaking, broaching racism as a structural and social phenomenon is met by dismissal and de-legitimization.

Obvious exceptions aside, when a clear case of racism is identified in America, amidst the usual loud but inconsequential denial from the far right, a collective shame and embarrassment is expressed, even if correction and redress are denied or contested. In Britain, there is no acknowledgement of racism, of post-imperial xenophobia, of a tiered citizenship and a concentric circle of privileges and rights, in which black Britons and African immigrants occupy the barren outer ring. Without acknowledgement, embarrassment and shame are impossible, let alone redress. Moreover, a powerful, socially operational narrative of African immigrant ability analogous to the American social myth of the model Nigerian—and African —immigrant does not exist in Britain to mitigate the impact of structural racism and xenophobia

The ways in which aggressive British proclamation of equality and subtle investments in the existing hierarchies constrain and condition the black immigrant British experience find evocative expression in the autobiographical narrative of an obscure but insightful book with the misleading title of *The Law, the Lawyers, and the Lawless*.[56] It is the story of Dele Ogun, a Nigerian-born Briton who, since migrating to London as a child, has been fighting for space and socioeconomic fulfillment in Britain in the midst of undeclared but powerful racial strictures and barriers.

In this brilliant little book, Dele Ogun, who had to shorten his last name from Oguntimoju to Ogun to make it easier for British interlocutors to pronounce and to tamp down the exotic foreignness that the name might advertise, crafts the tapestry of a life journey that begins in the small, informal universe of a Nigerian village and terminates for the time being in the world of low-end English lawyering. In between these two signposts of life in Africa and Britain, Ogun takes the reader through the intriguingly uncompromising world of African diasporic parenting; the racially charged and xenophobic underbellies of British post-imperial cosmopolitanism; and the starkly debilitating limits placed on African and Caribbean immigrants in a British society that, on the surface, appears at racial and cultural peace.

The story begins in Aiyede, Southwestern Nigeria, stalls momentarily in post-independence Lagos, then zigzags through Britain in the period in which the Crown and the British people were still twitching from the loss of their African empire: the 1970s and 1980s. Ogun's journey of self-discovery then winds its way through a moment of anti-immigrant ferment in Britain, the late 1980s and 1990s. Thrust into the British legal profession, Ogun navigated not just the exclusionary racial politics of the British Bar but also, tragically, the disappointment of lingering economic non-integration in the acclaimed bastion of post-imperial racial and cultural diversity: London.

Navigating these forces necessitated guile, persuasive power, persistence, shrewd interpersonal skills, and, more than all these, the embrace of unconventional paths to the British legal mainstream. It also required the mastery of minority activism and politics at the elite end of legal practice in England. Ogun was a leader in the struggle for operational space and professional empowerment for minority lawyers in Britain. His search for the British dream entailed an immersion in a multiracial, multicultural socialization process and in a peculiarly African form of educational discipline administered by his father. In the end, however, Ogun finds that the unspoken rule of British professional circles is that black immigrant professionals, credentialed and intellectually prepared they may be, have to find and accept their marginal space, content and thankful at being allowed a piece of British life at all. The attitude seems fairly discernible: you can come to Britain but you should not try to encroach on coveted professional heights, which are reserved, through the unspoken rule of hierarchical citizenship, for white native Britons.

Ogun's tale is a sad, depressing commentary on the external, predetermined forces that shape the African and Caribbean immigrant's life in Britain, and his futile, life-long struggle to find operative space commensurate with his training, aptitude, and ambition. Dele Ogun's story is only personal to the extent that his experiences as an African immigrant in Britain derive from the willful choices and agency that underpin his actions and in-actions. Other than that, his story is an approximation of the sto-ry of every postcolonial immigrant in the country: constrained and challenged by the aftermaths of colonialism, by the conceit and self-indulgence of metropolitan institutions, and by the unseen, discriminating hands of post-imperial racial backlash against the children of the Empire who now call Britain home.

One moment we catch the author reflecting on his internal battles with that perennial immigrant's liability: pride. Not pride from accomplishment, but pride that stands in the way of the immigrant's humiliating acceptance of second-class citizen-ship in a society sold to him as color-blind, equal, and fair. It is a particularly teachable moment when Ogun decides to swallow his pride and stoop to a professional superior of lower education, training, and ability—all in a seemingly doomed effort to pay his dues, secure the validation of his adopted country, and access its opportunities. Another moment, we see him resisting the humil-iating and Othering claims of a haughty apologist for a racially exclusive Britain.

Ogun's sharp retort to an Oxford Don who was enunciating the propriety of excluding immigrants from the political life of Britain is a classy yet piercingly effective refutation. Here is a sample of Ogun's response, at a public function in Oxford Uni-versity, to the bigoted Professor, who was fuming about the elec-tion of "heathen" Asians to the British parliament:

> When you speak of heathens in your parliament, you seem to have overlooked the fact that these hea-thens were happy in their own countries until your grandfathers...took it upon themselves to go and vis-it them. I need to share something with you, which is that in cultures like mine, if you decide to come and visit me, it would be regarded as rude if I didn't return the visit and that is what we immigrants are doing.[57]

This commentary on post-imperial migration to Britain calls attention to the absence of an ethic of reciprocal hospitality and accommodation on the part of British officialdom. You introduced your subjects to the glories of the metropole, using violence and persuasion in the process. Now, these former subjects and their descendants have responded and trudged peacefully to the metropole to behold and partake in its advertised glories. In this scenario, you should, according to the basic law of reciprocity, allow them to avail themselves of your society's privileges and glories if they are willing to fulfill the educational conditions you have prescribed. This, Ogun says, is what Britain refuses to do. The absence of this reciprocal hospitality in post-imperial Britain is at the heart of Britain's tense relationship with immigrants from the defunct Empire, argues Ogun.

The author's narration of his struggles with the familiar immigrant's burden of the "exotic" name is simultaneously depressing and inspirational, especially for African immigrants in Euro-America who have "exotic" names of their own and must make themselves and their children's names acceptable or tolerable to the arrogant nomenclatural preferences of host societies by tweaking or Anglicizing the inflections and cadences of these names.

At many junctures in the book, the author packages into readable personal narratives sophisticated commentaries on the unacknowledged tensions of race relations, racism, xenophobia, and structural discrimination in Britain—and the elaborate narratives and nationalist infrastructures that are created and lubricated to conceal them.

This culture of concealment helps to further entrench the marginality of African and Caribbean immigrants in the economy and professional circles of Britain. The African immigrant's name screams "foreign" and "outside," a person to be excluded without guilt. The African immigrant is thus the perversely perfect target of Britain's normalized structural racism. Sanitized through proactive revisionist discourse, this racism targets the bodies, aspirations, epistemologies, and rights of African immigrants in particular, and blacks in general. It is also institutional. I work in the field of African studies. In the US, educational institutions and the government, mostly for various admittedly political reasons, provide support for the study of African peoples, cultures, and institutions. Even here, the field is grossly marginalized in funding, importance, and recognition. The larger field of black studies fairs only a little better. Over the pond in Britain, however, these fields barely exist, as attested to by a recent clamor by black Britons for the introduction of Black Studies in British universities.[58]

The number of African immigrant academics and advanced students working in the British educational system is minuscule compared to America, even when the smaller size of the British higher education system is taken into account. Only 5 percent of professors in the British university system, which is almost wholly state-funded, are black.[59] Many black British actors and artists have to migrate to America to find roles, recognition, and success. And when it comes to profiling, Africans and especially African Muslims are treated like second-class citizens even as British officialdom boasts about the country's status as a post-imperial cosmopolis of unencumbered self-fulfillment. Somali-born British journalist, Jamal Osman, has protested against this uneasy coexistence between British rhetoric about openness, cosmopolitanism and equality and the practical reality of officially sanctioned xenophobia against African immigrants.[60]

It is not that in these various indicators, the US is much better or is necessarily a model. That is a valid countervailing point. However, the US is not the country whose leading historians and some of its statesmen engage in the revisionist enterprise of declaring its global imperial hegemonies a net positive. It is not the country that, unwilling to confront its racist history and the persistence of that history in contemporary times, goes around the world lecturing others about how cosmopolitan, fair, and tolerant it is. Britain is that country. Britain is the country whose prime minister says "there's an enormous amount to be proud of in what the British Empire did and was responsible for,"[61] a sentiment routinely thrown in the face of black immigrants from former colonies who identify and criticize the lingering negative legacies, at home and in the former empire, of Britain's imperial system.

CONCLUSION

African and Caribbean "voluntary" migrants to Euro-America are often plunged into preexisting and in some cases fairly normalized systems of social exclusion and cultural devaluation. Although this is truer for a post-imperial metropolis like the United Kingdom than it is for the Unites States where immigration is more integral to the social fabric, both societies present the "foreign" black immigrant with choices constrained by forces with roots in national self-definitions and anxieties about the black foreign Other.

The African immigrant's struggle against these social formations is complicated by the fact that key identifiers such as culture and name announce his difference and foreignness even more loudly than the nomenclatural and cultural identifiers of a Caribbean immigrant might. Although in both Britain and America, the black immigrant is forced to make hard choices that will, to the extent possible, shape his place in the adopted country, the choices and their outcomes are not necessarily the same in both countries.

In America, the bizarre logics of racial and ethnic stereotypes can work in reverse, sometimes benefitting the African and Caribbean immigrant victim of racism and xenophobia, thus mitigating or erasing their negative consequences. In Britain, the absence of a countervailing narrative and a deserved or undeserved reputation of black immigrant competence translates to a socioeconomic victimhood without recourse, buffers, and filters. What's more, the culture of pretense, silencing, and denial in racial matters, and of proactive claims about Britain's equal opportunity cosmopolitanism denies black immigrants in Britain legitimate spaces to articulate their plights and spark conversations on them.

CHAPTER 25

NOLLYWOOD AND THE FUNCTIONAL
LOGIC OF MEDIOCRITY

As a Nigerian who is now infinitely proud of the ingenuity and creative improvisation that are at the heart of Nollywood, Nigeria's thriving home-video industry, I confess that I was an unsparing critic of the industry's artistic credentials. I criticized its stories, plotlines, dialogue, acting, and the technical quality of its films. Then I had a conversation about Nollywood with my friend Farooq Kperogi, a professor of communications and citizen media at Kennesaw State University. He shared my basic critique of Nollywood but cautioned me against dismissing the industry on account of its many "levels of badness." He had talked to a film scholar who is passionate about Nollywood and celebrates its unassuming genius. The scholar had asked Kperogi if he had given a thought to the possibility that the popularity of Nollywood might in fact be derived from its indisputable lack of aesthetic and technical sophistication. His theory congealed to a single poignant question: What if the badness of Nollywood is its selling point? What if what we perceive as filmic mediocrity is a quality that Nollywood's audience treasures?

Kperogi proceeded to tell the story, relayed to him by his interlocutor, of a Westerner who, motivated by haughty notions of artistic messianism, set out to save Nollywood and to help the industry realize its potential, which he thought was being stifled by the technical deficiencies of its productions. His philosophy was simple if naïve: If one preserved the cultural appeal of Nollywood storylines and combined this with sophisticated, expensive production, Nollywood would explode to a different stratosphere of cinematic success.

The Western artistic do-gooder set out to make a film along those lines. He used a Nollywood script and a typical Nollywood story line but tweaked it for suspense and complexity. He then shot the film on celluloid and subjected it to sophisticated Hollywood editing and postproduction. When he was done he screened the movie for free in select Nigerian theatres. Very few Nigerians showed up despite an aggressive publicity campaign. The movie was a commercial disaster. Nigerians found the movie too sophisticated for their aesthetic palates. Its story was not relatable and was riddled with twists and suspense that Nigerian viewers found confusing. His theories of Nollywood deficiencies thoroughly confounded, the disillusioned Western artistic savior packed up and sauntered away, thoroughly reeducated on the contextual determinants of aesthetic value.

The anecdote got me thinking. Here is a home video industry that is as crude as many of its stories are amateurish. Here is an industry that thrives on technical mediocrity. Yet thrived it has. Mediocrity apparently has an audience. Badness must have its appeal. Crudity can be a virtue. Nollywood has shrewdly and profitably catered to the aesthetic appetite of Nigerians for films considered mediocre by the aesthetic standards of Western filmmaking. Perhaps not everything has to be sophisticated and technically elevated, just as not everyone has to be an overachieving workaholic. Excellence is overrated, perhaps, and is unrewarding in contexts that define excellence in counterintuitive ways.

To characterize the Nollywood movie industry as an incubator of cinematic mediocrity is, of course, to privilege, perhaps subconsciously, the hegemonic standards of value set by the Euro-American movie industry emblematized by Hollywood. It is to use as a baseline the standards of high culture, which devalue non-Western and lower class artistic productions. However, to the extent that there are aspirational standards, regardless of their identity, that have shaped a fairly global aesthetic of taste and artistic value, the failure to aspire to that standard, as opposed to a deliberate and heroic rejection of it, ought to be highlighted. Moreover, I am not sure that the antidote to the aesthetic tyranny of high culture is to simply revalue artistic productions devalued as "trashy." Nonetheless, the argument that every society deserves the right to construct its own standards of artistic value and that this process should mirror local aesthetic ferment is a compelling one. Perhaps, as Kenneth Harrow argues, the response should be the establishment and defense of alternative aesthetic values.[62] Even so, since Nollywood clearly operates within the commercial and artistic paradigms of Hollywood and has not articulated a rejection of the normative logics of dominant aesthetic and technical metrics, it is valid to call attention to the ways in which the Nigerian movie industry fails woefully in this effort to mimic and replicate Hollywood in Nigeria and Africa.

Beyond these issues, however, are larger questions of how the categories of mediocrity and laziness on one side and excellence and vigor on the other are produced, disseminated, and normalized in multiple contexts. The debate on Nollywood and its aesthetic and technical output is a microcosm of a larger philosophical conversation over seemingly contradictory entwinements and symbioses that are rarely acknowledged although almost always posited indirectly in narratives of value.

At a generic philosophical level, one is compelled to ask: Is mediocrity the greatest sin in the world? Why are badness and laziness vilified in such unforgiving terms in most societies? I mean, everybody can't be an overachieving hard worker in a world of zero-sum equations, can they? It's a matter of simple logic. Badness sustains the value of excellence. Without mediocrity, achievement would be diminished in worth and the world would be a bland, undifferentiated playground of overachievers. Without badness, we would not recognize goodness. Although the opposite proposition is also true, badness and mediocrity are not normative aspirational standards, so they are not the paradigms that need to be reinforced or defended.

Please follow my logic carefully. The Protestant work ethic has socialized us into thinking that work and achievement constitute the only markers of noble humanity. Don't get me wrong; I like my job as an academic. No, I love my job. If I didn't work, I would suffocate from boredom. But as I reflect on it, I am not entirely sure if that's what nature intended or if I am simply an unwitting victim of the capitalist denunciation of laziness, badness, and mediocrity and its simultaneous recommendation of work, excellence, and achievement. Those who are fanatical campaigners against mediocrity ought to pause and temper their intolerance with a sober acknowledgement of how their intolerance may have been formed by forces outside them—by the work-obsessed capitalist system.

A graduate school professor of mine patented a phrase of critique that was stinging or entertaining, depending on whether you were a spectator or a target. He would examine a piece of writing or presentation and conclude that the product had two, three, four, five, or six "levels of badness." That phrase was magical. It caught on among graduate students of our cohort. We used it to entertain ourselves, to laugh at our work, and to preempt and laugh off critiques of our papers. It was therapy in the harsh, depressing world of graduate school. We even invented our own variation on the phrase. A piece of writing, art, film, musical production, or theater might have three major levels of badness and two minor ones. That was our self-consolatory take on the idea.

As we made our way through graduate school, and as I reflected on the "levels of badness" thesis, it occurred to me that the phrase encapsulates a mindset that does not tolerate mediocrity, however defined—a mindset that refuses to recognize how mediocrity is ultimately constitutive of and indispensible to excellence. Without mediocre engineers, we cannot recognize or appreciate engineering excellence; in fact we would not have the category of "engineering excellence" to begin with. If all engineering is excellent, then "excellent" loses its function as an adjective of value.

Capitalism is partly to blame for our obsession with excellence and our disdain for mediocrity. The stigmatization of mediocrity is a product of the culture of obsessive work, which is itself the culture of capitalism. Disciplined work has a history, which is intertwined with the history of capitalism. Capitalists, socialists, and everyone in between make it seem as though work is natural to humans. It is not. Scavenging, harvesting, and consumption are. The transition from scavenging and other consumption-based modes of existence to capitalist work discipline was not a "natural" evolutionary progression as modern social science claims. It took the conscious, contested, chaotic, and unevenly successful effort of shrewd, self-interested groups to institute the culture of regimented work and accumulation and to normalize it as the standard of success.

The notion that everyone has to be a worker or producer, and that this ethos of production and productive excellence, however defined, should be the central defining feature of human progress, is not natural, nor even upheld by capitalism itself. That's the ultimate contradiction. Capitalism is supposedly about working and producing, but it depends for its survival on a nonproductive activity that requires little or no work: consumption. Consumption is not a capitalist activity. Yet it helps sustain the entire edifice of capitalism—work, profits, pursuits of excellence, and other idioms of capitalist ascent.

This brings me back to the dilemma confronting Nollywood. Like every industry, it is driven by consumption. This consumption is in turn lubricated by a particular aesthetic appetite, defined as a taste for stories, motifs, and plots that Hollywood and those claiming sophisticated artistic sensibilities would describe as mediocre, trashy, and undiscerning. The dilemma that Nollywood is wrestling with is whether to aspire to the normative standards of moviemaking and lose a critical mass of its consumers or stick to that which may be mediocre but which will guarantee steady patronage for the industry.

Nollywood is a metaphor for a larger reality of how systems come to define themselves, over time, by their ability to pander and cater to the prevailing value systems and moralities of their environment. These systems, whether they are political, economic, or social, assume the moral and aesthetic identity of the environment that nurtures them. It is futile to insist on some abstract aspiration toward standards and values invented and nurtured outside that environment without first deconstructing these alternative value systems and their lack of purchase in this cultural environment.

In many parts of Africa, political mediocrity exists because dysfunction and chaos have their functions. Political disorder works, however bizarrely, to create opportunities and gaps that political actors can fill and exploit. As Patrick Chabal and Jean-Paschal Daloz argue, dysfunction and disorder provide a lucrative field for political actors who desire to take advantage of institutional absences, legal and moral ambiguity, and crude populism to line pockets and enhance individual status.[63] Mediocrity in this context may serve to underscore the superiority of political excellence, but over time it may acquire its own functional logic, preventing any movement towards professed and valued political ideals. Mediocrity, nurtured and operationalized in a political or cultural arena, can thus become its own justification, making it unrewarding to aspire to a higher standard defined by an external political or aesthetic logic.

Nollywood may be aesthetically dysfunctional by normative and hegemonic standards of audio-visual artistic production, but within this dysfunction is a powerful, pragmatic convergence of societal and industrial priorities, a confluence of intermeshing factors that sustains lucrative artistic entrepreneurship. Is it adequate to condemn this coincidence between the financial and technical limitations of Nollywood (which compels moviemakers to cut corners and compromise quality) and the audience's pragmatic desires for cheap, accessible cinematic entertainment without recognizing how integral to Nigeria's national cultural economy Nollywood has become? Badness and mediocrity, broadly defined as features of Nollywood, have become embedded in the industry. Exhibiting and perfecting this cultural entrepreneurship may continue to inspire critiques of artistic deficiency and mediocrity, but such critiques will not dent a compelling reality: that badly produced movies with predictable plotlines now have a growing symbiotic relationship with Nigerians who desire recreational artistic escape in uncomplicated—some might say unsophisticated—genres of audiovisual entertainment.

CONCLUSION

In many African contexts, the dysfunctions of postcolonial life compel people to find the good, the salvageable, and the redeemable in the miasma of sociopolitical and economic regression they routinely encounter and engage with. This pragmatic appreciation of items of supposedly low value often entails a revaluation of that which is considered substandard in popular discourses of high culture and excellence. The case of Nollywood, a paradoxical success story undergirded by an aesthetic vision dispensing purportedly mediocre products and catering to allegedly mediocre tastes, is illustrative of this functional goodness of badness, this entwinement of mediocrity and excellence in postcolonial Africa. The enduring question is, of course, whether we might apply this logic of productive mediocrity to the political arena, and at what cost.

CHAPTER 26

TOWARD A NEW AFRICAN RENAISSANCE

As the twenty-first century trudges on, Africa appears to stand at a crossroads marked by two parallel developments. The first of these two seminal forces is the resurgence of existential, nationalist, and political questions left unsettled by the messy march to independence and decolonization. Although variegated and complex, taking on regional and sub-regional identities and patterns, one may characterize these questions collectively in one general rubric as the residual complications of postcolonial nation building.

The second instrumental development is the dizzying circulation of ideas, peoples, technologies, and vocabularies between Africa and the West on the one hand, and within physical and virtual African worlds on the other. These two events continue apace, aided by new, informational organs of sociability, debate, and discussion.

Africa's future will be determined in large measure by how it manages and responds to these ongoing processes.

In October 2013, Nigeria's president, Goodluck Jonathan, inaugurated a committee to craft the modalities of a national conference that would bring representatives of Nigeria's multiple ethnic, religious, occupational, and gender constituencies together to discuss the existential and structural problems plaguing a Nigerian union that many agree has stifled the aspirations and hopes of its constituent peoples. The announcement set off a nationwide debate on the motives, trajectory, and scope of such a dialogue.

But national dialogues are not new in Africa. In fact, when the Soviet Union collapsed in 1991 and along with it the Cold War rivalries that actuated and sustained autocracies and authoritarianism on the continent, it unleashed a wave of national stocktaking and deliberative assembly that Western advocates of democracy and political accountability jumped on with funding and intellectual endorsement. From Benin Republic to Zaire (now Democratic Republic of the Congo) to Zambia, political actors were consumed with the quest for a catchall national conversation on unsettled foundational questions previously subsumed under hurriedly packaged decolonization agendas. Africans sought to rebuild nations ravaged by Cold War-subsidized dictatorships, corruption, and festering national discord. The questions that bubbled to the surface in these national conferences all indicate the failure of postcolonial African nation-states to address the evolving aspirations and agitations of ethnic, regional, and religious constituents. At a broader level, these questions also point to the failure of the totalizing nation-state structure crafted by departing colonial regimes to accommodate the competing idioms of solidarity, belonging, and identity that those regimes clumsily lumped into it.

Many African states have embraced in principle the idea of revisiting the questions left unresolved by colonial regimes, but they have balked at attempts to have holistic conversations that include any and all aspirations, no matter how constructive or disruptive. This is not surprising, for it is in the nature of the nation-state to guard its claim to sovereignty jealously against alternative political and territorial aspirations. Moreover, the guardians of African states prefer the familiar structural status quo, however broken and unsatisfying, to the uncharted path of searching for a more functional alternative. In that spirit of waffling between acceptance of national dialogue and a rejection of its rupturing possibilities, the Nigerian government left the breakup of Nigeria and the self-determination of ethno-regional nations off the menu of topics to be discussed in the national conference.

The problem with this approach is that you cannot inaugurate a political conversation on the many existential questions plaguing the Nigerian state and declare the breakup option off-limits. Such restrictions undermine the very essence of convening national dialogues that seek to reexamine the terms of a union. It is difficult to corral political conversations into preferred boxes or outcomes while avoiding uncomfortable questions that depart from predetermined trajectories.

African states facing similar existential threats and questions as Nigeria ought to move away from the Nigerian model of declaring the union, a colonial product of messy, arbitrary amalgamation, an inviolable baseline of national structural and constitutional reform. Instead, they will do well to give those who want to pursue their political aspirations outside the inherited state framework and those who simply see that political architecture as an insufferable drag on their ambitions a deliberative platform to convince their compatriots. It is the civilized, democratic thing to do.

All over Africa, separatist and centrifugal pressures continue to mount on increasingly fractured and dysfunctional postcolonial nation-states. The problem, for now, is that instead of embracing and productively engaging these pressures, most African states are shooing them underground or reacting with paranoid aggression. It is the wrong approach, especially in a twenty-first-century geopolitical order in which self-determination, decentralization, and political consent have become paradigmatic cornerstones of nationhood.

In pre-colonial Africa, the process of forming, dissolving, reforming, reimagining, reconstituting, fragmenting, replacing, and founding new nations was an accepted routine of political life. In today's Africa, centrifugal pressures are regarded as potentially fatal challenges to nation-states. They need not be. If properly managed, these pressures can become regenerative, creative ingredients in nation building, for they serve to shake stakeholders from their complacency, and to prevent citizens from taking the nation as a settled, sacrosanct, final product. Moreover, providing a platform for those who desire separate states will afford African states an opportunity to understand the depth and breadth of the disenchantment of many African peoples with the existing structures and functions of their countries. Additionally, it is a way to redirect the more virulent forms of these separatist political imaginations into political mediums that would tame and mainstream them before they morph into something threatening and violent.

As I think about the national conference idea, I am struck by interrelated problems that need to be deconstructed, understood, and resolved. The first is that there are several unfinished or truncated nationalisms and decolonizations all over Africa. The second is the reality that, across the continent, there seems to be a growing fetish of the nation-state as a final, linear end-point of political organization and state formation, which in turn reduces the possibility of revising and, when necessary, undoing the territorial political bequests of colonizers.

On the first point, a cursory survey of the continent reveals many spots in which the postcolonial state finds itself dealing with the pesky burden of its illegitimacy in the eyes of a growing number of malcontents. More disturbingly, this narrative of il-legitimacy is increasingly being articulated in the claims of eth-no-regional entities that never bought into the nation to begin with. In Cameroon, the peoples of the former British colony of Southern Cameroons, English speaking and Anglophone in man-nerisms and outlook, want out of the postcolonial nation state of Cameroon. They have refused to accept their place in the state since independence from France and a 1961 referendum put them under the territorial jurisdiction and administrative orbit of French Cameroon.

In the Western Sahara, the people's struggle for a separate state or at least for substantial autonomy from Moroccan rule is all but forgotten. In Nigeria, a resurgent Biafra movement is now one of several movements of ethno-nationalist self-determina-tion. In the Central African Republic, the Democratic Republic of the Congo, Sudan, Senegal, Mali, Uganda, Kenya, Angola, Ivory Coast, and several other African states, seemingly settled nation-al configurations are bursting at the seams with unaddressed pressures and alternative political narratives, and the work of colonial state building is unraveling. Regions and peoples that colonial state makers threw into strange national cauldrons are increasingly voting with their feet against such arrangements.

Africa's postcolonial nations have been reluctant to recognize, let alone engage this growing phenomenon. Reacting to an ear-lier, shorter version of this essay, a colleague of mine, a special-ist in international history and a historian of America's foreign relations, said perceptively that "nations don't like doing such things."[64] That's the crux of the matter. Given their origins in anti-colonial nationalist struggles, one would expect postcolo-nial states to be less committed to the boundaries and political cartographies drawn up by colonizers, and to be more willing to revisit and redo these boundaries. But they are not. It is one of the enduring ironies of postcolonial nationhood, but it is understandable. Regardless of their origins, once imagined national communities become actual sovereign nation-states, it is almost impossible for such states to willfully revisit their boundaries or allow legitimate challenges to their territorial sovereignties. Moreover, no state wants to entertain, subsidize, or preside over a process that might lead to its weakening or demise. And, although it was successful in the cases of Eritrea and South Sudan, I'm not entirely sure that the human cost of a violent self-determination struggle is worth the satisfaction of forging alternative, more legitimate nations out of colonial creations.

Having stated that, I do think that what many of Africa's separatist political movements and agitations really desire is not secession and separation per se but local autonomy, which the *de facto* and *de jure* unitary, all-conquering colonial state model bequeathed to postcolonial African states does not accommodate. The mere expression of this desire for regional autonomy, decentralization, and devolution is often severely punished, as it is outlawed in many countries. This is the real problem.

Although in a country like Mali, given the racially charged politics, entertaining secession talk or allowing a secession clause in the constitution has not worked, in most African countries without the racial variable, a secession clause would have a reassuring, calming effect on the polity, forcing separatists to explore less radical options in the knowledge that secession is already available to them as a last resort. It would not make sense to begin the process of articulating a grievance and seeking redress by putting this already guaranteed last resort first. Dizzying ethnic plurality, interethnic and interregional intermarriages, and deeply entrenched socioeconomic interdependencies mean that, as a practical matter, secession is almost impossible. Some people say they want secession, but if actually given the option, they likely will not act on it because it would do them more harm than good. This is why the violently intolerant disposition of postcolonial African states toward movements for self-determination and local autonomy within their borders is befuddling. Instead of allowing them or even engaging these movements, the general attitude has been to contain or crush them.

It is precisely because of this intolerance, which is expressed through paranoid laws and violent crackdowns, that separatist movements are proliferating. If you let people express their aspirations in a civil manner, they will feel treasured and will work for redress within existing national boundaries rather than seek an out. In fact, in most cases, the demand for autonomy or outright secession is merely an expression of disillusionment with a dysfunctional, oppressive state, not really a desire for secession. Secessionist sentiment is a symptom of postcolonial dysfunction; it is this dysfunction that needs to be addressed, not the sentiments coalescing in response to it. Most postcolonial African states are insecure, paranoid, and illegitimate entities. This identity crisis informs the way they react to alternative political imaginations within them, and that is the problem.

One of the things that fascinate me about America is that, despite fighting a civil war to keep the union together (among other things), there have been and still are literally hundreds of secessionist movements in the United States. They are scattered across the country, operate legally, and have membership drives and activities in the open without molestation from the government. In fact, I recently came to understand that there is an annual convention of all secession movements in the US. It is a huge, eclectic gathering of old and new secession movements that imagine political alternatives to the American union, which they detest. My theory is that the American union is secure precisely to the extent of this openness and tolerance toward open challenges to its sovereignty and legitimacy. By being so open to them, the American government and people have not only reduced these secessionist movements to the minority, fringy sideline of American politics but they have also consigned them to the status of a largely irrelevant political subculture of malcontents. These secessionist movements are little more than objects of political curiosity for other Americans. They pose no serious threat to the union. This would not be the case if the US were to outlaw or crack down on them. The lesson for African states dealing with secessionist movements is apparent.

The other aspect of the existential problem plaguing postcolonial African states is the need to locate where, when, and how, to quote master storyteller Chinua Achebe, the proverbial rain began to beat Africans. This quest for original causality leads logically to problems associated with the nation-state as a generic political archetype in Africa.

The nation-state as a form of disciplined territorial political space is a relatively recent idea, having its origins in the Treaty of Westphalia in the mid seventeenth century. In Africa, its origin is even more recent, dating only to the late nineteenth and early twentieth centuries. Yet Africans have become so wedded to this state form, seduced by its global popularity. This is in spite of the fact that, being a jealous and domineering entity that brooks little or no challenge to its claims, the nation-state continues to stifle alternative expressions of African nationhood and group political solidarity. Given the youth of the nation-state and the non-linear movement of human political evolution, the notion that the African postcolonial nation state is beyond negotiation or reconstitution and is a sacred baseline of political organization, debate, and governance is untenable, and retrogressive in the twenty-first century.

My feeling is that in addition to having a debate on whether the national houses that colonizers built can still accommodate the varying, divergent aspirations of their occupants, a parallel debate on how best to reeducate Africans on the artificiality, newness, and awkwardness of their nation-states needs to begin. Africans need to become more receptive to legitimate challenges to the existing nation-states of Africa, whether these challenges envisage new, more functional nations, supra-national regional blocs, or a continental government of equal member-states.

The second potential catalyst for Africa's development in the twenty-first century turns on the degree to which the continent's leaders harness and channel into productive endeavors the ideas, peoples, goods, intellectual capital, and technologies moving in and out of Africa. This effort to take advantage of new ideas and mediums to rebuild, reclaim, and revitalize Africa is as much an intellectual process as it is a political project. As thinkers on Africa's fate and future, African intellectuals must accept that certain aspects of their analytical toolkit are now simply outmoded, rooted as they are in struggles and constructs that were relevant to sociopolitical moments that have expired. For instance, the old utopian pan-Africanist vision that sought to dissolve rather than understand intra-African difference is no longer tenable. Without explicitly intending it, some of these outmoded constructs shut off discussions on communal fissures, contentious relations between contiguous African peoples, internal hegemonies of class, race, and ethnic privilege, and the ugly underbellies of a frayed Afro–Arab relationship.

As the shine of anti-colonial victories have worn off and the failures of Africa's rulers have manifested themselves, African youths, armed with new critical tools and empowered by informational innovations of the twenty-first century, are constructing new outlines of what it means to be African and act African, rejecting old definitions for new, dynamic ones. African modes of intellectual reflection have been slow to capture this shift. This needs to change.

Meanwhile, Africans are moving in and out of the continent at a pace previously unseen, carrying new techniques for tackling old problems and new vocabularies for discussing the challenges of various countries. Young, restless, continental and diasporic Africans alike are taking technologies and ideas patented in the global North and adapting them to distinctly African needs. These constant physical and virtual movements between Africa and the world and between different African nodes will ensure that Africa's increasingly visible dynamism is replenished by new energies coming from its roving intellectual diasporas. The ways in which Africa taps this circulating set of ideas and technologies will go a long way in determining its twenty-first-century status in the world.

Furthermore, as the spaces for discussing, brainstorming, and troubleshooting on Africa's slate of challenges increasingly take on informal characteristics with the popularity of social media and others organs of democratized punditry, African leaders and intellectuals have to engage with nontraditional African discursive communities nurtured on informal technologies of expression and problem solving.

All of this throws up larger, more consequential questions. How can African leaders and intellectuals reckon with increasingly mobile African bodies, ideas, and objects? How can they keep up with the narratives that are animating the lives of African communities in fixed, situated locales and in shifty information landscapes such as Internet forums and social networks? How do we write African stories that are proliferating in cyber-spaces into our rendering of African realities, into our descriptions of African ways of seeing and structuring the world, and, ultimately, into our prescriptions for an African renaissance?

Africa's future depends on the extent to which these ideational, human, and technological flows between Africa and the world and within Africa intersect to create new economic, political, and intellectual paradigms. The first imperative is a basic existential one of remaking the territorial, constitutional, and political contours of postcolonial African nation-states in the diverse, complex images of their constituents.

CONCLUSION

Running stealthily through the preceding essays is an important organizing question: What is a nation or continent, and how do the elastic meanings of these two terms constrain or animate discussion and debate about their physical referents? The essays in this volume consider questions and topics revolving around the relationship between nation, continent, peoples, and identities. Africa is at the heart of these reflections, but the question of what constitutes Africa and Africans and whether this Africanity is transferable and negotiable is the invisible framing device in these essays.

Because Africa is a fragmented entity, it can sometimes be understood from the vantage point of its units and in terms of the relationships between the fragments and the whole. Although written and published independently of one another, the essays in this volume speak to the tensions and connections between Africa and its fragments, between Nigeria and Africa, and between the two and a globalizing world in which Africans, continental and diasporic, have emerged as both preeminent actors and disempowered stragglers. While Africans continue to struggle to break into the global mainstream in many sectors, they are visibly rejecting their marginality and are increasingly challenging the terms of their existence on the periphery.

I have tried here to upend some established ways of seeing and representing Africa. This is a deliberate, provocative challenge to certain visions and explanations of Africa and its variegated realities. As we struggle to make sense of Africa and Africans everywhere, our terms for talking about the continent need to reflect the bewildering pace of shifts and change in the communities we claim to explain. As I argued in the last chapter of this book, the old utopian pan-African mode of thought, which stressed commonality and unity not as an organic process of evolution but as a top-down elite project, is no longer tenable; nor should an exploration of intra-African debates and squabbles be seen, in the current moment, as an assault on pan-Africanism.

Pan-Africanist constructs, because of understandable political efforts to reclaim an Africa homogenized by the Eurocentric
colonial library,[65] shoved aside images, idioms, claims, grievances, and discourses that disturbed their overly neat narratives on
Africa. This displacement of uncomfortable questions about certain aspects of Africa's long dysfunction endured for the period
of postcolonial triumphalism. But as triumphalism gave way to
a cold, sober acknowledgement of Africa's postcolonial deficits,
new questions and crises emerged on the ground to undermine
taken-for-granted national and continental consensuses. These
consensuses, which emerged along with the natural solidarities
of the post-independence afterglow, foreclosed the interroga-
tion of the problematic foundations of many African nations and
the pre-colonial and colonial-era conditions that came to haunt
postcolonial states. The essays on the existential crises of Nigeria and Sudan re-posed these old foundational questions of ethnicity, citizenship, and nationhood. Hopefully, these essays will
function as catalysts for new, iconoclastic questions on nation,
ethnicity, boundaries, race, and concepts of home, autochthony,
and exile.

On the global, diasporic front, African peoples, problems, and
issues have shifted radically as trans-national human mobility
has intensified in a globalizing world. The resulting cosmopolitanism challenges familiar terms of identity such as "African,"
"black American," "native-born blacks," "diaspora," "African
American," and "black." These terms shift meanings as people of
African descent and those in solidarity with them explore new
spaces and engage in new kinds of politics. But as Stuart Hall
and Simon Gikandi have argued, cosmopolitanism has not simply collapsed the cultural boundaries of identity and localized
claims to modernity and authenticity; it has also produced unintended outcomes.[66] In some ways, cosmopolitanism made Africans, wherever they are, return to brands of politics, narratives,
and cultural practices that seek to reestablish the blurring lines
of difference in both inter- and intra-racial contexts.

Increased mobility of Africans within and outside Africa has
been critical to this ambivalent engagement with globalization.
This to-ing and fro-ing has the capacity to produce two equally
profound outcomes for Africa. One is that Africa's participation

in globalized processes will grow, aided by the agency of its mobile youth who, increasingly displaced in the political and social spaces at home, see travel, mobility, and international economic and epistemic transactions as a potential springboard to earn a reckoning.

The other effect of increased African mobility is paradoxical. As African peoples are increasingly sucked into institutions dominated by the global North, and as they are exposed to the bland homogeneity of global capital and consumption patterns, they will ultimately seek avenues to escape globalization's cultural erasure and retreat more and more into cultural and aesthetic forms deemed authentically African. This ability to choose when, where, and how to engage with globalization will prove decisive for Africa, for it will insulate the continent from the worst aspects of global flows while harvesting their tangible and intangible benefits.

Some analysts and scholars have begun writing the story of Africa's brain gain, locating instrumental intellectual and economic capital in the returning diaspora and African immigrant returnees who are plunging into new ventures and pioneering new economic sectors in various corners of the motherland. The brain gain narrative is a powerful one, and it documents an ongoing process that is easy to miss. I would argue, however, that the narrative's casting of global Africans as those who merely return with expertise and ideas to power economic change in Africa is reductive. It does not fully account for how returnees are increasingly being joined in these transformative endeavors by Africa-domiciled professionals for whom migration is not an option, but who travel from and between African nodes to access and adapt ideas to local problems. The narrative of brain gain also does not account for how this diverse group of Africans is changing the very terms upon which Africa engages with globalization.

It does appear then that lamentations about Africa's victimhood in the global cultural industry and about the negative effects of cultural imperialism on Africa is premature. In the long term, the proactive and reactive agency of young, mobile, and self-conscious Africans will ensure that Africa's marginality in global processes is complemented by the opportunities that only marginal global communities can create and exploit in a globalizing world, opportunities that peripheral communities have to seek in order to be economically relevant in increasingly zero-sum global interactions.

The process I am signaling is not new. Perceptive scholars like Simon Gikandi and Stuart Hall have identified similar responses to cosmopolitanism, itself an outgrowth of various phases of globalization.[67] In responding to cosmopolitan influences, communities in the global South and those with origins there adopt an ambivalent attitude. They reap the benefits of cosmopolitan openness while embracing and, at times, recreating culturally parochial signs, symbols, and objects that can root them in specific locations, experiences, memories, and traditions. The celebration of cosmopolitanism proceeds in tandem with a retreat to parochially grounded identities that confer certitude in a world in flux—a world in which cosmopolitanism and globalization mask hegemonic Western cultural ascendancy. No one wants to be globalized out of existence, so globalization paradoxically generates its own contradictions, its own antithesis, as globally disadvantaged communities who feel threatened by the economic and cultural hegemony of capital seek recognition and secure identities in parochial economic and cultural innovations.

In the next few decades, Africans will continue to search for their place in global processes, but they will resist complete assimilation to the cultural and economic imperatives advanced by such processes. Africa's future will be partially animated by this creatively deliberate ambivalence towards globalization. Specifically, a key transformative trend will grow in the next few decades of the twenty-first century: African cultural and economic markers and techniques will be exported abroad, naturalized and recalibrated and then re-exported back to the continent in a process that one may call Afroglobalization—a fascinating process of cultivating and exporting African authenticity only for the human and material cultural bearers of that authenticity to find their way back to Africa in new, potentially inspirational forms.

We can no longer take Africa, Nigeria, Africanity, and diaspora for granted, nor can we discuss the familiar sociopolitical and economic problems associated with these entities with old analytical bromides. As nations morph into amorphous regional groupings and as the set of conditions and realities that constitutes what one calls global Africanity shifts with remarkable regularity, the vocabularies for capturing the struggles, anxieties, aspirations, and expressive outputs of self-identified black communities around the world must shift in tandem with this experiential fluidity. Conceptual instability is thus a virtue in the effort to explain the condition of blackness and black nationhood, not a burden. This is one takeaway from this volume.

Another takeaway comes as a set of open questions. As scholars and chroniclers of African experiences, how do we recalibrate our methodologies, protocols of understanding, and reflections to better account for the migration of identity, entitlement politics, and debates to cyber platforms and other arenas that collapse space and distance? Communities that replicate and mimic Africa's familiar fragmentations are reconstituting themselves on Facebook and Internet discussion groups, redefining the boundaries and terms of traditional identity markers. They are writing new rules of inclusion and exclusion and demanding a different, punchier, and more polemical engagement with Africa. The ensuing debates retain old forms, but they also introduce new, more virulent and elastic lexicons for talking about African realities.

This trend calls for experimentation with new styles of provoking debate and disseminating insights on Africa's many issues. This collection is intended as an installment in a growing medium of polemical essaying on Africa. The old template of fence-sitting analysis driven by methodological scripts now seems incapable of carrying the weight of new debates and discussions going on in and about Africa and its many diasporas. More than anything else at this critical juncture, Africa needs an open, elevated debate on its challenges and opportunities, and on the openings and closures that confront Africans in a globalizing and digital world.

SELECT BIBLIOGRAPHY

Adi, Hakim. *West Africans in Britain 1900-1960: Nationalism, Pan-Africanism and Communism.* London: Lawrence & Wishart Ltd, 1998.

Adichie, Chimamanda Ngozi. "The Dangers of a Single Story," TED Talk, July 2009. http://www.ted.com/talks/chimamanda_adichie_the_danger_of_a_single_story.html. Accessed on February 4, 2014.

Anderson, Benedict. *Imagined Communities: Reflections on the Origin and Spread of Nationalism.* London: Verso, 1991.

Appiah, Kwame Anthony. *In my Father's House: Africa in the Philosophy of Culture.* Oxford: Oxford University Press, 1993.

Azikiwe, Nnamdi. Address to the NAACP Convention on the Organization's Fiftieth Anniversary, 1959. http://www.blackpast.org/?q=1959-nnamdi-azikiwe-addresses-national-association-advancement-colored-people-organizations-50th-ann. Accessed on November 21, 2013.

Bayart, Jean-Francois. *The State in Africa: The Politics of the Belly.* New York, NY: Longman, 1993.

Bonilla-Silva, Eduardo. *Racism without Racists: Color-Blind Racism and the Persistence of Inequality in America,* Third Edition. Lanham, Maryland: Rowman and Littlefield Publishers, 2006.

Patrick Chabal and Jean-Paschal Daloz, *Africa Works: Disorder as Political Instrument.* Bloomington: Indiana University Press, 1999.

Chua, Amy and Jed Rubenfeld, *The Triple Package: How Three Unlikely Traits Explain the Rise and Fall of Cultural Groups in America.* New York, NY: Penguin Press HC, 2014.

Cooper, Frederick. *Decolonization and African Society: The Labour Question in French and British Africa.* Cambridge: Cambridge University Press, 1996.

Diamond, Jared *Guns, Germs, and Steel: The Fate of Human Societies.* New York: W. W. Norton and Company, 1999.

Diouf, Sylviane "Introduction" in Sylviane Diouf ed., *Fighting the Slave Trade: West Africa Strategies.* Athens: Ohio University Press, 2003.

Ekeh, Peter. "Colonialism and the Two Publics: A Theoretical Statement," *Comparative Studies in Society and History* 17: 1 (1975), 91-112.

Fraser, Nancy and Axel Honneth, *Redistribution or Recognition? A Political-Philosophical Exchange*. London: Verso Books, 2003.

Garang, John. "Pan-Africanism and African Nationalism: Putting the African Nation in Context—the Case of the Sudan," in *Pan-Africanism/African Nationalism: Strengthening the Unity of Africa and its Diaspora*, ed. B. F. Bankie and K. Mchombu. Trenton, NJ: Red Sea Press, 2008.

Gikandi, Simon. "Race and Cosmopolitanism," *American Literary History* 14:3 (2002),

593–615.

Gilroy, Paul. *Black Britain: A Photographic History*. London: Saqi Books, 2007.

Hall, Staurt. "Cosmopolitan Promises, Multicultural Realities" in R. Scholar ed.,

Divided Cities: The Oxford Amnesty Lectures 2003. Oxford: Oxford University Press,

2006. 20–51.

Harrow, Kenneth. *Trash: African Cinema from Below*. Bloomington: Indiana University Press, 2013.

Ibn Khaldun. *The Muqaddimah, an Introduction to History: A Classic Islamic History of the World*. Abridged Edition. Translated by Franz Rosenthal. Princeton, NJ: Princeton University Press, 2004), 63.

Jefferson, Cord. "Ivy League Fooled: How America's Top Colleges Avoid Real Diversity," *GOOD*, August 31, 2011, http://www.good.is/posts/ivy-league--fooled-how-america-s-top-colleges-avoid-real-diversity. Accessed on November 12, 2013.

Kane, Ousmane. *Muslim Modernity in Postcolonial Nigeria: A Study of the Society for the Removal of Innovation and Restatement of Tradition*. Amsterdam: Brill Academic Publishers, 2003.

Kperogi, Farooq."Insults Africans and African Americans Hurl at Each Other," Blogpost February 16, 2013. http://www.farooqkperogi.com/2013/02/insults-africans-and-african-americans.html. Accessed on May 20, 2014.

Last, Murray. "From Dissent to Dissidence: The Genesis and Development of Reformist Islamic Groups in Northern Nigeria," paper presented at the African History Seminar, School of Oriental and African Studies (SOAS), University of London, March 6, 2013, 2.

Mamdani, Mahmood. "The Politics of Naming: Genocide, Civil War, Insurgency," *London Review of Books* 29, no. 5 (March 2007): 5–8.

Mudimbe, V.Y. *The Invention of Africa.* Bloomington: Indiana University Press, 1988.

_____.*The Idea of Africa.* Bloomington: Indiana University Press, 1994.

Mazrui, Ali. A. "Towards Understanding the Causes of Terrorism: The Culture, the Mission, the Motive and the Target," a short paper commissioned by the United Nations Foundation as part of Secretary-General Kofi Annan's call for an evaluation of new challenges to the "architecture" of international security, February/March, 2004.

Nkrumah, Kwame. *Ghana: The autobiography of Kwame Nkrumah.* New York: Thomas Nelson and Sons, 1957.

Nwanze, Cheta. "A Short History of Boko Haram," *Saharareporters.com*, March 31, 2014, http://saharareporters.com/article/short-history-boko-haram. Accessed on March 31, 2014.

Ogun, Dele. *The Law, the Lawyers, and the Lawless.* London: New European Publications, 2009.

Olaniyan, Tejumola. "On 'Postcolonial Discourse': An Introduction," *Callaloo* 16:4 (1993), 743–749.

_____ *Arrest the Music: Fela and His Rebel Art and Politics.* Bloomington and Indianapolis: Indiana University Press, 2004.

Prah, Kwesi Kwaa. "The Politics of Apologetics: Genocide Denial, Darfur Version," *Pambazuka.com*, no. 305, May 22, 2007. Accessed May 9, 2013.

Przeworksi, Adam, and Fernando Limongi. "Political Regimes and Economic Growth," *Journal of Economic Perspectives* 7:3 (1993), 51–69.

Salkida, Ahmad. "Genesis and Consequences of Boko Haram Crisis," *Kano Online*, http://kanoonline.com/smf/index.php?topic=5429.0;wap2. Accessed on September 8, 2013.

Selvon, Samuel. *The Lonely Londoners.* London: Penguin Books, 1966 [1956].

Walid, Dawud. "Fellow Humans Are Not 'Abeed,'" *The Arab American News*, September 20, 2013. http://www.arabamericannews.com/news/news/id_7486. Accessed February 19, 2014.

_____. "Responses to My Calling Out the Term "Abeed,'" Weblog of Dawud Walid: http://dawudwalid.wordpress.com/2013/11/24/responses-to-my--calling-out-the-term-abeed/. Accessed February 19, 2014.

Zeleza, Paul Tiyambe. "Rewriting the African Diaspora: Beyond the Black Atlantic," *African Affairs* 104: 414 (Jan. 2005), 35-68.

NOTES

1. Tejumola Olaniyan, "On 'Postcolonial Discourse': An Introduction," *Callaloo* 16:4 (1993), 743–749.

2. I borrow this term from Benedict Anderson's seminal reflections on nations and nationalism. See Benedict Anderson, *Imagined Communities: Reflections on the Origin and Spread of Nationalism* (London: Verso, 1991)

3. Author's note: this essay was written before the convocation of a national conference by the Goodluck Jonathan administration, and some of the issues raised here are, as of the time of this book going to press, being discussed in this forum. Whether the final recommendations of this conference will reflect the positions and arguments articulated here or whether they will be implemented remains to be seen.

4. The so-called security vote is a budgetary set aside of up to a billion naira (about 6.5 million dollars) a month for each of Nigeria's 36 states. As the name suggests, it is designed to fund security operations, and for paying the cost of curbing security challenges, responding to security threats, and maintaining law and order in states. However, because there is little or no oversight over this money and little accountability is required of governors, and because most states do not suffer from serious security challenges requiring expenses beyond the federally funded operations of security agencies, state governors treat this monthly allocation as political slush funds to be spent as they please. Governors typically keep the bulk of the money to themselves and use some of it for political purposes, courting new allies and rewarding existing ones with largesse.

5. Jean-Francois Bayart, *The State in Africa: The Politics of the Belly* (New York, NY: Longman, 1993).

6. The basic outlines of this postulation was sketched by political scientists Adam Przeworksi and Fernando Limongi. See Przeworski and Limongi, "Political Regimes and Economic Growth," *Journal of Economic Perspectives* 7:3 (1993), 51–69. Other scholars and authors have since elaborated and expanded the evidentiary scope of the argument.

7. "Leaders of Change," *South2North* (TV show), http://www.aljazeera.com/programmes/south2north/2013/01/201315819281981.html.

8. This summation of the material and symbolic objects of social and individual

struggles was posited by Philosopher Nancy Fraser in the introduction to her published exchange with philosopher colleague, Axel Honneth. See Nancy Fraser and Axel Honneth, *Redistribution or Recognition? A Political-Philosophical Exchange* (London: Verso Books, 2003).

9. Peter Ekeh, "Colonialism and the Two Publics: A Theoretical Statement," *Comparative Studies in Society and History* 17: 1 (1975), 91–112.

10. Jared Diamond, *Guns, Germs, and Steel: The Fate of Human Societies* (New York: W. W. Norton and Company, 1999).

11. See www.utexas.edu/conferences/africa/ads/915.html (accessed on February 5, 14).

12. Mahmood Mamdani, "The Politics of Naming: Genocide, Civil War, Insurgency," *London Review of Books* 29, no. 5 (March 2007): 5–8.

13. Kwame Anthony Appiah, *In my Father's House: Africa in the Philosophy of Culture* (Oxford: Oxford University Press, 1993).

14. John Garang, "Pan-Africanism and African Nationalism: Putting the African Nation in Context—the Case of the Sudan," in *Pan-Africanism/African Nationalism: Strengthening the Unity of Africa and its Diaspora*, ed. B. F. Bankie and K. Mchombu (Trenton, NJ: Red Sea Press, 2008).

15. Kwesi Kwaa Prah, "The Politics of Apologetics: Genocide Denial, Darfur Version," Pambazuka.com, no. 305, May 22, 2007.

16. Ibn Khaldun, *The Muqaddimah*, 63.

17. Ibid.

18. Dawud Walid, "Fellow Humans Are Not 'Abeed,'" *The Arab American News*, September 20, 2013. http://www.arabamericannews.com/news/news/id_7486. Accessed February 19, 2014.

19. Ibid.

20. Dawud Walid, "Responses to My Calling Out the Term "Abeed,'" Weblog of Dawud Walid: http://dawudwalid.wordpress.com/2013/11/24/responses-to-my-calling-out-the-term-abeed/. Accessed February 19, 2014.

21. Ali. A. Mazrui, "Towards Understanding the Causes of Terrorism: The Culture, the Mission, the Motive and the Target," a short paper commissioned by the United Nations Foundation as part of Secretary-General Kofi Annan's call for an evaluation of new challenges to the "architecture" of international

security, February/March, 2004.

22. Ousmane Kane, *Muslim Modernity in Postcolonial Nigeria: A Study of the Society for the Removal of Innovation and Restatement of Tradition* (Amsterdam: Brill Academic Publishers, 2003).

23. Murray Last, "From Dissent to Dissidence: The Genesis and Development of Reformist Islamic Groups in Northern Nigeria," paper presented at the African History Seminar, School of Oriental and African Studies (SOAS), University of London, March 6, 2013, 2.

24. Ibid.

25. Ibid, 18.

26. Ibid., 19.

27. Ibid., 18.

28. See "Radical Zaria Islamic Preacher 'Albani Zaria' and Wife Killed by Unknown Gunmen," Saharareporters.com, February 1, 2014, http://www.saharareporters.com/news-page/radical-zaria-islamic-preacher-albani-zaria-and-wife-killed-unknown-gunmen. (Accessed on February 6, 2014).

29. Ibid. Sheikh Albani was gunned down along with his wife and son by gunmen believed to be Boko Haram members on February 1, 2014. Boko Haram had targeted many moderate clerics opposed to its ideology. It is believed, however, that Albani's anti–Boko Haram stance posed a particularly formidable challenge to the insurgency movement, given the clerics large following in the Zaria–Kano axis of Northern Nigeria.

30. Ahmad Salkida, "Genesis and Consequences of Boko Haram Crisis," *Kano Online,* http://kanoonline.com/smf/index.php?topic=5429.0;wap2. Accessed on September 8, 2013.

31. Cheta Nwanze, "A Short History of Boko Haram," *Saharareporters.com,* March 31, 2014, http://saharareporters.com/article/short-history-boko-haram. Accessed on March 31, 2014.

32. Ibid.

33. Ibid.

34. For a full text of Nyako's speech, see "We Must Look Deeper for Answers to Boko Haram," by Murtala Nyako, *Daily Trust,* Tuesday, March 25, 2014: http://dailytrust.info/index.php/columns/tuesday-columns/19838-we-must-look-

deeper-for-answers-to-boko-haram.

35. *Daily Trust Interview: What Boko Haram Fighters Told Me—Governor Kashim Shettima*: http://saharareporters.com/interview/dailytrust-interview-what-boko-haram-fighters-told-me-about-sect-governor-kashim-shettima. Accessed on May 4, 2014.

36. Ibid.

37. Ibid.

38. Sylviane Diouf, ed., *Fighting the Slave Trade: West Africa Strategies* (Athens: Ohio University Press, 2003).

39. Sylvian Diouf, "Introduction," in Sylvian Diouf, ed. *Fighting the Slave Trade*, xviii.

40. See http://www.ted.com/talks/chimamanda_adichie_the_danger_of_a_single_story.html. Accessed on February 4, 2014.

41. See Frederick Cooper, *Decolonization and African Society: The Labour Question in French and British Africa* (Cambridge: Cambridge University Press, 1996).

42. Kwame Nkrumah, *Ghana: The autobiography of Kwame Nkrumah* (New York: Thomas Nelson and Sons, 1957).

43. Nnamdi Azikiwe's address to the NAACP Convention on the Organization's Fiftieth Anniversary, 1959. http://www.blackpast.org/?q=1959-nnamdi-azikiwe-addresses-national-association-advancement-colored-people-organizations-50th-ann. Accessed on November 21, 2013.

44. Drew Tewksbury, "Fela Kuti's Lover and Mentor Sandra Smith Talks About Afrobeat's L.A. Origins, as Fela! Musical Arrives at the Ahmanson" (Interview with Sandra Isidore, nee Smith), LAWeekly Blogs December 13, 2011. http://blogs.laweekly.com/arts/2011/12/fela_kuti_los_angeles_sandra_i.php. Accessed on November 21, 2013. See also Tejumola Olaniyan, *Arrest the Music: Fela and His Rebel Art and Politics* (Bloomington and Indianapolis: Indiana University Press, 2004), 29–30.

45. Amy Chua and Jed Rubenfeld, *The Triple Package: How Three Unlikely Traits Explain the Rise and Fall of Cultural Groups in America* (New York, NY: Penguin Press HC, 2014).

46. Farooq Kperogi, "Insults Africans and African Americans Hurl at Each Other," Blogpost February 16, 2013. http://www.farooqkperogi.com/2013/02/

insults-africans-and-african-americans.html. Accessed on May 20, 2014.

47. "Akata...Fishing Treasures of Benue," *The Guardian Life Magazine*, edition 187, June 12, 2009, http://theguardianlifemagazine.blogspot.com/2009/06/akata-fishing-treasures-of-benue.html. Accessed on September 9, 2013.

48. See https://mail.google.com/mail/u/0/?shva=1#search/akata/140bc9428b2d9b5f. Accessed on September 30, 2013.

49. Cord Jefferson, "Ivy League Fooled: How America's Top Colleges Avoid Real Diversity," *GOOD*, August 31, 2011, http://www.good.is/posts/ivy-league-fooled-how-america-s-top-colleges-avoid-real-diversity. Accessed on November 12, 2013.

50. See Paul Gilroy, *Black Britain: A Photographic History* (London: Saqi Books, 2007).

51. Samuel Selvon, The Lonely Londoners (London: Penguin Books, 1966 [1956]).

52. Hakim Adi, *West Africans in Britain 1900–1960: Nationalism, Pan-Africanism and Communism* (London: Lawrence & Wishart Ltd, 1998).

53. Paul Tiyambe Zeleza, "Rewriting the African Diaspora: Beyond the Black Atlantic," *African Affairs* 104: 414 (Jan. 2005), 35–68, 55.

54. "Ed Miliband: Nigel Farage is 'Not a Racist,'" Skynews.com, Sunday, May 18, 2014: http://news.sky.com/story/1263755/ed-miliband-nigel-farage-is-not-a-racist. Accessed on May 27, 2014.

55. Eduardo Bonilla-Silva, *Racism without Racists: Color-Blind Racism and the Persistence of Inequality in America*, Third Edition (Lanham, Maryland: Rowman and Littlefield Publishers, 2006).

56. Dele Ogun, *The Law, the Lawyers, and the Lawless* (London: New European Publications, 2009).

57. Ibid., 128.

58. William Ackah, "British Universities need Black Studies," *The Guardian*, Wednesday, May 14, 2014. http://www.theguardian.com/commentisfree/2014/may/14/british-universities-need-black-studies?CMP=twt_gu. Accessed on May 30, 2014.

59. "Why Isn't my Professor Black?," *Blackbritishacademics.co.uk*, March 14, 2014: http://blackbritishacademics.co.uk/2014/03/12/why-isnt-my-professor-

black/ (Accessed on May 30, 2014).

60. Jamal Osman, "I am a British Citizen—Not a Second Class Citizen," *The Guardian*, Sunday May 25, 2014. http://www.theguardian.com/ commentisfree/2014/may/26/british-citizen-passport-control. Accessed on May 30, 2014.

61. "We Should be Proud of Empire Rule, Says Cameron," *Daily Express* February 21, 2013. http://www.express.co.uk/news/uk/379138/We-should-be-proud-of-our-Empire-rule-says-Cameron Accessed on May 30, 2014

62. This phenomenon of revaluing art forms devalued by high culture is the subject of Kenneth Harrow's brilliant book. See Kenneth Harrow, *Trash: African Cinema from Below* (Bloomington: Indiana University Press, 2013).

63. Patrick Chabal and Jean-Paschal Daloz, *Africa Works: Disorder as Political Instrument* (Bloomington: Indiana University Press, 1999).

64. Conversation with Thomas Schwartz.

65. The colonial library is a term coined by V. Y. Mudimbe to denote the body of texts, claims, labels, discourses, and designations that colonizers and Eurocentric commentators on Africa developed over centuries. These texts shaped subsequent knowledge about Africa, and came to constitute the baseline for many of the debates and discussions on Africa in the colonial and postcolonial periods. Even more tragically, some Africans appropriated the contents of this colonial library of Eurocentric texts for their own epistemological and instrumental purposes. See V.Y. Mudimbe, *The Invention of Africa* (Bloomington: Indiana University Press, 1988); See also *The Idea of Africa* (Bloomington: Indiana University Press, 1994).

66. Stuart Hall, "Cosmopolitan Promises, Multicultural Realities" in R. Scholar ed., *Divided Cities: The Oxford Amnesty Lectures 2003* (Oxford: Oxford University Press, 2006), 20–51; Simon Gikandi, "Race and Cosmopolitanism," *American Literary History* 14:3 (2002), 593–615.

67. Ibid.

INDEX

A

Abuja   14, 21-6, 29-30, 47, 58, 87
accountability   13, 22, 29-30, 55-8, 60, 123, 129, 192, 234
activism   215-16, 240
actors, political   184, 263, 268
Africa
  black   142, 146-7
  pre-colonial   190, 269
  continent of   v, viii, xii, xx, 110, 115-16, 121-4, 126-8,
    179-80, 189, 235, 238-41, 269-70, 277, 279-80
African agency   184, 186
African American affairs   210
African American families   243
African American freedom struggles   210
  large-scale   211
African American names   243
African American relationships   225
African Americans (*see also* African descent)   xix, 79,
    147, 209-12, 214-19, 221-4, 226-9, 243, 278
  and African immigrants   xii, 209
  Afrocentric   79
  devalue   219
  grievances animating   211
  interlocutors   213
  outperform   219
  race-infused social relations vis-à-vis   211
  upper class   218
  victimized   215
African ancestry   135, 207
Africans and African Americans   183, 209, 212, 223
African and Caribbean immigrants   246, 253, 255
  victims of racism   257
African chiefs   190

African colonial subjects   206
African communities   xviii, 187, 207, 274
  global   vii, ix
African continent   vi, xi
African corruption   121-3
African countries   xvi, xix-xx, 59-60, 116, 199, 231
  indebted   231
  North   140
African crisis   xvi, 241
African critics   110
  corruption of   119
African culpability   127, 185
African cultural inclination   123
African cultural orientation   157, 159
African culture   58, 118, 133, 152-3
  and Islamic practice   158
African descent   xiii, 278
African economies   122, 231
African emigration   195-6, 200
African governments   xx, 231-2, 234
African groups   140, 188, 191, 193
African heritage   244-5
African identities   125, 158
African immigrants   xix, 196, 200, 202-3, 205, 207,
    210-19, 221-7, 229, 245, 247, 252, 255-6
  African American relations   183, 209, 218, 221-2, 224, 229
  Community life   207, 212
  community in North America   221, 255
  community in Britain   254
  indifference   218
  names   255 *see also* African name(s)
  stories (of escape)   200, 202
  success in North America   219-21
  struggles   257
African involvement   184-6
African Islam   xiv, 151, 158, 181
African Islamists   181
African languages   133, 138-9
African leaders   50, 123, 127, 149, 234, 274

African migrants   199, 220, 222, 229 *see also* African immigrants
African migration   iii, 195-6, 212
African Muslims   151-3, 159, 180-1, 256 *see also* African Islam
African name(s)   243, 245, 247
African nations   xii, 116, 127, 268, 275, 278
African nodes   274, 279
African peoples   ix, 4, 137, 181, 189, 241, 255, 269, 278-9
African polities, powerful   190
African postcolonial nation state   273
African predicament   231, 238-40
African pride   241
African progress   110
African realities   125, 275, 281
African scholars   110, 232
African slave-trading states   192
African slavery   183, 191
African societies   xvi, 142-3, 147, 179-81, 195
African states (*see also* African nations)
    xv, 53, 116, 231, 236-7, 268-72
    powerful   xviii
African stories   201, 275
African Union (AU)   149
African victimhood   183, 187
African World   xix, 142, 183-4
African youths   179, 274
Africanity   277, 280
Africanization of corruption   120
Africanized terms   17, 139
Africans   vii-ix, xvi-xviii, 115-23, 131-4, 137-8, 140, 142-5,
    152-3, 180, 195-6, 201-2, 214-16, 234-6, 240-1, 277-8
    diasporic   v, 274
    enslavement of   137-8, 143-4
    global   iii-iv, 279
    group of   246, 279
Africa's poverty problem   232
Africa's problems   128-9, 232, 238
Africa's resource poverty   123
Africa's underdevelopment   126-8
Agbenu   243-6

aid, increased   231, 235-6
aid-corruption-Swiss bank accounts racket   233
akata   225-6
Al Qaeda in the Islamic Maghreb (AQIM)   154, 179, 181
Al-Shabaab   154, 179, 181
alibis (excuses)   11, 30, 116, 122-3, 129, 183-4
alien   152-3, 156, 158, 181
alienation   4, 197-8
  political   174-5
America   xii, 50-1, 55, 79, 144, 147, 157, 187, 209-17,
    219-21, 226, 228-9, 243-6, 251-2, 256-7
American dream   245
American society   215, 217, 219, 227, 229, 243-4
American union   272
Americans   54, 57, 93, 125, 129, 163, 214, 222, 243-4, 248, 251, 272
  white   222-3
analysts   vi, xvi, 174-6, 220, 250, 279
Arab countries   131, 140-1
Arab culture   132-3, 135, 138-9
Arab identity   133, 135, 137-8
  claims of   138
Arab racism   132, 139, 145-7, 149
Arab slavery   143-4
Arab-speaking world   145
Arab states   146-7
Arab superiority   136, 138
Arab world   131, 137, 140-3, 145-7, 149
Arabization   133-4, 137-9
Arabized countries of North Africa   141
Arabs   131-7, 139-40, 142, 144, 146-9, 193
aspirations   xv, 2-8, 31, 33, 99, 216, 255, 267-8, 272, 281
Atlantic slave trade   v, xviii, 183, 186-7, 190-1
  African participation   iii, 183, 185-6, 188-9, 191, 201, 212
  enslaved Africans in   144-5
African Union (AU)   149
autonomy   4, 6, 32, 270, 272

B

basis, historical   7
bearer   75, 93, 96-7, 99
beliefs   7, 12, 33, 35, 121-2, 137, 163, 169-70, 177-8
benevolent dictatorship   53-4, 59
benign   144, 226
Benue State   224-5
black Africans   132, 134-5, 143, 146-9 *see also* Africans
Black Arabs   135, 145-6
black communities   xiii, xix, 209, 215, 226
black immigrants   xix, 217, 223, 227-9, 252, 256-7
blackness   v, xi-xii, 212-14, 245-6, 281
blacks   132, 135, 141, 145-9, 214, 226, 228, 246, 248, 250, 255, 278
   native-born   209-10, 217, 222, 228, 278
Boko Haram   151-2, 161-78, 181
Bongos   87-91
book knowledge   82-3, 85, 169
boundaries   94, 270-1, 278, 281
Britain   1-6, 8-9, 184, 187, 246-8, 250-7
   modern   250-1
   West Africans in   246
British/Britons   1-6, 8-9, 93, 160, 253, 256
British society   246, 248, 250-1, 253
bureaucrats   17, 19, 35-7, 42, 65, 115, 239

C

capacity   xvii, 11-12, 16, 18, 21, 36, 119, 222, 228, 278
capitalism   262-3
challenges (in the African world)   iii, 1, 42, 89, 146, 179, 215, 274, 281
children (in Nigeria)   99, 143, 236, 244, 252
choices   7, 36, 54, 56, 58, 88, 176, 200, 203, 208, 220-1, 236, 245, 254, 257
Christians   32, 155, 160, 163, 167
church   12, 117
citizens   xiv, xvii, 2, 11, 22-3, 26, 29-30, 37-8, 41-2, 52, 54, 56, 66-7, 75-6, 116-17
civil society   60, 231, 237, 239
civil war   xiv, 3, 272

class   104, 127, 228, 244, 246, 274
  political   23, 26, 47, 69
colonies   5, 206, 256
colonization   5, 246
colonizers   248, 250, 270, 273
commentaries   vii, ix-x, 107, 142, 209, 228, 243, 253-5
communities   v, xix, 38, 55, 76, 88, 98-9, 178, 189, 191, 193, 207, 223, 246, 280-1
complexities   vii, x, 125, 128-9, 186, 259
concepts   viii-x, xii, 6, 52, 76, 79, 89, 144, 196, 232-3, 241, 278
conference   13-14, 21, 195
  national   33, 40, 267-8
conflicts   ix, 14, 135, 138, 213, 219, 226, 229, 239
consequences   xix, 43, 120, 122, 189
constituents   xiv, 2-3, 5-9, 24, 30, 89, 275
consumption   x, 77, 169, 200, 262-3
contests   29, 71, 134
continuity   70, 223
control   22, 69, 71, 102, 181, 199-200
conversations   22, 59, 171, 209, 229, 243-4, 259
conversion (religious)   141, 144
corruption   iii, ix, xvi-xviii, 11-16, 18-19, 22, 24-6,
  37, 48, 52, 55, 115-24, 126, 176, 231-5
  democratized   48
  moral consequences of   xviii, 121
  political   115, 120, 153
  public   xvii, 121
  scandals   16-17
corruption discourses   xvi-xvii
corruption problem   122, 124, 128
  national   18
cosmopolitan   43, 88-9, 247-8, 251-2, 256
cosmopolitanism   ix, 248, 256, 278, 280
Council on American-Islamic Relations (CAIR)   147
counterargument   24, 27
country   xiv-xv, 1, 3, 16-17, 25-6, 47, 49-54, 56-9, 81,
  107-9, 122-6, 139-41, 247-8, 256-7, 271-2
  love of   107
crimes   16, 18, 22, 24, 37, 144, 146
criminals   190-1

crises   vi, 24, 42-3, 132, 233, 278
critics   xx, 1, 107, 109, 183, 187, 231, 233, 235-6 *see also* African critics
critique   xiii, 53, 105, 107, 126, 175, 182-5, 188, 237, 262, 264
culpability   14, 127, 129, 184-6, 188, 192-3, 233, 239
   white   184-5, 187
cultures   v, ix, 2, 4-5, 30, 84, 132-3, 139-41, 152-3,
   210-11, 220-1, 245, 251, 254-5, 262
   high   260, 264
cynicism   35, 37, 104, 109-10

D

Darfur   131-2, 134, 138, 147, 149
daughter   243-5
debt cancellation/relief   231-3, 235-6, 241
debts   53, 127, 232, 234-5
Delaware State University (DSU)   209, 211
Dele Ogun   252, 254
democracy   iii, ix, 23-6, 47-60, 67-70, 166, 267
   critique of   53, 55
   liberal   51, 55-57, 59-60
democratic practice   48, 51-3, 58, 60
   recalibrate Nigeria's   58
democratic rules   53-4
democratic system   26, 56
desperation   21, 23, 68, 71, 196
   political   67, 70-1
diasporas   ix, xii, 77, 84, 214, 246, 278, 280-1
dictatorships   53-4, 59
distribution (of political office)   23, 40-1
diversity   228-9, 251
dysfunctions   51, 53, 263-4, 272

E

East Africa   179
Economic Backwardness   63, 65

economic success   197-9

economies   v, xvi, 51, 192-3, 255 *see also* African economies

el-Rufai   14-15

elections   21-4, 56, 145, 174, 254

electoral
  laws   68, 70
  malpractice   21, 23
  process   67, 69-70
  reform   21-3, 67-71
  system   23-4, 67, 69-70

elites   56, 63, 66, 133-4, 139, 253

emergence, historical   135-6

empire   5, 249-50, 254, 256

entrepreneurs   59-60, 84

equality   39-40, 146, 213-14, 251-2, 256

equity   26, 39-41

Euro-American
  culpability   183-4, 186
  economies   192
  friends   77-8

Europeans   188, 191, 193, 195-6

evidence   69, 103, 128, 131, 142, 144, 157, 159, 163, 172, 174, 184, 190, 211

excellence   x, 42, 45, 136, 260-4

executive power   25, 58, 68-71

exile   v, 200-1, 222, 228, 278

existential   31, 267

exotic   201-2, 245

expertise   41, 68, 82-4, 279

explanations   vi, 11, 115-16, 126-7, 129, 165, 173, 175-7, 197, 219, 224, 277

extremist   xiii-xiv

F

faculty
  increasing African American   210
failure (of state and society)   iv, xv, 9, 12, 35-6, 38,
    50, 53, 58-9, 63, 81, 104, 187-8, 215, 268
fairness   39-40

families   15, 98-9, 115, 129, 178, 190, 217, 220, 245, 247
Familoni, K. A.   225-6
federal character   39-43, 45
federal government   29, 32
followers   154-5, 164, 167-8, 190
fragments   vi, viii-x, 277
France   128, 184, 205-7, 270
freedom   33, 133, 144, 220, 225, 249
French   2, 205-8

G

Gates, Henry Louis   xviii, 183-8, 190, 193
  article   184, 187
  fault   186-8
Geldof, Robert   240-1
gestures   36, 89, 222-3, 229, 231-2
global Africanity   iii, x-xi
globalization   v, 233, 278-80
globalizing world   iii, 277-9
governance   22, 24, 48, 53-4, 273
government   xx, 3, 11, 17, 26, 28, 30, 35-8, 42, 50, 99, 102-5, 107-8, 139, 172-3
  bad   125-6
  failure of   37
  federal executive   69
  small   38
governors   21, 25, 49, 95, 172, 177-8
gun-slave cycle argument   189-90

H

Harik, Iliya   132, 135, 140-2, 149
Hausa   94-7
Hausaland   94-5, 153
Historically Black Colleges and Universities (HBCUs)   210
history   xviii, 1-2, 6, 42, 64, 79, 81, 124, 127, 132, 136-7, 159, 180, 205, 262
  of Islamic dissent   160-1
  romanticize African Islamic   181

Hollywood   260-1, 263
home countries   219, 221
homogeneity   xiv, 6, 9, 31, 206-7
honor   78-9, 96, 153, 241

I

Identity (*see also* African identities)   viii-x, xiii, 5, 32, 75,
     88, 91, 95, 133, 135, 137, 144, 211, 277-8, 280-1
  ethno-national   4-5
ideologies   xiv, 144, 158, 164, 167, 174-5, 177-8, 181
Idoma   87-91
images   x, 176, 198, 238, 241, 249-50, 278
immigrants   xii, 77-8, 199, 203, 205, 208, 213-14,
     219-21, 226, 228, 243, 245-8, 250-2, 254-5
imposition   2-3, 33, 139
incompetence   22, 24-5, 37, 43, 103, 105, 123, 153
industry   x, 88, 259-60, 263-4
infrastructures, social   103, 105, 121
institutions   xiv, xix-xx, 4, 15, 22, 27, 29, 35-7, 44, 56, 67, 69, 71, 179, 210
insurgencies   165, 171, 173-4
interests   v, 3, 5-8, 12, 14, 27, 33, 36-7, 56, 70, 93, 108-9, 127, 140, 149
Irish   3-6
Islam   xiv, 137-9, 144, 151, 155-6, 159-60, 163-4,
     167-8, 179-80, 227 *see also* African Islam
Islamic practice   157, 162
Islamic traditions   152, 156, 180-1
Islamist groups, violent African   171
Islamization   138-9
Ivy League institutions   228

J

Jellaba   136-7

K

Kanamma 165
Khartoum 131-2, 134
kings 77, 79, 96-7
kingdoms 7, 184, 189-92
knowledge 24, 37, 47, 81, 83, 85, 95, 168, 176, 191-2, 196, 271

L

languages 17, 89, 132, 138-40 *see also* African languages
Last, Murray 159-61, 176
laws 15-16, 23, 26, 44, 48, 68-9, 78, 123, 252
leaders 27, 29, 35, 37, 58, 66, 109, 147, 154, 161, 164, 170-1, 234, 236, 253
leadership argument 27
legacies (of slavery and colonialism) 64, 123, 140, 161, 209-10, 249
literate 16, 18
Live Aid 231, 237, 240-1
  initiative 238-9
loss 64, 121-2, 253
love 78, 88, 109-10, 126, 128-9, 261
luxury 35, 38, 41, 51, 53, 65

M

Maiduguri 165-6
mainstream xiv, 94, 160-1, 166-7, 210, 217, 243, 269
Maisuna 96-7
Marshall Plan 233-4
martyrdom 151-3, 156, 165, 180
matter 8, 23-4, 26, 31-2, 37, 49, 52, 69-70, 80, 82-3, 94, 108, 159, 196-7, 270-1
Mazrui, Ali 152-3
mediocrity x, 25, 41-2, 45, 84, 259-62, 264
merchants 188-90
Middle East 137, 144, 146, 152, 157-8, 163
migration ix, 195-6, 200-1, 219, 246, 279, 281 *see also* African migration
Militant Islam 158-9

military rule   48, 51, 54-5, 58
ministers   14, 41, 256
modernity   78, 160, 166, 168, 170, 181, 248, 278
money   13, 17, 66, 83, 96, 102-3, 159, 231, 233-4, 249
Morocco   131, 141
motivations   67, 109, 195-6
   economic   181, 196
mounds   17-18
movements   xi, 29, 31-2, 38, 155, 160, 162, 165, 171, 177, 238, 241, 263, 270-1
Muslims   32, 94, 147, 155, 157, 160, 166, 168, 171-2,
   207, 227 *see also* African Muslims
Mutallab, Abdul   151-2, 154, 156, 158-9
myths   xvii, xx, 7, 63, 200, 205, 207, 252

N

naira (Nigerian currency)   13, 17-18, 49
name(s)   11-12, 15, 42, 56-7, 93-100, 116, 148, 153,
   170, 209, 224, 243-5, 248, 252, 255
   exotic   244-5, 255
   last   93, 95-7, 244-5, 252
   legal   94, 96
naming   11-12, 15, 93, 95, 98, 184, 243
narratives   v, xii, xviii, xx, 77, 102, 117, 136, 138, 142, 144, 173, 192, 200, 203
nation   xv, 2-9, 23, 27, 30-1, 33, 39, 42, 54, 75, 228, 234, 269-70, 277-8
   ethnic   4, 7
nation building   xvi, 8-9, 269
nation-state   xvi, 1, 4, 6, 8, 107, 268-70, 273 *see also* states
national conversation   45, 268
national dialogues   267-8
nationhood   1-2, 5, 9, 269, 278
Niger Delta   3, 40, 172, 176, 179
Nigeria   iii-xi, 1-4, 6-9, 12-16, 23-8, 31-3, 37-43, 49-51,
   53-8, 67-70, 80-4, 95-9, 107-9, 161-3, 224-5
   democratic   26
   destabilize   171-2
   northwestern   164, 170
   postcolonial   39, 80

regions of   17, 29-32, 39, 41-2, 63-4, 66, 94, 138-9,
    157, 161, 172, 177, 179, 189, 270
  southern 42, 63-6, 95, 132, 138, 155
  unity of   7, 31
Nigeria and Africa   vii-viii, xiii, 170-1, 176, 261, 277
Nigerian-American socioeconomic ascendancy   221
Nigerian
  and African immigrant distinction   221
  and African phenomena   vii
  democracy   26, 51, 67, 69
  economy   99, 104
  elites   9, 85
  English names   98
  government   128-9, 168, 268 *see also* African government
  immigrants   77, 221
  languages   17-18, 99
  model   xv, 268
  names   93, 99-100
  nationhood   3, 7
  politicians   47, 68, 76
  ruling elites   85
  society   17, 55, 101-2
  state   iii, xv, 3, 23, 31, 68, 70, 104, 167, 170, 268
  superrich   101, 103-4
  Taliban   165
  union   x, xiv-xv, 1, 4, 8-9, 22-3, 25, 41, 54, 267-9, 272
Nigerian Muslims
  privileged Northern   156-7
  young Northern   158-9
Nigerians   iv-v, vii-ix, 1-3, 6-7, 11-16, 18-19, 21-3, 26-8,
    31-3, 35-41, 47-55, 67-8, 78-81, 103-5, 108-10
  groups of   109
  rich   101
nigeriavillagesquare.com   1, 12
Nigeriens   51
Nollywood   80, 259-61, 263-4
non-Africans   110, 116, 243
non-Arabs   133-4, 138
non-patriots   108-9

North Africa   137, 140-1, 149, 179
North African
  and Northwest African   141
  African Arabs   132
  Islamic identity   152
Northern Nigeria   42, 44, 63-6, 95, 97, 154-5, 157-62, 165-6, 169, 171-4
  Islam   156, 161
  Muslim   167, 169
Northern Sudan   133, 136
nuances   vii, xiv, 11, 125, 187-8, 218, 239

O

Obasanjo presidency   69-70
office   24, 27-8, 49, 96
Ogahood   75, 77-80
Ogun   252-5
oil-producing states   29-30
oil revenue   40, 66
optimists   64, 108-9
orthodoxy, liberal democratic   58-9
outlaws   190-1, 272
outrage   xvii-xviii, 16-18, 43, 93, 118, 122

P

palace   96-7
pan-Africanists   186, 213
paradise   157, 177-8
participation   xviii, 23, 43, 185, 193, 212, 216 *see also* African participation
patriots   9, 50, 107-9, 110-11
  self-declared   107-9
patronage politics   52, 65, 115-17
perceptions   xix, 38, 51, 126, 222-3, 229, 232
  uninformed African American's   223
personal importance   78-80
pessimists   107-10

PHCN (Power Holding Company of Nigeria)   14, 36
philosopher   75, 88
Plateau State   93
policy   4, 42, 44, 50, 54, 108, 139, 175, 206-7, 228, 239
political crises   54, 125, 246
political elites   xv, 41, 55, 59-60, 63, 65
Political Islam   155-7, 162
political power   65, 69
  attainment of   21, 155
politicians   17-18, 21, 29-30, 32, 36, 40-1, 44, 67-8, 71, 82-3, 115, 118, 177, 234-5
politics   v, x, xviii, 11, 32, 41-2, 50, 52, 68, 71, 81-3, 93, 155-6, 213, 278
population, black   145-7, 215-16, 246
post-imperial   247-8, 251-4
postcolonial states   xvi, 270
poverty   iii, 36-7, 52, 56-7, 101, 115, 122-5, 127,
  176-7, 195, 197-9, 205, 207, 227, 239
power   iii, xii, xiv, 18, 21, 23-5, 27-9, 44, 50, 58, 68-71, 99, 109, 133, 136-7
presidents   12, 24-5, 28, 67, 69-70, 84, 213
  messianic   27-8
prices   53, 149, 207, 244
princes   77-8
privileges   xii, 35, 38-9, 68, 103-4, 137, 142, 159, 181, 200, 218, 222, 252, 260
projects   xx, 8, 79, 84, 117, 119, 185, 218, 234-5
prophet   95, 160, 163, 166
protest   205, 209, 214-18
puritanical   156, 160-3, 167

Q

quality of life   197-9, 219, 259

R

race   v, ix, 131-3, 135-6, 211-13, 227, 229, 243, 248, 252, 274, 278
racial claims   133, 137
racial terms   135
racism   131-2, 141, 144, 149, 210-12, 214-18, 243-4, 247-8, 251-2, 255, 257

anti-African   140, 146
anti-black   147-8, 215
white   211, 215-16
racists   131, 140, 142, 218, 223, 244, 250-1
rationalizations   12, 14-15, 126
reforms   21-3, 43, 53, 58, 67-70, 161, 231
rejection   166, 168, 170, 260-1, 268
relief   239-41
religion, national   2-3
religious practices   139, 153, 156, 180
reparations   152, 185-6
resources   x, 4, 12, 21-2, 25-6, 43-4, 53, 55, 58, 69-71, 104-5, 116, 155, 193, 210
revelations   12-13
revenues   22, 27, 29-30, 64
rewards   3, 5, 35, 43, 78, 81, 85, 144, 177, 195, 206, 220
rhetoric   8, 26, 40, 52, 107, 119, 132-3, 138, 147, 175, 196, 206, 238, 240-1
Rhodes, Cecil   249-50
risk   4, 175, 177, 180, 218

S

sacrifices, historical African American   229
sayings (proverbial)   99, 160
schools   49, 55, 121-2, 144, 154-5, 210
secession   8, 271-2
sects   155, 160, 162, 178
sectors, informal   236-7
secular   162, 164-5, 167
self-determination   192, 268-9, 271
sermons   163, 168-9
servitude   xii, 76-7, 133, 140, 146-8
settlers   43-4
Sharia   31-2
Shekau, Abubakar   165-6
slave trade   iii, xviii, 138, 184-9, 191-3, 234 *see also* Atlantic slave trade
   accounting   xviii, 187-8, 234
slave-trading polities, powerful African   191
slavers   188-9

slavery   xii, 127, 143, 147, 183, 185, 187, 190-3   *see also* Atlantic slave trade
slaves   xviii, 79, 141, 144-6, 148, 189, 191, 224   *see also* enslaved Africans
social group   136
songs   79, 87-8, 90
state
  corruption   118 *see also* corruption
  failure   105
  level   22-3, 25, 29
  resources   65, 70, 116-17
statistics   64, 225
stories   12, 63, 77, 95, 100, 145-7, 153, 193, 200-2,
    209, 221, 225, 247, 252-4, 259-60
  single   201
struggles   viii-x, xiv, 2, 15, 17, 21-2, 26, 30, 75, 99, 101, 138, 152-3, 214-17, 277
  black   214-17, 226
students   127-9, 164, 210, 213, 225
Sub-Saharan Africa   137, 149
Sudan   xi, 131, 133-4, 136-9, 146-7, 227, 270, 278
Sunna   154, 164, 166, 168
superrich   102-3

T

tactics   132, 151-3, 214
Taimiyya, Ibn   163, 166-7
teachings   116, 157, 160, 163-4, 167
technologies   160, 267, 273-4
tensions   iii, v, ix-x, xii-xiv, 87, 89, 132, 155, 193, 209, 219, 227, 277
terminologies   viii, x-xiii, xvii, 2, 29, 49, 51, 75,
    84, 108, 148, 197, 212, 224-6, 277
theft   13, 16, 18, 24, 26, 48, 116, 122
theologies   xiv, 162-3, 171, 179, 181
trade   xii, xviii, 38, 93-4, 137, 145, 186-91, 193, 236
traffic   54, 102
Tunisia   131, 141

U

unitary   6, 21, 23
United Kingdom   246-7, 257 *see also* Britain
United States   38, 147, 212, 215-16, 224, 238, 255-6, 272 *see also* America
   and African Americans   xix
USAfricadialogue   183, 188

V

values, cultural   x, 31-3, 75-6, 81, 84, 88-9, 140, 245
victims   42, 59, 146, 167, 178, 186, 188-9, 191-2, 214, 250, 261
violence   xiv, 41, 151-3, 159, 166, 171, 176, 201, 269
virtual African worlds   267

W

waste   xx, 25, 125, 128-9, 231, 235, 237
waves   156, 159, 162, 234, 246, 267
wealth   57, 80, 95, 97-9, 117, 124, 190, 198
West, the   iii, vi, xx, 51, 53, 56, 68-70, 78, 121-4,
   151-2, 156-8, 195-200, 202, 232, 234-5
Western
   actors   xx, 233-4
   antipoverty movements   239-40
   commentators   123
   countries   xx, 77, 121, 127, 234, 241
   education   42, 160, 162-3, 165-8, 178
   governments   xix-xx, 233
   knowledge   168
   politicians   239, 241
   trade practices   231, 233
Westerners   51, 118, 120-2, 125, 129, 196, 240, 259
women   80, 101, 191, 219-20, 238-9
Wonders of the African World (documentary)   183-4, 188

X

xenophobia   227, 229, 244-5, 251-2, 255, 257

Y

Yobe State   165-6
Yusuf, Muhammad 162-4, 166-9

CPSIA information can be obtained at www.ICGtesting.com
Printed in the USA
BVOW04s2129140915

417937BV00001B/25/P